The Twentieth Century Pulpit

The Twentieth Century Pulpit

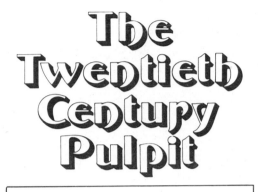

Edited by James W. Cox

Abingdon
Nashville

THE TWENTIETH-CENTURY PULPIT
Copyright © 1978 by Abingdon
Second Printing, 1978
All rights reserved

\

Main entry under title:

The Twentieth-century pulpit.

1. Sermons. I. Cox, James Williams, 1923-
BV4241.T93   252   77-21997

\

ISBN 0-687-42715-0

MANUFACTURED BY THE PARTHENON PRESS AT
NASHVILLE, TENNESSEE, UNITED STATES OF AMERICA

CONTENTS

FOREWORD

Approximately thirty years have passed since Andrew W. Blackwood compiled his *Protestant Pulpit,* a collection of sermons from the time of the Protestant Reformation to the mid-1940s. Blackwood's book did contain a number of notable sermons from the twentieth century; yet the selection was limited, and the book is now out of print. The present volume is designed to increase the number of sermons from this century, to broaden the scope to include sermons by Roman Catholics, and to bring matters up to date. None of the sermons in this book was included in Blackwood's volume.

While it is anticipated that *The Twentieth-Century Pulpit* will be of interest primarily to ministers and students for the ministry, it is hoped that many laymen may profit from reading it. The former will, of course, find suggestions for sermons. More important, they will find models that will help them learn or improve their own craft of sermon-making. To that end, I have included in the Appendix an instrument for the homiletical study of a sermon. Also, I have included in the biographical sketches a listing of certain of the preacher's books in order to encourage further study of their other sermons.

Laymen will find in this book much that is informative and edifying on the Christian faith and life. The wide variety of backgrounds will, no doubt, bring some readers into contact with viewpoints with which they are unfamiliar and, in some cases, with which they will sharply disagree. No matter! The book could hardly be representative of the preaching of this century and at the same time be uniform in expression. Each preacher bears his own witness to truth as he sees it. The reader will judge for himself or herself what is helpful.

In most cases, the content of the sermon—as well as its style—is typical of the preacher. In some cases, the content, in particular, is special. That is, it is especially expressive of the preacher's faith or outlook. This is true of sermons like "The Sacred and the Secular Are Inseparable," by Harry Emerson

Fosdick, or "The Revelation of God in Human Suffering," by Wayne E. Oates.

It goes without saying, this volume does not contain all the worthy sermons that might have gone into it. Limits were set by the twentieth-century time span, by space considerations, by availability of the sermons, and obviously by the editor's knowledge and tastes.

P. T. Forsyth said that "with its preaching, Christianity stands or falls." If these sermons are representative, we have, it seems to me, every reason to be encouraged.

James W. Cox
The Southern Baptist Theological Seminary
Louisville, Kentucky

D. M. BAILLIE

The Doctrine of the Trinity

*In the name of the Father, and of the Son, and of the
Holy Ghost.*

—Matthew 28:19

On this Trinity Sunday I wish to speak about the doctrine of the Trinity. That sounds formidable and uninviting. But surely we ought not to shirk the task of understanding it. We sing "God in three Persons, blessed Trinity." What do we mean? Perhaps we couldn't say. Perhaps we are just mystified. Perhaps this doctrine of three in one, of Trinity in Unity, conveys nothing to our minds but the sense of sheer mystery.

Well, even that is something. The sense of mystery is quite wholesome, in all our thoughts of God, for no human mind can comprehend Him. But mystery is not enough. We need a positive Gospel. And I believe we can find the whole Christian Gospel summed up in this mysterious doctrine, of three Persons, Father, Son and Holy Spirit, in one God. Let us try.

(1) First of all: *One God.* That is very important. It is part of the good news. When Christianity first went out into the pagan world with its Gospel, many people were tired of the old religions, and this was one of the really splendid things about the new Gospel: that instead of a whole host of gods it offered them ONE true God. To us that is so familiar that we don't realize what good news it is. But we would realize it if we had been brought up in a religion which had many gods. You can read in missionary books today of how it comes as a tremendous relief to heathen people when they learn from Christian missionaries that, instead of a whole host of gods and spirits to be propitiated, there is one great God over all, and that they have to do with Him alone.

From *To Whom Shall We Go?* by Donald M. Baillie (Edinburgh: The Saint Andrew Press, 1955), pp. 73-79.

9

A famous divine of the middle ages said wittily that the Devil was the first grammarian, when he taught men to give a plural to the word God. It ought not to have a plural. For if you have more than one God, you never know where you are. To put it into modern terms: if you divide your heart between different loyalties, if you idolize many things, if you believe not only in Providence, but also in blind Fate, and in lucky numbers and charms and mascots, and in the Almighty Dollar above all, then life is distracted, your heart is torn asunder, because you have too many gods. Anything more than One is too many. For there is only one true God. That is what the great prophets of Israel told the world, when the world had gone astray after many gods. They said: All that is based on a lie, and a tragic lie, which destroys all justice and truth and trust among men, and turns the universe into a chaos of conflicting forces and claims. It is a lie. And the truth is far better. It is the good news of One God who governs the world in righteousness and mercy; and to trust in Him alone is salvation. "Look unto me and be ye saved, all the ends of the earth. For I am God, and there is none else."

That was something gained once for all in the education of the human race, and never to be lost or forgotten: the good news that *God is One.* That is fundamental.

Why wasn't that enough? Why did Christianity have to go on to say something more, and something so complicated and mysterious—that in the Unity there is a Trinity? It was not because God, as it were, dropped down from heaven a ready-made doctrine for our acceptance, a mathematical doctrine of three in one and one in three. That is not how God reveals His truth, and if He did, it wouldn't help us much, but would simply leave us guessing. Why then did Christianity have to go on from the One God to the Three-in-One?

Well, it was because something happened, and then something else happened. There were two new facts of history and experience. Let us think what they were.

(2) *The fact of Jesus Christ.* About nineteen centuries ago there appeared among the Jews in Palestine a new religious leader, a working-man called Jesus. His career did not last long, for He got into trouble with the authorities and was condemned to death. But on His followers He had made such an impression that they were faced with a quite new task of explanation. Who and what was this Jesus? He had come into their lives and made everything different. He had brought God into their lives in a

way they had never known before, and He had brought
forgiveness and joy and power and victory over sin and death.
He had been put to death Himself, yet somehow they were
convinced that His very death had been the greatest victory of
all, reconciling sinners to God; and to complete the victory, He
had risen from the dead.

But how could Jesus accomplish all that? What was the
meaning of it? The only possible meaning, they felt, was this:
that God was in Christ. This was not just Jesus of Nazareth.
Somehow, it was God. Yet how could that be? Was Jesus simply
identical with God? Was "Jesus" just another name for God?
No, that could not be quite right. For Jesus was a real Man, in
both body and mind. Jesus talked about God, and He used to
pray to God; and He was tempted, as all men are, and He
suffered pain, and then He died on the Cross. But not one of
these things could be said without qualification about God the
Father Almighty.

Then was Jesus a kind of second God, alongside of God the
Father? No, that was impossible, for there could not be two
Gods. God is eternally one. Then was Jesus a kind of demi-god,
something between God and Man, half and half? No, that would
be of no use, for then you would lose both the divine and the
human. Jesus would be neither God nor Man, but a
mythological figure, like the demi-gods that were so plentiful in
other religions. That was not a bit like the Christ they had
known: and what could such a figure do for man's salvation? It
was not a demi-god, but the very God Himself, that they needed
and that they found in Jesus.

What then were they to say about it? Well, they had to go on
and find new expressions, and say things that had never been
said about God before. They said that God became incarnate in
Jesus; and yet somehow God did not become wholly, absolutely
incarnate, for they knew that God also remained all the time the
eternal invisible omnipotent God in Heaven. They had to make
further distinctions. So they said it was the Word of God that
became incarnate. "The Word was made flesh." But there was
another expression still more natural. Jesus Himself had
continually spoken of God as His Father, and He had a deep
continual sense of sonship to God. So they began to speak of the
Son of God. It was not God the Father, but God the Son, that
was incarnate and became Man. They did not mean that there
were two Gods, or that God the Father and God the Son were

two quite separate individuals like a human father and son, for there can only be one God. Really they meant something they could not adequately put into words at all. For in Jesus Christ something new and tremendous had come into their lives, and it stretched all their thoughts of God to find new expressions. So they came to speak of the Father and the Son; and even if they couldn't quite explain it or think it out, it was at the very heart of their faith.

It was all because of this tremendous new fact in their experience—the fact of Jesus Christ.

(3) *The fact of Pentecost.* But something else happened, and there is another historic fact that went to the making of the doctrine of the Trinity. We may indicate it by the word Pentecost.

Remember that the disciples of Jesus had their Master with them in the flesh for only a few brief years, and that no other Christians ever since have had that experience at all. To the disciples it was an infinitely marvellous experience. Jesus had brought God into their lives. And if they ever faced the thought that He might be taken away from them suddenly, the prospect of such a bereavement was overwhelming. How could they ever get on at all without Him? Their whole faith in God would collapse.

But if a few months after the departure of Jesus you had asked these disciples whether they missed their Master very badly, and whether they had lost God out of their lives altogether, they would have replied with a joyful and unanimous NO. Indeed they would have told you that somehow the Divine Presence was far more real and powerful in their lives now than ever it had been while their Master was with them in the flesh. It was expedient, they now saw, that their Master should have departed in order that this new experience should come to them.

There was one great day in particular when the experience came home to them. It was on the date of a Jewish festival called Pentecost. The disciples and some others who had become Christians were assembled in a large room in Jerusalem for fellowship and prayer, when they had a marvellous experience, an overwhelming sense of the presence and power of God. And now they were quite sure that they had lost neither God nor Jesus. Jesus seemed nearer than ever. Though they could not see Him with their eyes, it was only now that they began really to understand Him. And God had come into their lives as never before—far more marvellously than even while their Master was on earth—so that now they could go anywhere and witness for Him. Moreover, they very soon found that this great experience need not be confined to those who had known Jesus in the flesh. This was a thing that could happen to anybody anywhere, through the story of Jesus. A new power was abroad in the world; and wherever the apostles went with the message, the new thing kept on happening, in the lives of all sorts of people, just as it had come to the apostles themselves on the Day of Pentecost.

What was it? Was it simply the Jesus they had known, now come back to them unseen? Yes, in a way. They did sometimes speak of it as the presence of Christ. And yet it was not just the same. It was something greater and more universal than what they had known when Jesus was with them in the flesh—the same, yet different, deepened and widened and freed from all limitations of space and time. Was it, then, simply the presence of the Eternal God Himself? Yes, and yet it was something new, something beyond what men had ever known of God before, something that could not have happened but for the work of Jesus.

What was it? How were they to define it? Well, they remembered that in the Old Testament, whenever such a power came into the lives of certain outstanding and exceptional men, it was described as the Spirit of the Lord coming upon them. They remembered also that a prophet called Joel had once foretold the coming of a time when the Spirit of God would be poured out, not on a few exceptional people, but on all sorts of ordinary men and women. And they remembered that their own Master Jesus had said God would give His Holy Spirit to those who asked Him. So now on the Day of Pentecost they said: "This is what Joel predicted. This is what Jesus promised. And God our Heavenly Father, who came to us in His Son Jesus, is with us now, and for evermore, in this new and wonderful way, through His Holy Spirit."

And that is how Christians have come to speak of Father, Son and Holy Spirit, One God.

Can you see now why I said that the doctrine of the Trinity sums up the whole Christian Gospel? I began by saying that it is good news to learn that God is One. But, as you see, there is still better news in the message that the One God is Father, Son and

Holy Spirit, when you really understand it. Of course to say merely "three in one and one in three"—that in itself means nothing. But when it comes at the end of the story, it tells you everything. It tells you of what God is, in His eternal and infinite love; and of what God did in Jesus Christ for our salvation; and of what God does still today, dwelling with us as truly as He dwelt among men nineteen centuries ago, and the same for evermore. So to those who know the story, the doctrine of the Trinity sums up the whole Gospel. And the Church never tires of singing in gratitude: "Glory be to the Father, and to the Son, and to the Holy Ghost: as it was in the beginning, is now, and ever shall be, world without end."

KARL BARTH
translated by Marguerite Wieser

Look Up to Him!

*Look up to him, your face will shine, and you shall
never be ashamed.*—Psalm 34:5

My dear brothers and sisters, *"Look up to him!"* This is what
we commemorate on Ascension Day: the urgent invitation, the
permission and the command, the freedom we enjoy as
Christians and the obedience that is expected from us to look up
to him, to Jesus Christ, who lived for us, died and rose again. He
is our Saviour who watches over us like an older brother
watches over his younger brothers and sisters, yet in his
protection is also their example and their master.

He is above, in *heaven*. We are below, on earth. When we
hear the word "heaven" we are inclined to think of the great
blue or grey sphere arching over us with its sunshine, its clouds
and its rain, or of the even higher world of the stars. This is
what we may have in mind right now. In the vocabulary of the
Bible, however, this "heaven" is nothing but the sign of an even
higher reality. There is a realm *above and beyond* the world of
man, which is lost to our sight, to our understanding, to our
penetration, and even more to our dominion. It is way above
and beyond us. In biblical language heaven is the dwelling
place, the throne, of God. It is the mystery encompassing us
everywhere. *There* Jesus Christ lives. He is in the centre of this
mystery beyond. Of all men, he alone went there, all by himself,
in order to be there and from there, from the throne of God, the
Lord and Saviour of us all. Therefore: *Look up to him!*

To "look up" alone would not do. "Chin up!" we are wont to
say to a friend in distress. You may have heard this "chin up!"
yourself. But this is somewhat of a problem. Could it not be that
above and beyond us, in heaven, we are confronted with a stark

and merciless mirror, reflecting our own human affliction? We might see once more the wrong done to us by our neighbours and the wrong done by us to them, but now magnified and projected into the infinite. We might see our guilt, our inner anxieties and our outward affliction, all we call fate, and finally death itself. All these could be included in the mystery beyond, in heaven! This heaven would lie like a dark cloud over our heads, or like one of those dungeons where they used to keep prisoners in centuries gone by, or even like a coffin lid, burying us alive under its weight. Does anyone wish to look up there? No, we'd better forget about such a menace from above! But what is the use of trying not to think of it if it is nevertheless real? Things could even be much worse. God himself could be like this heaven: a Holy Being, rightfully turned against us, a sinister tyrant, the very enemy of mankind, or perhaps simply an indifferent God who willed for unknown reasons to set us under this cloud, under this dungeon, under this coffin lid. Many of us, even all of us in our desperate moments and years, hold on to this mental picture of heaven and of God. No, "look up" by itself would be no help at all.

But to look up to him, to Jesus Christ—this is our help! He is over us. He is in the centre of that encompassing mystery. He is in heaven. Who is Jesus Christ? He is the man in whom God has not only expressed his love, not only painted it on the wall, but put it to work. He is the principal actor who has taken upon himself and has overcome our human affliction, the injustice done by ourselves and by everybody else, our guilt and anxiety, our fate, even our death. These evils no longer threaten us from above. They are below us, even under our feet. He is the Son of God, who was made man in our likeness, who became our brother, in order that we may be with him children of the Father, that we may all be reunited with God and may share in his blessings: in his severe kindness and in his kind severity, and lastly in the eternal life for which we are meant and which is meant for us. This Jesus Christ, this mighty man, this Son of God is in heaven. And so is God. In the face of the Son the face of the heavenly Father is made to shine.

"Look up to *him!*" This means: Let him be who he is, above us, in heaven. Acknowledge and believe that he is up there and lives for us! Keep firmly in mind that he intervenes with all his power in your behalf, but keep firmly in mind also that you belong to him and not to yourselves. Say very simply "yes." Say that he is right and wants to make things right for you, indeed has already made them right for us all. Is this an exaggerated claim? Has he really made things right for all of us? Even for the most miserable, the most afflicted and the most embittered of human beings? Yes! Even for the most grievous offenders? Yes! Even for the godless—or those pretending to be godless, as may be the case with some of your fellow-prisoners who declined to be with us this morning? Yes! Jesus Christ has made things right for them and for us all. He is willing to do it time and again. To look up to Jesus Christ means to accept his righteousness and to be content; not to question any more that he is right. This is the message of the Ascension: we are invited to look up to him, to this Jesus Christ, or, to use a more familiar expression, to believe in him.

"Look up to him *and your face will shine!*" What an announcement! What a promise and assurance! People, very ordinary human beings, with illumined faces! Not angels in heaven, but men and women on earth! Not some lucky inhabitants of a beautiful island far away, but people here in Basel, here in this house! Not some very special people among us, but each and every one of us! Might this be the true meaning of promise? Yes, this is the true meaning. But is this the only real meaning? Yes, this is the only real meaning. Look up to him, and your face will shine!

When a man, any one of us, obeys this imperative and looks up to him, to Jesus Christ, a momentous change takes place in him. The greatest revolution is unimportant by comparison. The transformation cannot be overlooked. It is manifest, quite simply, in so much as he who looks up to him and believes in him, here on earth, here in Basel, here in this house, may become a child of God. It is an inward change, yet it cannot possibly remain hidden. As soon as it occurs, it presses forcefully for outward manifestation. A great and enduring light brightly dawns on such a person. This light is reflected on his face, in his eyes, in his behaviour, in his words and deeds. Such a person experiences joy in the midst of his sorrows and sufferings, much as he still may sigh and grumble. Not a cheap and superficial joy that passes, but deep-seated, lasting joy. It transforms man in his sadness into a fundamentally joyful being. We may as well admit it: he has got something to laugh at, and he just cannot help laughing, even though he does not feel like it. His laughter is not bad, but good, not a mockery, but an open and relaxing laughter, not a diplomatic gesture as has recently become so fashionable in politics, but honest and sincere laughter, coming from the bottom of man's heart. Such light and joy and laughter are ours when we look up to him, to Jesus Christ. He is the one who makes us radiant. We ourselves cannot put on bright faces. But neither can we prevent them from shining. Looking up to him, our faces shine.

Dear brothers and sisters, why is it then that our faces are not bright? If they were, we would feel fine, would be glad to live uprightly and contentedly in spite of adversities, wouldn't we? Just because we would feel fine, we would be radiant. But something more important has to be considered here. If the light, the joy and the laughter of God's children really pressed for outward manifestation and became visible, our fellowmen around us would notice it in the first place. Don't you agree with me that such a change would make a quite definite impact on them? It would be a sign that there are different and far better things in store than they are wont to see. It would give them confidence, courage and hope. They would be relieved, as we have been relieved this last week by the sun after a long winter. Why relieved? Because such a bright face would be the reflection of heaven on earth, of Jesus Christ, of God the Father himself. What a relief that light would be for them and for us! Do we not all together long for its appearance?

We should get the simple truth straight, dear friends. We are in the world not to comfort ourselves, but to comfort others. Yet the one and only genuine comfort we may offer to our fellowmen is this reflection of heaven, of Jesus Christ, of God himself, as it appears on a radiant face. Why don't we do it? Why do we withhold from them the one comfort of mutual benefit? Why are the faces we show each other at best superior looking, serious, questioning, sorrowful and reproachful faces, at worst even grimaces or lifeless masks, real carnival masks? Why don't our faces shine?

Let me say only one thing here. It could easily be otherwise. We could greet each other with bright faces! We could comfort each other. We, here, today! Where the Spirit of the Lord is, there is freedom for man to comfort his neighbour. "He who believes in me," says Jesus Christ himself in another Scripture passage, "out of his heart shall flow rivers of living water." This happens when we look up to him. No one has ever looked up to him without this miracle happening. No one who gets slowly used to looking up to him has failed to glimpse light around him. The dark earth on which we live has always become bright whenever man looked up to him, and believed in him.

"Look up to him, your face will shine, *and you shall never be ashamed.*" I just mentioned the "dark" earth. Reading the newspapers, looking around at the world and into our own hearts and lives, we can't possibly deny that the earth is really dark, that we live in a world to be afraid in. Why afraid? Because we all live under the threat of being put to shame, and rightly so. This would not only imply that we have blundered here and there, but that our whole life, with all our thoughts, desires and accomplishments, might be in truth, in God's judgment and verdict, a failure, an infamy, a total loss. This is the great threat. This is why the ground shakes under our feet, the sky is covered with clouds, and the earth, so beautifully created, darkens. Indeed we should be put to shame.

But now we hear the very opposite. "You shall never be ashamed." What I would like to do, dear brothers and sisters, is to ask you, each and all, to get up together and like a choir repeat: "We must never be ashamed!" Each one would have to repeat it for himself and lastly I would repeat it for myself: "I must never be ashamed!" This is what counts. We shall not be, I shall not be ashamed, not when looking up to him. Not because we deserve to be spared the shame! Not even because our faces shine when raised to him. Our radiance will be and must be a sign that we will not be put to shame. It is an evidence of the relationship established between God and ourselves. And this is the power of the relationship: What is true and valid in heaven, what Jesus Christ has done for us, what has been accomplished by him, man's redemption, justification and preservation, is true and valid on earth also. The Father does not put us, his children, to shame when we look up to Jesus. In consequence we, his children, may never be ashamed. This we may know, this may be our strength, this may be our life, if only we look up to him, fearlessly and rightly. May each one repeat in his heart: "Bless the Lord, O my soul; and all that is within me, bless his holy name! Bless the Lord, O my soul, and forget not all his benefits, who forgives your iniquity, who heals all your diseases, who redeems your life from the Pit, who crowns you with steadfast love and mercy." [RSV] With these words let us go to the Lord's Supper. Amen.

FREDERICK BUECHNER

The Hungering Dark

*O that thou wouldst rend the heavens and come
  down,
that the mountains might quake at thy presence—
as when fire kindles brushwood and the fire
  causes water to boil—
to make thy name known to thy adversaries,
and that the nations might tremble at   thy
  presence! . . .
There is no one that calls upon thy name,
  that bestirs himself to take hold of thee;
for thou hast hid thy face from us,
  and hast delivered us into the hand of our
iniquities.*—Isaiah 64:1-2, 7 RSV

*And there will be signs in sun and moon and
stars, and upon the earth distress of nations in
perplexity at the roaring of the sea and the waves,
men fainting with fear and with foreboding of what
is coming on the world; for the powers of the heavens
will be shaken. And then they will see the Son of
man coming in a cloud with power and great glory.
Now when these things begin to take place, look up
and raise your heads, because your redemption is
drawing near.*   —Luke 21:25-28 RSV

About twenty years ago I was in Rome at Christmastime, and
on Christmas Eve I went to St. Peter's to see the Pope
celebrate mass. It happened also to be the end of Holy Year,
and there were thousands of pilgrims from all over Europe who
started arriving hours ahead of when the mass was supposed to

begin so that they would be sure to find a good place to watch from, and it was not long before the whole enormous church was filled. I am sure that we did not look like a particularly religious crowd. We were milling around, thousands of us, elbowing each other out of the way to get as near as possible to the papal altar with its huge canopy of gilded bronze and to the aisle that was roped off for the Pope to come down. Some had brought food to sustain them through the long wait, and every once in a while singing would break out like brush fire—"Adeste Fidelis" and "Heilige Nacht" I remember especially because everybody seemed to know the Latin words to one and the German words to the other—and the singing would billow up into the great Michelangelo dome and then fade away until somebody somewhere started it up again. Whatever sense anybody might have had of its being a holy time and a holy place was swallowed up by the sheer spectacle of it—the countless voices and candles, and the marble faces of saints and apostles, and the hiss and shuffle of feet on the acres of mosaic.

Then finally, after several hours of waiting, there was suddenly a hush, and way off in the flickering distance I could see that the Swiss Guard had entered with the golden throne on their shoulders, and the crowds pressed in toward the aisle, and in a burst of cheering the procession began to work its slow way forward.

What I remember most clearly, of course, is the Pope himself, Pius XII as he was then. In all that Renaissance of splendor with the Swiss Guard in their scarlet and gold, the Pope himself was vested in plainest white with only a white skullcap on the back of his head. I can see his face as he was carried by me on his throne—that lean, ascetic face, gray-skinned, with the high-bridged beak of a nose, his glasses glittering in the candlelight. And as he passed by me he was leaning slightly forward and peering into the crowd with extraordinary intensity.

Through the thick lenses of his glasses his eyes were larger than life, and he peered into my face and into all the faces around me and behind me with a look so keen and so charged that I could not escape the feeling that he must be looking for someone in particular. He was not a potentate nodding and smiling to acknowledge the enthusiasm of the multitudes. He was a man whose face seemed gray with waiting, whose eyes seemed huge and exhausted with searching, for someone, some *one*, who he thought might be there that night or any night, anywhere, but whom he had never found, and yet he kept looking. Face after face he searched for the face that he knew he would know—was it this one? was it this one? or this one?—and then he passed on out of my sight. It was a powerful moment for me, a moment that many other things have crystallized about since, and I have felt that I knew whom he was looking for. I felt that anyone else who was really watching must also have known.

And the cry of Isaiah, "O that thou wouldst rend the heavens and come down, that the mountains would quake at thy presence . . . that the nations might tremble at thy presence! . . . There is no one that calls upon thy name, that bestirs himself to take hold of thee; for thou hast hid thy face from us, and hast delivered us into the hand of our iniquities."

In one sense, of course, the face was not hidden, and as the old Pope surely knew, the one he was looking for so hard was at that very moment crouched in some doorway against the night or leading home some raging Roman drunk or waiting for the mass to be over so he could come in with his pail and his mop to start cleaning up that holy mess. The old Pope surely knew that the one he was looking for was all around him there in St. Peter's. The face that he was looking for was visible, however dimly, in the faces of all of us who had come there that night mostly, perhaps, because it was the biggest show in Rome just then and did not cost a cent but also because we were looking for the same one he was looking for, even though, as Isaiah said, there were few of us with wit enough to call upon his name. The one we were looking for was there then as he is here now because he haunts the world, and as the years have gone by since that Christmas Eve, I think he has come to haunt us more and more until there is scarcely a place any longer where, recognized or unrecognized, his ghost has not been seen. It may well be a post-Christian age that we are living in, but I cannot think of an age that in its own way has looked with more wistfulness and fervor toward the ghost at least of Christ.

God knows we are a long way from the brotherhood of man, and any theory that little by little we are approaching the brotherhood of man has to reckon that it was out of the Germany of Goethe and Brahms and Tillich that Dachau and Belsen came and that it is out of our own culture that the weapons of doom have come and the burning children. Yet more and more, I think, although we continue to destroy each other, we find it harder to hate each other.

Maybe it is because we have seen too much, literally *seen* too much, with all the ugliness and pain of our destroying flickering away on the blue screens across the land—the bombings and the riots, the nightmare in Dallas, the funeral in Atlanta. Maybe it is because having no cause holy enough to die for means also having no cause holy enough to hate for. But also I think that is because as men we have tried it so long our own grim way that maybe we are readier than we have ever been before to try it the way that is Christ's—whether we call upon his name or not.

Out there beyond this world there are more worlds and beyond them more worlds still, and maybe on none of them is there anything that we would call life, only barrenness, emptiness, silence. But here in this world there is life, we are life, and we begin to see, I think, that negatively, maybe nothing is worth the crippling and grieving of life. We begin to see that, positively, maybe everything glad and human and true and with any beauty in it depends on cherishing life, on breathing more life into this life that we are. However uncertainly and ambiguously, something at least in the world seems to be moving that way. I cannot believe that it is just fear of the bomb that has kept us as long as this from a third world war, or that it is just prudence and political pressure that slowly and painfully move the races and the nations to where they can at least begin to hear all the guilt and fear that have kept them apart for so long. I cannot believe that it is just a fad that young men in beards and sandals refuse in the name of love to bear arms or that it is entirely a joke that, with Allen Ginsberg and Humphrey Bogart, Jesus of Nazareth is postered on under-graduate walls. Call it what you will, I believe that something is stirring in the hearts of men to which the very turbulence of our times bears witness. It is as if the moral and spiritual struggle that has always gone on privately in the consciences of the conscientious has exploded into the open with force enough to shake history itself no less than our private inner histories.

Maybe it will shake us to pieces, maybe it has come too late, but at least I believe that there are many in the world who have learned what I for one simply did not know twenty years ago in Rome: that wherever you look beneath another's face to his deepest needs to be known and healed, you have seen the Christ in him; that wherever you have looked to the deepest needs beneath your own face—among them the need to know and to heal—you have seen the Christ in yourself. And if this is what we have seen, then we have seen much, and if this is what the old Pope found as he was carried through the shadow and shimmer of his church, then he found much. Except that I have the feeling that he was looking for more, that in the teeming mystery of that place he was looking not just for the Christ in men but for the Christ himself, the one who promised that the son of man would come again in a cloud with power and great glory.

"There will be signs in sun and moon and stars," he said, "and upon the earth distress of nations in perplexity at the roaring of the sea and the waves, men fainting with fear and with foreboding," and then, at just such a time, we are tempted to say, as our own time, "look up and raise your heads," he said, "because your redemption is drawing near." And the words of Jesus are mild compared with the words of a later generation. The Son of Man with face and hair as white as snow and eyes of fire, the two-edged sword issuing from his mouth. The last great battle with the armies of heaven arrayed in white linen, and the beast thrown into the lake of fire so that the judgment can take place and the thousand years of peace. Then the heavenly city, New Jerusalem, coming down out of heaven like a bride adorned for her husband, and the great voice saying "Behold. . . ." The New Testament ends, of course, with the words, "Come Lord Jesus," come again, come back and inaugurate these mighty works, and I always remember a sign that I used to pass by in Spanish-speaking East Harlem that said simply, "Pronto viene, Jesus Cristo."

Surely there is no part of New Testament faith more alien to our age than this doctrine of a second coming, this dream of holiness returning in majesty to a world where for centuries holiness has shone no brighter than in the lines of a certain kind of suffering on faces like yours and mine. Partly, I suppose, it is alien because of the grotesque, Hebraic images it is clothed in. Partly too, I suppose, it is alien to us because we have come to associate it so closely with the lunatic fringe—the millennial sects climbing to the tops of hills in their white robes to wait for the end of the world that never comes, knocking at the backdoor to hand out their tracts and ask if we have been washed in the blood of the lamb.

But beneath the language that they are written in and the cranks that they have produced, if cranks they are, I suspect that what our age finds most alien in these prophecies of a second coming, a final judgment and redemption of the world, is their passionate hopefulness. "Faith, hope, love," Paul wrote, "these three—and the greatest of these is love," and yes, love. We understand at last something about love. Even as nations we have come to understand at last something about love, at least as a practical necessity, a final expedient, if nothing else. We understand a little that if we do not feed the hungry and clothe the naked of the world, if as nations, as races, we do not join forces against war and disease and poverty in something that looks at least like love, then the world is doomed. God knows we are not very good at it, and we may still blow ourselves sky high before we are through, but at least maybe we have begun as a civilization to see what it is all about. And just because we have seen it, if only through a glass, darkly, just because maybe love is not so hard to sell the world as once it was, perhaps Paul would have written for us: "Love, yes, of course, love. But for you and your time, the greatest of these is hope because now it is hope that is hardest and rarest among men."

We have our hopes of course. This election year especially, jaded as you get after a while, the hope that out of all these faces that we come to know like the faces of importunate friends there will emerge a face to trust. The hope that if the lives of a Gandhi, a Martin Luther King, cannot transform our hearts, then maybe at least their deaths will break our hearts, break them enough to let a little of their humanity in. The hope that even if real peace does not come to the world, at least the worst of the killing will stop. The hope that as individuals, that you as you and me as me, will somehow win at least a stalemate against the inertias, the lusts, the muffled cruelties and deceits that we do battle with, all of us, all the time. The hope that by some chance today I will see a friend, that by some grace today I will be a friend. These familiar old hopes. No one of them is enough to get us out of bed in the morning but maybe together they are, must be, because we do get out of bed in the morning, we survive the night.

There is a Hebrew word for hope, *gāwāh*, whose root means to twist, to twine, and it is a word that seems to fit our brand of hoping well. The possibility that this good thing will happen and that that bad thing will not happen, a hundred little strands of hope that we twist together to make a cable of hope strong enough to pull ourselves along through our lives with. But we hope so much only for what it is reasonable to hope for out of the various human possibilities before us that even if we were to play a child's game and ask what do we hope for most in all the world, I suspect that our most extravagant answers would not be very extravagant. And this is the way of prudence certainly because to hope for more than the possible is to court despair. To hope for more than the possible is to risk becoming the ones who wait, helpless and irrelevant in their white robes, for a deliverance that never comes. To hope for more than the possible is a kind of madness.

For people like us, the reasonably thoughtful, reasonably reasonable and realistic people like us, this apocalyptic hope for the more than possible is too hopeful. We cannot hope such a fantastic hope any more, at least not quite, not often. It is dead for us, and we have tried to fill the empty place it left with smaller, saner hopes that the worst possibilities will never happen and that a few of the better possibilities may happen yet. And all these hopes twisted together do make hope enough to live by, hope enough to see a little way into the darkness by. But the empty place where the great hope used to be is mostly empty still, and the darkness hungers still for the great light that has gone out, the crazy dream of holiness coming down out of heaven like a bride adorned for us.

We cannot hope that hope any more because it is too fantastic for us, but maybe if in some dim, vestigial way we are Christians enough still to believe in mystery, maybe if beneath all our sad wisdom there is some little gibbering of madness left, then maybe we are called to be in some measure fantastic ourselves, to say at least maybe to the possibility of the impossible. When Jesus says that even as the world writhes in what may well be its final agony, we must raise our heads and look up because our redemption is near, maybe we are called upon to say not yes, because yes is too much for us, but to say maybe, maybe, because maybe is the most that hope can ever say. Maybe it will come, come again, come pronto. Pronto viene, Jesus Cristo.

Where do they come from, the Christs, the Buddhas? The villains we can always explain by the tragic conditions that produced them—the Hitlers, the Oswalds—but the births of the holy ones are in a way always miraculous births, and when they come, they move like strangers through the world. History does not produce holiness, I think. Saints do not evolve. If we cannot believe in God as a noun, maybe we can still believe in God as a verb. And the verb that God is, is transitive, it takes an object, and the object of the verb that God is, is the world. To love, to judge, to heal, to give Christs to. The world. The thousand thousand worlds.

Certainly a Christian must speak to the world in the language of the world. He must make the noblest causes of the world his causes and fight for justice and peace with the world's weapons—with Xerox machines and demonstrations and social action. He must reach out in something like love to what he can see of Christ in every man. But I think he must also be willing to be fantastic, or fantastic in other ways too, because at its heart religious faith is fantastic. Because Christ himself was fantastic with his hair every whichway and smelling of fish and looking probably a lot more like Groucho Marx than like Billy Budd as he stood there with his ugly death already thick as flies about him and said to raise our heads, raise our heads for Christ's sake, because our redemption is near.

Maybe holiness will come again. Maybe not as the Son of Man with eyes of fire and a two-edged sword in his mouth, but as a child who had maybe already been born into our world and beneath whose face the face of Christ is at this moment starting to burn through like the moon through clouds. Or if even that is too supernatural for us, maybe it will come in majesty from some other world because we have begun to take seriously the fantastic thought that maybe we are not alone in the universe.

Who knows what will happen? Except that in a world without God, in a way we do know. In a world without God we know at least that the thing that will happen will be a human thing, a thing no better and no worse than the most that humanity itself can be. But in a world with God, we can never know what will happen—maybe that is the most that the second coming can mean for our time—because the thing that happens then is God's thing, and that is to say a new and unimaginable and holy thing that humanity can guess at only in its wildest dreams. In a world with God, we come together in a church to celebrate, among other things, a mystery and to learn from, among other things, our ancient and discredited dreams.

It is madness to hope such a hope in our grim and sober times, madness to peer beyond the possibilities of history for the impossibilities of God. And there was madness among other things in the face of the old Pope that gaudy night with Hitler's Jews on his conscience maybe and whatever he died of already on its way to killing him. There was anxiety in his face, if I read it right, and weariness, and longing, longing. And to this extent his face was like your face and my face, and I would have had no cause to remember it so long. But there was also madness in that old man's face, I think. Like a monkey, his eyes were too big, too alive, too human for his face. And it is the madness that has haunted me through the years. Madness because I suspect that he hoped that Christ himself had come back that night as more than just the deepest humanness of every man's humanity, that Impossibility itself stood there resplendent in that impossible place.

He was not there, he had not come back, and as far as I know he has not come back yet. It is fantastic, of course, to think that he might, but that should not bother too much the likes of us. It is fantastic enough just that preachers should stand up in their black gowns making fools of themselves when they could be home reading the papers where only their children need know they are fools. It is fantastic that people should listen to them. It is fantastic that in a world like ours there should be something in us still that says at least maybe, maybe, to the fantastic possibility of God at all.

So in Christ's name, I commend this madness and this fantastic hope that the future belongs to God no less than the past, that in some way we cannot imagine holiness will return to our world. I know of no time when the world has been riper for its return, when the dark has been hungrier. Thy kingdom come . . . we do shew forth the Lord's death till he come . . . and maybe the very madness of our hoping will give him the crazy, golden wings he needs to come on. I pray that he will come again and that you will make it your prayer. We need him, God knows.

"He who testifies to these things says, 'Surely I am coming soon.' Amen. Come, Lord Jesus!" [RSV]

Lord Jesus Christ,
Help us not to fall in love with the night that covers us but through the darkness to watch for you as well as to work for you; to dream and hunger in the dark for the light of you. Help

us to know that the madness of God is saner than men and that nothing that God has wrought in this world was ever possible.

Give us back the great hope again that the future is yours, that not even the world can hide you from us forever, that at the end the One who came will come back in power to work joy in us stronger even than death. *Amen.*

GEORGE A. BUTTRICK

Is It the Golden Rule?

Whatever you wish that men would do to you, do so to them.—Matthew 7:12 RSV

How often have you heard people say, "My religion is the Golden Rule"? Sometimes they speak with a superior air as if to tell us that there is no need for the Church, the Hallelujah Chorus, or even for the agonized prayer of Christ in Gethsemane. No, religion has been brought to one clear beam of light: "My religion is the Golden Rule." No need for deep thoughts about God (which these men are apt to call "the hair-splitting of theology"), or about the enigma of pain, or about life after death, much less about sin and forgiveness, for, "My religion is the Golden Rule." What do you think about that kind of "religion"? I suppose it is better than, "My religion is to get all I can get," but it is not likely to suffer from brain-fever from too much thinking. Some one of these all-too-confident men will say, "My physics is H_2O." So what about the Golden Rule?

I

Maybe the Rule of itself is blind, until . . . It cannot mean "whatever" we wish. The context denies us that interpretation. Suppose a man wishes to be invited to all the neighboring cocktail parties. All right: he throws a superduper cocktail party and invites the whole neighborhood. Has he therefore done to others as he wishes them to do to him? Yes, literally; no, actually, for on his basis the Rule can mean trade for trade, or even lust for lust. "Whatever you wish" means "whatever you should wish" or "whatever you may wisely wish." It cries aloud for some standard of wishing. If we were in jail or in shame or in sorrow, what would we wish from others? So when we wrench the Rule away from the Bible, it is *blind* unless and until . . .

Why do we credit the Rule to Christ? Confucius spoke it some centuries before Christ, and Hillel the famous rabbi spoke it a generation earlier than Christ, and the Stoic philosopher Epictetus a generation later than Christ. These latter gave it negative form: "Whatever you wouldn't wish," et cetera. Then why credit the Rule to Christ? Not alone because he gave it positive form, though that change is important, but because in himself he gave us a norm for wishing. For what should we wish? For what do we deeply wish? Not for *cash*. That is necessary, but if it is our central wish we become as hard as the coins we hoard. Not for *fame:* it is a flashlight bulb. Not for *peace of mind:* we wonder how that wretched heresy found its way into the Church, for Christ himself had little peace of mind, because of the trouble we caused him. Of course he did have the *peace of God*, but that is another item!

Do we deeply wish the peace of God? How do we get it? We don't get it. We *will* to do evil, even though we will to do good. How can a cleft will contrive its own unity, or a cripple turn handsprings in the back garden? Now we are asking, "What is God like? Does he care about us? Is he like Christ?" Now we are deep in theology. Now we have gone far beyond the Golden Rule, which of itself is blind until the Lord Christ gives it light.

II

Once again, the Golden Rule is a grievous burden of itself, unless and until . . . Now where does our simplistic man stand? He doesn't: he falls. Has anybody kept the Golden Rule for even half a day? All right: the Rule convicts us. As a matter of fact we do not keep even the Ten Commandments. "Thou shalt not covet," but none of us will reach sundown today without some coveting. "Thou shalt not kill," but there is slow killing and swift killing, and we may ask in a restaurant, "Who is our waiter?" and, if we have hardly noticed him, isn't indifference to our neighbor a slow way of killing him? What shall we do now? What can we do? We have blood on our hands.

In preaching class one of my students took as a topic, "Can we keep the Golden Rule?" His answer was a confident, "Yes, for the Rule is quite clear, as clear as the sign in the park: 'Keep off the grass': we can keep off or we can trespass." Well, a sermon is a piece of a man's life, so I didn't take issue with him before his classmates. But I did speak to him privately after class. I did not confess to him that the sign in the park always makes me wish to walk on the grass, but I did say, "Son, I haven't really kept the Rule for one hour. How about you?" A certain gasoline station calls itself The Golden Rule Station. That means fair measure for a fair price. Such trade is needed, for a recent survey showed that many gasoline pumps are "rigged." But the Golden Rule goes far beyond a mutual common honesty, though such honesty is far from common: it means my putting myself in my neighbor's place, and then and there treating him as I would wish to be treated.

So suppose I am a peasant in India living in a drought area? Suppose I am a Black in Mississippi? Suppose I am in the army in Vietnam, or in jail because for conscience' sake I refuse to go, what would Christ wish "others" to do, since he has given us a standard of wishing? Now the questions deepen. Can a mortal man rid himself of self-concern, especially in a nuclear age? There is a sharper question, namely, the whole issue of past failures. These are not "past": They are in the stream of history, like poison in a river from which all our neighbors drink. . . . No man can cleanse history, or even his own memory. The Golden Rule is burden indeed, the whole burden of man's transgression! Unless . . .

Unless Christ gathers it in grace! He said, "Your sins are forgiven." Frequently in the Gospels the verb used is even more wonderful: "Your sins have already been and are now forgiven." Our faith is this: since God was in Christ's being raised from the dead, God was in Christ's dying on the cross. Doing what? Exposing himself in love to our transgressions, bearing them and bearing them away, as only he can! That is why a Gallows has crossed an ocean, and set itself in the chancel to bless our worship. That is why we raise a Gallows over the graves of our dead, an act which would be the world's worst repugnance unless . . . unless! Now where has the Golden Rule led us? To a profound doctrine of the Atonement! The Golden Rule of itself is a dark burden which no man can bear, until Christ gathers it in grace. So we mustn't be content to say, "My religion is the Golden Rule"!

III

We try once more: the Golden Rule of itself sets the teeth on edge, unless . . . Why? Not only because the Rule *of itself* gives us no power to keep the Rule, but because all rules tend to alienate us. A rule if it is wrongly understood may even provoke us to disobedience, as in the case of the small girl who turned on her mother with, "Don't say 'You must' to me. It makes me feel 'I won't all over.' " Once in an ethics class a group of students was asked this examination question among others: "What do *you* feel about the Sermon on the Mount?" A particularly bright lad wrote, when summarized, as follows: it is a counsel of perfection, and therefore it mocks our best endeavors, for its heaven is too high for our upreaching; so, since it tempts us either to self-righteousness (if we appallingly claim to keep it) or to despair (if we know we can't), it is a blunder or shame that it was ever spoken. Nothing wrong about that answer! Except the initial assumption! The Sermon on the Mount, which includes the Golden Rule, is not a counsel of perfection. Even if it were, it would not be misfortune: we cannot reach the sun, but it gives us light, warmth and power.

But the problem of its being a Rule still besets us. We can measure a man for a suit of clothes by means of a ruler, but we cannot or shouldn't so measure a man. Human beings have no right to command and compel one another, and the attempt nearly always provokes some sort of rebellion. Has Christ himself any such right? Would he ever claim it? He doesn't give us a manual of directives, as if we were junior executives or "hands" in some mammoth corporation. He doesn't bark at us as if he were our drill sergeant, and we were privates in his army. If he tried it, there would be little love lost—on either side. He said, "No longer do I call you servants . . . but I have called you friends." Again He said, "This is my commandment, that you love one another as I have loved you." Without that last phrase a commandment to love is a contradiction in terms. So an Indian chief when he first heard the Golden Rule said, "It is impossible. But if the Great Spirit who made man would give him a new heart, he might do as you say."

So imagine a floundering vessel. You and another man are the only two left on board, and there is only one vacancy in the lifeboats. The other man insists that you take that one chance at life. He says to you as the lifeboat pulls away, "Do as much for somebody else some day." That would be a command, yet not a command, for any seeming coercion would be lost in self-giving love. It would speak from *within* you, not simply from *outside* you. It would be *your own* wish, not simply the word of a neighbor. So with the commands of Christ: "We love because he first loved us." Therefore the Golden Rule no longer sets our teeth on edge, for Christ gathers it into our will and his power. We are no longer "under the law." His love provoking our glad love for him is "the fulfilling of the law."

That is why artist after artist tries to depict Christ, and why they all fail. The pictures are too mushy or too stern, too high above us or far-too-like ourselves. How do we know? Well, a German theologian has written that though we cannot know Jesus "there is no one whom we know half so well." How? By the gift of his Holy Spirit Whose presence and power are always beyond our best art in word, music or color. Once in awhile a picture seizes us, such as that which shows a Cross in the sky with Jesus looking down on our planet. There far below is a little boat drawn up on the beach, and children running along the sand. Yes, Jesus sees them. He sees our squirming politics, our sputnik journeys, our stuffy power-stript churches. He speaks. He doesn't say, "Keep the Golden Rule," but, "Do you love me?" The wonder is that despite our sins, and even though we fail him day by day, we can say with truth, "Lord, you know everything: you know that I love you." Thus the rule no longer sets our teeth on edge because in Christ it has won our hearts.

IV

So what about the Golden Rule? We have no right to lift it from its setting in what we call the Sermon on the Mount. The man who dismembered the scriptures into snippets called verses, thus ghoulishly cutting arms and legs into slices, was no benefactor. The Bible comes in creative paragraphs. There are no separated verses in the original manuscripts. Meanwhile we have no right to lift the Sermon on the Mount from the context of the whole Gospel. In Matthew there are five double panels set between Christmas on one side and Calvary and Easter on the other side. The first half of each panel is narrative; the second is the living word from the lips of our Lord. So the Golden Rule (in the second half of the initial panel) is set between Christmas and Calvary-Easter. That is why it is blind without Christ, and burdensome without Christ. We should pity the simplistic man who dares to say, "My religion is the Golden Rule." Hasn't somebody warned us that we cannot explain astronomy by "Twinkle, twinkle, little star"?

If you wish to know how this poor sermon began, here is the occasion. I was speaking at a luncheon club, and arrived late because my plane was late. As I entered the room they were singing, "Tiptoe through the tulips." It was an unnerving experience from which I have never really recovered. The president of the club who, as I afterwards learned, had not troubled the church in many a moon, greeted me with, "Reverend, my religion is the Golden Rule." What could I answer? I was tempted to say, "I must be speaking to one of the cherubim," but refrained: I wouldn't want anyone to speak thus to me: I remembered the Golden Rule just in time. The next word that sprang to mind was, "Brother, you've bitten off far more than you can chew." But again the Golden Rule restrained me. So I settled for, "Fine, if you remember who spoke it." Then I went home and wrote this attempt at a sermon.

We must not pick and choose among the kindling words of Christ except to say that there are other "rules" in our Gospel, such as, "This is my commandment that you love one another as I have loved you." In one version that last phrase almost begins a new sentence: "As I have loved you that you love one another." A lad was caught stealing from automobiles outside a church on Sunday morning. A well-meaning woman, who nevertheless had not learned of Christ, seeing him standing between two policemen, said, "Why don't you come inside and learn what is right." He replied, "Lady, I already know what is right." Did he? He did not know what is love, and she did not greatly help him to know. Do we ever know until we stand before the Cross remembering that its shadow falls on us by the light of the Resurrection? Yes, the Golden Rule is indeed the Golden Rule, but only because the Rule is held in the life and love of him who spoke it, who has said also: "Love one another as I have loved you." You will remember, won't you? Christ will always remember you!

ERNEST T. CAMPBELL

No Faith, No Church

Lord, I believe; help thou mine unbelief.
Mark 9:24

A man made his way to the southwest corner of 42nd Street and Fifth Avenue to visit the central building of the New York Public Library. He passed the sculptured lions that keep their vigil at the gates, climbed the marble stairs that would do a palace justice, walked between those two towering renaissance pillars and through the doors. He was ill-prepared for what he saw inside: Glass covered display cases, mounted stamp collections hanging from the walls, busts of notable benefactors, a store, rest-rooms, checkrooms, telephones, stairs and elevators. Finally, in a dark mood of rising desperation, he turned to a member of the staff and cried, "Where do they keep the books?"

To many outsiders, and not a few insiders, The Riverside Church must seem like a bewildering assortment of unrelated projects, causes and activities. What one is likely to see when she comes to The Riverside Church depends on the day and hour and the door through which she enters.

People can be forgiven for coming into this place, seeing its theatre and tower, its gymnasium and cafeteria, its parking facilities and radio station, its many halls and elevators and asking, "Where do they keep the faith?"

What books are to a library, faith is to a church. No books, no library! No faith, no church! Because it is expected that the first sermon of the new season will have a key-note quality about it, I have deliberately set aside a host of other options and chosen to speak to you today of faith.

* * *

Used by permission of Ernest T. Campbell.

The scriptures say some tall things about faith. "Without faith it is impossible to please God" (Heb. 11:6 RSV). "All things are possible to him who believes" (Mark 9:23). And perhaps most astoundingly of all, that sweeping word of St. Paul's, "Whatsoever is not of faith is sin" (Rom. 14:23). We are told in the Bible that faith can move mountains. It can set a man straight with God. If can generate enormous reserves of hope and love.

How shall we define this elusive desirable, this critical quality called faith? The writer of Hebrews defined it as, "The assurance of things hoped for, the conviction of things not seen" (Heb. 11:1 RSV). John Calvin defined it as "a steady and certain knowledge of the divine benevolence towards us, which being founded on the truth of the gratuitous promise in Christ is both revealed to our minds and confirmed to our hearts by the Holy Spirit." Gerhard Ebeling, a contemporary German theologian, says simply, "Faith is man's participation in God."

Defined in these or similar ways, it is no exaggeration to say that without faith, whatever else a church may have, it is nothing. Yes, without faith it is impossible *even for a church* to please God.

* * *

Let me move on now to make and amplify three statements about faith. Faith is always mixed with doubt. Faith is always tied to life. Faith's chief resource is Jesus.

Faith is always mixed with doubt. Faith and doubt are nourished by the same inner energies. They are, as it were, two sides of the same coin. Only man who doubts can believe and only the man who believes can doubt. The scripture read today bears this out (Mark 9:14-29). Jesus and the "A" team, Peter, James and John, had gone up into the mountain of Transfiguration in the north country near Caesarea Philippi. Meanwhile, the "B" team, the remaining nine, on the flats below, were approached by a man who wanted healing for his epileptic son. The truth of the matter is that neither team fared well. As Hillyer Straton has put it, "One group of disciples did not know what to do on the mount, and the others were powerless to help in the valley."

Presently, Jesus came down from the mountain with the three disciples and and confronted the distraught father. The lad's condition was pitiable indeed. He had all the symptoms of

genuine epilepsy; spasms, foaming at the mouth, grinding of
the teeth, and motionless stupors. As Jesus faced the anxious
father, a soul-stirring dialogue ensued. Jesus asked the father,
"How long has he had this?" The father replied, "From
childhood . . . but if you can do anything, have pity and help
us." Jesus responded with some vehemence, "If you *can?*" A
leper, you will remember, had said to Jesus, "Lord, if you *will,*
you can make me clean" (Mark 1:40). Here, "if you can," is the
best the father can do. Jesus answered, "If you can? All things
are possible to him who believes." Immediately the father came
back with one of the most honest confessions to be found
anywhere in literature; "Lord, I believe; help Thou mine
unbelief."

There is the mix: "Lord, I believe; help thou mine unbelief."
We have here not one man saying, "Lord, I believe," and
another saying, "Help thou mine unbelief," but one and the
same man saying both. Faith and doubt are inseparable.
Wherever you find the one you are bound to find the other.

* * *

The second statement: Faith is always tied to life. History is
the sphere in which faith operates. The habitat of faith is time
and place. It is only as life interrogates us that we know *what*
we believe and *how deeply* we believe it. Indeed, it is only as life
interrogates us that we discover the need to believe.

It is not the case, then, that we get our faith all worked out
intellectually—perhaps in college, perhaps in a seminary,
perhaps in our own homes—and then go out to apply what we
have put together in life situations.

The structure of St. Paul's epistles is misleading at this point.
The apostle first formulated his convictions and then connected
them to life. This was the way Paul *expressed* his faith, but this
was not the way the apostle *got* his faith! He got it as he went.
To put it aphoristically, "You know as you go."

I had an interesting conversation with a young man this
summer around the shore of Lake Junaluska in North Carolina.
He is a choice young man who has finished three years of
college. His father is one of the abler preachers in the South. He
comes from a solid home where he is much loved and well
supported. He is flirting with the ministry but going through
what he described as a mild crisis of faith. As we walked

together, he confessed to this void in his life. "I'm not sure that I believe."

Suddenly it occurred to me to ask this attractive young man one question. Speaking in love and out of genuine concern I said: "What would you do with more faith now if you had it?" I went on to suggest that he really had few needs at present that required faith. His father and mother are financing his college life. He has a faculty that cares about him. He has a home to go back to. All things are being provided for him. "What would you do with more faith now if you had it? What do you need more faith for anyway?"

If I understand the Bible correctly, there is an economy with God regarding the gift of faith. It is only as we attempt great things for God that we can expect great things from God. If we are content to play the "money game" or the "status game" or the "pleasure game," we don't need faith for that! If we are playing "nine to five 'till 65 and then away," we don't need faith for that! But if we are trying to move some mountain of unbelief, apathy, prejudice, injustice, or hatred, it is then that God will give us faith. We know as we go. If we will not go we will not know.

A friend of mine was giving a series of lectures at an institution many miles from here. This man is known as much for his honesty as for his erudition and eloquence. It was his candor that prompted him to end his last lecture something like this, "I'd have more to say to you on this subject if I were clearer on the resurrection. But right now, frankly, I don't believe it." Later a colleague on the host faculty reprimanded him: "You shouldn't have said that. Where did you ever get the idea that you had to believe everything all the time?" He went on, "When you have to believe in the resurrection, you will." My friend said, "When will I believe it?" His host replied, "When you die, or when you die with someone else."

Job did not know how deeply he believed until his wife advised him to curse God and die. Under the provocation of that option, he found it in his soul to say, "Though he slay me, yet will I trust him" (Job 13:15). Faith is tied to life.

* * *

Finally, this word: Faith's chief resource is Jesus. To talk of faith in Christian circles is to talk of Jesus. We commonly think of Jesus as an *object* of our faith. And he is that, indeed. But he is also for us the *source* of faith. We believe *in* him but we also believe *through* him and *like* him.

The question that ministers face as they contemplate the paucity of faith in themselves and in their congregation is, "How is faith generated?" Only too well we know how unbelief and pessimism are generated. But what is it that generates faith? The answer, I believe, is that Jesus is the primary source of faith.

May I remind you that the predominant characteristic of Jesus was his consciousness of God. Virtually all of the critics are agreed on this. From first to last, in shine and shadow, Jesus was conscious of God.

Form critics have worked the gospels over time and time again. These scholars are generally agreed that at least three aspects of the gospel tradition are traceable directly to Jesus. What are these? They are the parables, the teachings about the Kingdom of God, and the Lord's Prayer. The outstanding characteristic of the parables, the teaching on the Kingdom of God, and the Lord's Prayer is Jesus' assumption that God is real and active.

As we draw near to Jesus we find that his basic trust in God is contagious. When we hang around some people we find ourselves drifting into dirty speech. When we hang around some other people, we find ourselves laughing more. When we hang around still other people, we tend to become cynical. *But when we begin to keep company with Jesus we start to believe.*

Jesus brings us to faith. He is faith's most reliable witness and most convincing spokesman. His life awakens faith. He inspires us to doubt our doubts and believe our beliefs. He provokes the questions that induce and evoke faith.

Faith, then, does not come by exhortation. It comes through exposure to Jesus who is the source of faith. This is why it is important for us to read the scriptures and avail ourselves of the sacraments, to sense His presence in other people, and to be open to His spirit in the world around us.

* * *

We are familiar with the term "identity crisis." Teenagers rebel, we are told, in part because they want to know who they are. Black separatism is a strategy by which America's largest minority may come to know itself in terms other than those imposed by a white majority. A woman who gives up a career in order to marry and have a home will begin to ask herself again, "Who am I?"

The church is caught in an identity crisis today. Who are we anyway, we whose work in so many ways and places is duplicated by others? Why are we here?

I am proposing in this key-note message that we are in essence those who believe in God through Jesus Christ. At bottom, we are what Paul called us in a remarkably felicitous phrase, "the household of faith" (Gal. 6:10). *It is our faith that constitutes us as Christian.* The richness of Riverside is its people. The richness of its people is their faith.

It is my judgment that we cannot do much for others, or for long, until we know who we are. The activist is right! We can't have what we will not implement. But it is also true that we cannot implement what we do not have!

The church is more than the sum of its parts. But we must not forget that the faith of a given congregation rests ultimately on the faith of its members in particular. Most of us shy away from what Karl Barth described as "I Hymns" and "I Piety." But Barth was wise in reminding us that our criticism of "I Hymns" and "I Piety" must always be relative and never absolute, for running through the scriptures are those attestations of faith in the first person: "The Lord is *my* Shepherd." "This one thing *I* do." "He loved *me,* and gave himself for *me.*"

Those who love this church can do nothing more or better for it now than to look to their faith. How is it with you and your faith? Do you prize your faith for the treasure that it is? Do you expose yourself to Jesus for the growth and enlargement of your faith? "Lord, I believe; help thou mine unbelief." Let this be our prayer.

JAMES T. CLELAND

The Unattractiveness of Jesus

When I was a boy in Glasgow, there hung in our living room a large print of a painting by Sigismund Goetze, entitled "Despised and Rejected." I know nothing about the artist. I know nothing about the merits of the painting. But I have never forgotten the picture. In the center was the Christ bound to a Roman Imperial altar, overshadowed by an angel with the Gethsemane Cup. On each side of the altar there streamed by a procession of men and women in modern dress. Here was the political agitator and there a common laborer; here a sportsman with the pink edition of the paper, there a scientist with his test tube. A newsboy shouted the latest society scandal and a woman went by in a widow's weeds. A soldier in uniform and a clergyman replete with clerical collar stalked by in unconscious company. Only one person had any look of surprise or wonder or sympathy for the Christ—a nurse.

What is the picture saying? For the artist, Christ is still "despised and rejected" by most folk in the everyday, work-a-day world.

That is a little hard to believe. For example, think of the church that is named for him. Church membership in the United States has increased at a faster rate than the population since 1900. Congregations love such hymns and anthems as "Fairest Lord Jesus," "Jesus Shall Reign," "All Hail the Power of Jesus' Name." Books on Jesus are legion, and often bestsellers. Three brand new "lives" of Jesus have been published since the middle of 1949. And we thank God for the congregations and the hymns and the books.

Yet the other side of the picture is also true. "He is despised and rejected of men; a man of sorrows, and acquainted with grief. . . . He was despised, and we esteemed him not" (Isaiah 53:3). These words were not penned originally to apply to Jesus; but it was a wise early Christian, maybe Peter, who applied them to him. (It may have been an illegitimate use of Scripture, but it was effective.) For many Christians Jesus fulfills Isaiah 53. The "unattractiveness of Jesus" was and is a fact. It may be a deplorable fact, but it is an authentic fact. One summer several of us took refuge from the rain in the Episcopal Cathedral on the island of Cumbrae in Scotland. Noticing a crucifix on the altar, instead of a cross, one low churchman began to complain. He was silenced by the remark of another: "The crucifix is *the* symbol of our modern civilization." Not an empty cross; that is the symbol of the church's resurrection faith. But a crucifix; the symbol of what the world did and does to Jesus. Despised and rejected. A man of sorrows. Acquainted with grief. So very unattractive. Why?

One reason is familiarity. That is a danger constantly besetting folk like us, churchgoers. It is the temptation that the average Christian is open to. Familiarity may not always breed contempt, but it often breeds indifference. That is the risk Jesus runs with us. We hear about him so much that our appreciative sense is dulled, atrophied. We become numb and insensitive to the things that pertain to Christ. He is a name; a religious name; a Sunday name.

The routine of church lulls us into an apathy. That is partly the fault of the pulpit, as can be seen in this story told by Harold Cooke Phillips in his Yale Lectures on Preaching. A minister once recognized as the most regular attendant at the worship service a hard-working washerwoman who Sunday after Sunday was observed in her pew. He wanted to find the reason for such fidelity and so asked: "Is it that you enjoy the beautiful music?" "Na, it's no that." "Perhaps you enjoy my sermons?" "Na, it's no that." "Then what brings you here every week?" "Well, it's like this. I work hard a' week, and it's no often I get sic a comfortable sate wi sae little tae think aboot." (Harold Cooke Phillips: *Bearing Witness to the Truth,* pp. 156-7.)

Yes, that's partly the cause. The pulpit gives the pew so little to think about. But it is partly the fault of the pew. You don't expect anything unusual. Therefore, you settle down to "thole" the sermon, to plan next week's affairs, to doze. It's all just the old, old story. You've heard it since you were in Sunday School. You aren't particularly excited about what a six year old called "this Jesus stuff." That was true in Jesus' day. His own folk were not enthusiastic about his point of view. "A prophet is not without honor, save in his own country, and in his own house,"

(Matthew 13:56a) was Jesus' way of summing it up. "He's crazy" (Mark 3:21b). That was his family's judgment.

Of course, we wouldn't kill him, as the Roman and Jewish authorities did. We just accept him indifferently or semi-seriously. Studdert Kennedy was worried by that fact, and wrote a poem on it:

> When Jesus came to Golgotha they hanged him
>   on a tree,
> They drove great nails through hands and feet,
>   and made a Calvary;
> They crowned Him with a crown of thorns, red were
>   His wounds and deep,
> For those were crude and cruel days, and human
>   flesh was cheap.
>
> When Jesus came to Birmingham they simply
>   passed Him by,
> They never hurt a hair of Him, they only
>   let Him die;
> For men had grown more tender and they would not
>   give Him pain,
> They only just passed down the street, and left
>   Him in the rain.
>
> Still Jesus cried, "Forgive them, for they know not
>   what they do,"
> And still it rained the winter rain that drenched Him
>   through and through;
> The crowds went home and left the streets
>   without a soul to see,
> And Jesus crouched against a wall and cried
>   for Calvary.

What can we do about it? What is the remedy for this indifferent familiarity? Get to know him.

Read the Gospels. If we know the King James Version, then read other translations. Read them in a foreign language. We shall be shocked and shaken by the pungency of much we have never really heard before.

Read the lives of Jesus. There are all kinds: orthodox and heretical; literary and historical; fictitious and critical; Jewish and Christian; psychological studies and environmental studies. There must be one that interests you. That will lead you to another. There will be a chain reaction.

Read the plays about him: "Family Portrait," "Good Friday," "The Trail of Jesus," "The Man Born to Be King." That will replace familiarity with knowledge and appreciation and a sense of wonder.

There is another reason for the unattractiveness of Jesus: the intellectual problems that are interwoven with the Church's estimate of him. This is an inevitable difficulty for thinking young people. It is partly due to their mental age. We are in college where the intellect is, at least in theory, given the primacy. We are expected to think; we are even trained to think. Life is an intellectual puzzle to be solved by reason. Therefore, we doubt. That is one of the privileges of being a matriculated student. And the first result of thought is destruction. Plato described the young philosopher as a puppy dog tearing things to pieces. And religion stands the major shock of our onslaught.

And that is aided and abetted by the scholarly-critical approach to the Bible, to the books of which it is composed, to the history in which it is set, to the characters of its men and women. And Jesus does not escape.

Moreover, the language of the creeds in endeavoring to interpret him is for many of us out-of-date, incomprehensible, self-contradictory, and unintelligible. That is a common estimate. And it is not altogether wrong. Listen to Dr. Van Dusen of Union Seminary commenting on the Chalcedonian Formula of 451 A.D. in which a Council of the Church sought to express its reasoned opinion of Jesus the Christ:

It mirrors with fair accuracy what the church wanted to say, though in terms which could not successfully embody its faith. To the logical mind, it sounds like distilled nonsense. There the phrases stand, side by side, in all their seeming contradiction and glorious incredibility: "Perfect in deity and perfect in humanity" . . . "acknowledged in two natures, without confusion, without change, without division, without separation . . . not divided or separated into two persons by one and the same Son and only begotten God Logos, Lord Jesus Christ." It is as though the Fathers were determined to affirm their certainties at whatever humiliation to reason. (Henry P. Van Dusen: *Liberal Theology: an Appraisal,* p. 208.)

The remedy is to bring understanding to bear on the language of the creeds. We should know the Greek philosophic vocabulary with which the Church tried to clothe its estimate of Jesus. But more than that we should try to discover why the Church made such contradictory statements about him. It was because he was apprehended spiritually by them, but not comprehended intellectually by them. The creed is a symbol of the Church's wondering-gratitude before the person of Jesus Christ, who seemed too great to be measured in terms less than divine. If we grasp that, we shall begin to understand, allow for, even appreciate, the confusion of statement.

The creeds of the Church are like frozen foods. They are neither palatable nor digestible until they are thawed out. So we must bring warmth to our analysis of the creeds—the warmth of sympathy, of insight, even of humour. Then we may begin to appreciate the kind of person Jesus Christ was who Gkcaused such elevated confusion of statements to be made about him, because he was such an unusual fact.

Then, having come to such an appreciation, we must rewrite the creeds in language fit for our time. This is constantly being done, sometimes with official ecclesiastical sanction. In a folder labelled "Creed" in my files I have five recent statements of faith. Two were issued by the Church of Scotland in 1926 and 1943. One is a statement by a Cornell student in 1932 and one the thought-through conviction of a professor of theology in 1940. The fifth was the work of "Group X" at Yale in 1933. The statement of faith adopted by our own Duke University Church (Interdenominational) is a re-phrasing of the truth enshrined in the Apostles' Creed.

Jesus the Christ must never be confused with any single credal statement about him. That is to confine him in a straight jacket, or even in grave clothes. Yet, he must be described in language that is valid for us. That is why we may rightly object to *a* particular credal statement about him, but must not object to the making of a credal statement about him. It is our job to interpret him for today with the guidance of the past, but without the need to repeat its formulations.

Then, intellectual problems will be tackled with intellectual enthusiasm and conviction, and an enlightened devotion will take the place of a militant objection or an embarrassed assent.

There is yet another reason for the unattractiveness of Jesus:

the ethical difficulties that confront his followers, or would-be disciples.

There are some folk who refuse assent to the ethical implications of some credal theology. Listen to George Bernard Shaw in his preface to "Androcles and the Lion":

Consequently, even if it were mentally possible for all of us to believe in the Atonement, we should have to cry off it, as we evidently have a right to do. Every man to whom salvation is offered has an inalienable natural right to say, "No, thank you: I prefer to retain my full moral responsibility: it is not good for me to be able to load a scapegoat with my sins: I should be less careful how I committed them if I knew they would cost me nothing." (George Bernard Shaw: *Prefaces,* p. 576.)

There are others who are frank to admit that they cannot understand Jesus' ethical teachings. They miss a legalism. They object to the amount of interpretation left to them. The "Love God and do what you like" that summed up Christian ethics for Augustine is just a source of bewilderment to more prosaic folk, who prefer the understandability of a religion that says "Thou shalt not," and is specific about the negative. "What would Jesus do?" is not easy of answer. Because, on the lowest estimate, he showed marks of genius.

There are others who understand the teaching but don't know how to follow it as the world is set up. There is a clash of loyalties, both good. In a debate in the House of Lords regarding a Divorce Bill just before World War II, the Archbishop of Canterbury is reported to have said, "As a Christian I am against it; as an Englishman I am for it. Therefore, I shall not vote." That is the raw material of tragedy: when two rights, both beloved, are in conflict.

The remedy is to admit the truth in the criticisms, but to go beyond them. Of course, the ethical implications of some interpretations of the Atonement are anathema to an ethically sensitive person. But there is no need to hold to a substitutionary view of the Atonement. Do some reading and some thinking on the Doctrine first. Doctrine should be prior to ethical action. Of course, Jesus' ethical teaching is hard to understand. That is because he doesn't begin by instructing the reason. He begins by converting the soul. We must be in agreement with his insights about the Fatherhood of God, the

Sonship of the Believer, the possible Brotherhood of Man, and the control of the indwelling Spirit before we may hope to understand the Beatitudes or the rest of the Sermon on the Mount, which someone has well described as a "post-graduate course in ethics" (Phillips, *op. cit.,* pp. 74-75). It is, in theory, through faith that one comes to understand love. Of course, Jesus' ethical teaching is hard to follow. It has led in the past to crucifixion, beheading, hanging. That is no pleasant path. There is a basic conflict between the Church and the World. But you and I live in both, partly in this, partly in that. Therefore, like the Archbishop, we compromise. But let us admit we compromise, and not pretend to ourselves that every act, or even any act, is in basic harmony with the ethical discernments and demands of our Lord and Master.

What we must do is to go on learning of him. We must get to know him. We must try to recapture the attitude of an early disciple who walked the dusty ways of Palestine with him. If we do that carefully, consistently, and sincerely, then we may come to love him. And in loving him we shall grow more like him and act more like him. That is the only way. It means keeping at it steadily until it becomes second nature—theologically, "rebirth."

Isn't that the meaning of Jesus' answer to Peter's question "Lord, how often is my brother to sin against me and be forgiven? Up to seven times?" "Seven times? I say seventy times seven" (Matthew 18:21-22). Jesus is not advising that we forgive four hundred and ninety times and get down to business on the four hundred and ninety-first. What he is suggesting is the need for that spontaneity of action which comes from cultivation, until the spirit of the Christ is formed in us and we almost automatically act as he would. That is the primary answer to the ethical difficulties.

Do you see where all this comes out? The reason for the unattractiveness of Jesus is not primarily found in him, but in his followers. It is we, who bear the name of Christian, who are in the main responsible for his rejection. Jesus still attracts folk. Listen to George Bernard Shaw again:

"This man" has not been a failure yet; for nobody has ever been sane enough to try his way. But he has had one quaint triumph . . . We have always had a curious feeling that though we crucified Christ on a stick, he somehow managed to get hold of the right end of it, and that if we were better men we might try his plan. (Shaw, *op. cit.,* p. 525).

"If we were better men." There's the rub. If we weren't so extraordinarily ordinary about the things of Christ. If we weren't so vaguely inaccurate about what we believe concerning him. If we weren't so consistently ambiguous about our following him. "If we were better men and women."

He is despised and rejected, chiefly because of us, his avowed followers. That need not be. He could be honored and accepted, in part, because of us, if we would allow him to reveal himself in us; through our careful knowledge of him, our intelligent understanding of him, and our loving devotion to him.

THEODORE P. FERRIS

Revelation and Response

One time when I was speaking to people about God, I said that in the long run the real issue is between those who think that they are struggling against a universe that is meaningless at best, hostile at worst, and those who think that the universe makes sense, and that at heart it is friendly. That, to my way of thinking, is the real issue of the existence of God.

Putting it that way, the question is raised, What is there to be said in favor of meaning and friendliness? If the issue is between those who quite honestly believe that they are struggling against a universe that is meaningless and possibly hostile, and those who think that it makes sense and at heart is friendly, what is there to be said in favor of meaning and friendliness?

I am going to speak to that question from my own experience, not because I think that my experience is unique, or that it may match yours; but rather, because the experience of one person sometimes helps another to interpret his own, whether by way of contrast or similarity.

I grew up in a small, friendly world. My father and mother loved each other, and they loved me. Even when I was a child, I had the sense to know that my father's and mother's love was not entirely lacking the friction which inevitably exists wherever two people live together under one roof, and a third, especially a small child, doesn't eliminate the friction. They were intelligent, but not intellectual; wise, but not sophisticated; religious, but not pious. The result was that at home I was safe and happy; things made sense, and were friendly.

Everything *outside* my home was not always friendly, not by any means. When I was a small boy my contemporaries weren't always friendly. I had no facility whatever with any kind of a ball—a baseball, hand ball, tennis ball, golf ball, football, any kind of ball. I couldn't throw one, catch one, or hit one. That made me something of an oddity, and small children can often

Used by permission of Trinity Church in the City of Boston and the Estate of Theodore P. Ferris.

be cruel to those who are different from themselves. So I had a taste of that.

My father, because of his profession, was completely surrounded by crime. All my growing life he was the District Attorney of our county, Westchester County, adjacent to New York, and you can imagine that, because of our proximity to the world's largest city, we had some large-sized criminals in our midst. I lived through many a murder trial, and I soon learned from the discussions and conversations at the dinner table that everyone was not to be trusted. But at home there was nothing to be afraid of, and I moved on quite naturally from one stage to another, always looking forward to the next one. I went to the public schools. First to the grammar school, then to the high school, with its generous mixture of races and nationalities. Then came college; and then the decision as to what I was to do with my life; then the theological seminary, and then the decision as to how I was going to exercise my ministry, in the academic world of teaching or in the more cosmopolitan world of the parish ministry.

One thing followed another quite naturally. I didn't stop to ask what the meaning of my life was, what the purpose of it was. I simply did each thing as it came and tried to make the best decision that I could. I never asked myself, "Who am I?" I knew. I was Theodore Ferris, Walter Ferris' son, of Port Chester, New York.

There were interruptions and heartaches along the way. While I was in the seminary as a student I lost a year because of illness, a long, serious illness. Later, while I was a tutoring fellow, my closest friend committed suicide. That was the first time that I was exposed to the depths of mental darkness through which thousands of people grope their way. Up to that time I knew nothing about it, and I can say now quite calmly that my first experience was a bitter one.

But at the center there was still love and meaning, and I projected that upon the larger screen of the universe. I could feel that there was a God who cared because my father and mother cared, and beyond them, as I went through life, people that I knew and trusted cared; people like the Dean of my seminary and my teachers and friends all along the way, and I projected that little local experience of mine upon the screen of the universe itself. Not conscious of it at the time, I'm sure, but it was as though I said to myself something like this: In spite of the terror that I sometimes see in the heavens, and the evil that I see around me in the world—gripping me, at times, in its cruel clutches—in spite of all that, I can believe that there is a God who cares.

I could believe that he had plans and purposes because my father and mother had them; and I had them, not self-consciously, not deliberately, but I had them. I did the thing that I was expected to do and I had the natural, human incentive that all normal people have to look forward to the next step along life's journey. I also knew as I grew a little older and was exposed to the opposition of those who think that Christian belief is sheer fantasy, that this was something more than projection. It was a response to something that was there, and I was able to make that response because I had been prepared to make it. My sophisticated friends from outside said to me, Well, you are simply projecting your little world onto the screen of the cosmos. How ridiculous! What right have you to think that your small, safe family and circle of friends gives you any indication of what is happening in this wild, furious universe of ours?

I finally came to the point where I could say, Now, hold on. Perhaps I am projecting; but may it not be true that I am responding to something that is really there? I didn't put it there; I found it there, and I found it because I had been prepared to see it and recognize it; I had been introduced to life by my father and mother, and that introduction made all the difference.

You know how it is when you go to a strange country. Your response to it may depend on the first people you meet. If you happen to meet rude, impolite, and inconsiderate people, you may be blinded for the rest of your life to the real nature of the people of that country. On the other hand, if you meet people who are gracious, who are glad you are there, who welcome you with open arms, you are then prepared to see the real warmth that is at the heart of the people of that nation.

I know that if I had been brought up in abject poverty, raised in a broken home, in a land like Algeria where life is dried out by the sun in thirty years, I might have been blinded to the meaning and friendliness of the universe. I know that. The shape of your early life has a great deal to do with the way you shape your thoughts about God, but not everything. Some people who are raised in a family very much like mine do not finally come to think of God in those friendly, meaningful terms, and others who are raised in terrible circumstances do. So, the shape of your early life has a great deal to do with the way you shape your thoughts about God, but not everything.

As I grew older, I began to think about these things. Because we are the creatures we are, we have to *think* about what we feel. At the beginning we don't think much. We take it as it comes, we enjoy it or we don't enjoy it, but we don't think much about it. But the time comes when we have to think these things through. Emotionally, I was slanted in the direction of God, and I think that that particular angle of mine was not only something that was given to me by my family; I think it was something given to me by God, something like a down payment of disposition and way of looking at things. But the question, of course, came, and sooner or later had to be answered, Could I find legitimate reasons for what I felt? Was I living in a world of fantasy or fact? That question comes to everyone.

I must be frank with you. It has never been easy for me to answer that question. By temperament and disposition it is much easier for me to doubt than it is to believe. This, I think, may be partly due to the fact that I can see more clearly than some the other side of every question. That is an enormous help at times, but at other times it can make decisions difficult.

Starting at that point, I went on to find the reasons, the best reasons I could, for what I felt. I have been more and more inclined to trust my intuition and my primitive response to things. For instance, I know that when I pick up a book, I assume that someone wrote it. I don't assume that it fell together by itself; I assume that if I read it even though it be difficult, if I put my mind to it, I will understand at least a part of what is contained in it, because the man who wrote it intended me to understand it. I make the same naïve assumption about the stars. If they are there, I assume that someone put them there, not a person like myself, not like the author of a book, but a mind and a love put the stars there, and made it possible for them to shine. I don't know what they are for; but they are there, and I see them, enjoy them, and I assume that they did not get there by chance.

I also know that beauty brings me to my knees, more quickly I think, and this may be another confession that I should not make, more quickly than either truth or goodness; that is, it moves me at the deepest levels. Beauty brings me to my knees, and never in my experience has the beauty been brought to pass by pure chance. It comes to pass only when the creative impulse of some human being imposes order on the existing disorder. I know of no instance, certainly none in the world of human activity, where beauty comes to pass by chance. Spontaneously—often, yes; but fortuitously—never. It is the result of the agony, the genius and the love of a human being who takes the disorder of life's raw material and imposes upon it the order that he sees before it ever comes into being. I naïvely assume the same about the universe. Order is imposed upon disorder, and where order is, beauty is not far behind.

Also, I know that human beings have an enormous capacity for hate. It is a shocking thing—the older we grow, the more evidence we see of it, not only for hate, but for jealousy, arrogance, pride and ambition—all the things that we dislike and despise. I know that, but I also know that they have an even greater capacity for love. At a time when you least expect it, some person who in spite of the fact that his own life may be in danger, and all of his own interests are at stake, does something which may cost him his life, because he loves someone else. This is the most spectacular thing about a human being.

You say that even an animal does that; a mother lion protects her cub. I know it, but animals do not do it with the same self-consciousness of danger and the same knowledge of what is in store for them that human beings have. The most spectacular thing about a human being is that he can deny the very basic law of his existence, namely, the law of self-preservation, when someone he loves greatly is in danger.

Can this come from a universe that is cold and heartless? Some think it can. I say that if it does, then the universe is more mysterious than ever. How a universe with nothing akin to that kind of self-giving love can nevertheless produce that kind of creature would be the greatest mystery of all.

I knew then, and I know now, that these are not intellectual arguments, but I also know that no argument can shake these things that I know. And I know, too, that most men and women do not live by their arguments, but by their commitments. Not by the arguments they may make in public, but by the commitments they make in secret do they live; and it is those secret commitments that give you the clue to their life.

H. G. Wells, the English novelist and historian, a professed agnostic, made it plain to the whole world that he believed in nothing because he did not know. Yet he wrote, "At times in the silence of the night and in rare lonely moments I experience a sort of communion of myself with Something Great that is not myself." He didn't live up to his arguments, but to his commitments.

Clarence Darrow, one of the heroes of the legal world in my younger life, once wrote this: "The outstanding fact that cannot be dodged by thoughtful men is the futility of it all." No one ever dodged the futility of it all more spectacularly than Clarence Darrow. He spent all his life defending the man or the woman who had been unjustly condemned. He did not live up to his arguments, or even by his arguments. He lived by his commitment, made in secret, manifest in public.

The real reason why I believe that the universe makes sense and that it is friendly is that I cannot get away from Jesus Christ. He speaks to me as a person. I don't know him as well as I wish I did, and the longer I live, the less I know about him, because the more mysterious he becomes. His humanity and his divinity mingle in such a way as to be an absolute mystery that the mind of man can never fathom.

But what I do know is this. If the universe were meaningless and hostile, the crucifixion would have been the end of him, the cross would have been the supreme example for the modern dramatist of the absurd; the man who gave himself for the good of all mankind was done to death by the very people for whom he gave himself. But the crucifixion was not the end of him. To put it in the vernacular, he is still around, still disturbing, still illuminating; still here and there, not in great institutions perhaps, but in individuals, sending people out to do extraordinary things, people whose minds have been lit by his greater mind and whose spirit fortified by his absolutely intransigent spirit, still around. And the cross on which he died has made all other suffering and evil capable of meaning, capable, that is, of being caught up into the tapestry of life and woven into the pattern in such a way as to make the pattern intelligible.

So I have come full circle, beginning with my early life, as you must begin with your early life, and ending with my life now. The Christ confirms my earliest response to life, that it can be trusted because at the center of it, at home, so to speak—not my home in Westchester County, but my real home, there is God, the God of all being who, like my father and mother, and infinitely more like my Lord and Master, both knows and cares about what I am doing.

HARRY EMERSON FOSDICK

The Sacred and the
Secular Are Inseparable

Human life can be differentiated into secular and sacred just as
water can be analyzed into hydrogen and oxygen. Water,
however, ought not to be so served to us—first, two parts
hydrogen and then one part oxygen; water ought to be taken as
a whole. So life is well lived only when the sacred and the
secular coalesce and blend, but we are not getting it that way.
To multitudes of people life is being served in its analyzed form,
first two parts secular, and then, if they are men and women of
faith at all, religion comes as an addendum.

Consider our daily life and see how true this is. On the one
side are science with its thrilling discoveries, statesmanship
with its critical problems, business, music, drama, literature,
homes, recreation, education—all conceived as constituting
man's secular life. Then, on the other side of an ever more
clearly marked boundary, is religion. So religion gets itself
segregated from the general body of human experience and
pushed into an ecclesiastical corner, until some day, from that
secluded area, religion looks over the ecclesiastical fence to see
human life as a whole passing it by as an irrelevance. That is the
situation in the world today.

Primitive man had no such division between secular and
sacred, and in all early cultures Paul's principle, "Whether
therefore ye eat, or drink, or whatsoever ye do, do all to the
glory of God," was literally practised. All art was sacred art, all
drama religious drama; even when men danced they danced,
like David, "before the Lord." There was no medicine apart
from religious rites, or ways of assuring crops without reliance
on the gods for rain, or education that was not saturated with
theology. As early man never dreamed that water was made up

A radio address presented on National Vespers, March 13, 1938. Used by
permission of Elinor Fosdick Downs.

of hydrogen and oxygen, so he never thought that life could be divided into sacred and secular.

Turn now from these early cultures to our own and how great the difference! Drama, that, whether in humbler eras or in the great days of the Greek theatre, was specifically centered in religion, became largely secular. Music, that once was religious, dedicated like Bach's major works "to the glory of God," is increasingly secularized now. Our major educational institutions were commonly founded from religious motives and for religious objectives, but for two long generations education has been increasingly withdrawing from that alliance and is more and more secular. Humanitarianism used to be the specific overflow of religion, but some of the most effective philanthropy we have today would never dream of acknowledging a religious background. And two of the most potent forces in our lives are science and democracy, but both would officially disclaim any religious allegiance whatsoever. I am not saying that all this is evil; I belong to a religious tradition one of whose major objectives was the separation of church and state; but, certainly, it is a towering fact. As the centuries have passed, the day-by-day interests of mankind have moved off by independent roads and left religion in its ecclesiastical corner.

Now, the consequence has been immense and, as some of us would think, appalling. Look, for example, at thousands of our churches to see what it has meant to religion to be thus pushed into ecclesiastical seclusion. Some things can be put into a corner. Collecting stamps, reading detective stories, playing golf—they can be put into the pigeonholes of living. But some things so essentially belong to the whole of life that, when they are segregated from it and forced to live, as it were, in a Ghetto, they are ruined. The central idea of religion certainly is God. But God is not the God of a corner. He is universal or he is nothing. As Lowell sang,

> God is in all that liberates and lifts,
> In all that humbles, sweetens, and consoles.

Such assurance is real religion, but it is not a kind of religion we are getting in many of our churches.

Sometimes we Christians pity the Jews because through the cruelty of their oppressors they are forced to live in Ghettos. But there is, as it were, an ecclesiastical Ghetto in which our

Christian churches have been crowded by the pressure that divides secular from sacred. When one goes down into this, shall I say Christian Ghetto? one does not hear the great interests of human life discussed with which we are most genuinely concerned and which hold in their hands the destiny of humankind but, rather, questions like this: Are we Methodists, Presbyterians, or Episcopalians? how much water was used when we were baptized? do we believe in this or that ancient miracle story? do we think that this or that theory of apostolic succession is necessary to constitute the true church? and so on. Sometimes I am appalled with the revelation of the quantity of such Ghetto religion there is in American churches. A man comes up from that Ghetto into the vivid and vital interests of human life again, crying out for air to breathe and wanting to shout from the housetops that this will never do and that somehow we must bring God and his revelation of life's meaning in Christ out of this corner into the thick of human life once more.

Moreover, consider not simply the consequence of this separation between secular and sacred upon religion but upon secular life itself. Do you like it? To watch the common body of man's day-by-day interests and activities progressively drained of the influence of great religion and the sacred meanings that are associated with it, and becoming ever more secularized—do you like it? Professor Montague of Columbia University has put into a single sentence what seems to me one of the most ominous facts about our modern world: "For perhaps the first time in history we are confronted with the prospects of a complete secularization of the opinions, the practices, and the emotions of mankind." So! They have even tried to make that official in Russia. They are trying something like that in Germany. Do you like the unofficial imitation of it in America?

If sometimes a man comes up out of the ecclesiastical Ghetto, feeling with inward agony how desperately religion needs the whole of life to operate in if *it* is to be wholesome, at other times one turns from watching the secularization of the rest of life, feeling that, unless we can bring back the high influence of religion into every-day affairs, our civilization, like a herd of swine possessed with devils, will plunge down the steep place into the sea.

Are there, then, some wise and true things that we can say about this crucial matter?

For one thing, in this separation of sacred and secular we have gotten far away from Jesus. We Christians need to keep ever more in our minds the fact that Christianity began in a carpenter's shop, surrounded by the common tools of daily life, and that Jesus was not an ecclesiastic—no, nor any of his apostles, but all of them plain men out of humble areas of living. When Jesus talked about religion how different from the official and conventional jargon his language was! He talked of fields ready for the harvest, flowers that were fairer than Solomon in all his glory, and about children at play. He talked about husbandmen and their vineyards, carpenters and their building, shepherds and their sheep. He talked about families where weddings are gaily celebrated or where a wayward boy has left home for a far country, or where new patches are sewed on old garments or where two sparrows may be bought for a farthing by the poor. He talked about business and money, about the varieties of soil that a farmer faces, about the unemployed standing in the market place waiting to be hired, about the powerful who oppress the poor, about friendship with its loyalties, and the changing colors of the evening sky. It doesn't sound like technical religion at all. It is not like any kind of official religion that ever existed or that exists now. It is the whole of human life lifted up into spiritual beauty and significance. No wonder the ecclesiastics of his day hated him. No wonder that our sectarian religion does not in the least resemble him. What has that kind of religion to do with this spirit of Jesus, this elevation of all life into dignity and worth, this seven-day-a-week, out-of-door way of seeing and loving and ennobling life? When we separate the sacred and secular, we are far away from Jesus.

Furthermore, in this separation of secular and sacred we are creating for ourselves a personal problem that on the basis of that separation never can be solved. The greatest single difficulty, I suspect, in the way of our best living is not our intellectual problems, important as they are, but rather the fact that, while in the sacred corner of our lives we do sometimes see high meanings in life to which we know we owe allegiance we must go out into a world, increasingly secularized, that scorns our insights. Sometimes after a high hour on Sunday, when we have faced great matters of faith and character and felt together how rightly our loyalties belong to them, I go out into the world only to run headlong into some prevalent paganism, some utter secularity, that denies everything that we have thought. And I say to myself, That is what the people face to whom I have been trying to preach. How can the flame of spiritual life that has been lighted in a kindling hour burn brightly in the stifling atmosphere of that secularized world? Abraham Lincoln's principle is everlastingly true: this world can no more abide, half sacred and half secular, than this nation could remain half slave and half free. A house divided against itself shall fall. Either we will elevate the secular into the sacred or the sacred will be dragged down into the secular until its sacredness is gone.

The most important thing going on in Christian churches today is the way they are drawing together into a more ecumenical mind and a more cooperative spirit. That is not chiefly due to some sudden access of kindliness, tolerance, and magnanimity. That is mainly due to what we are talking about today. The churches of Christ around the world begin to see, as they had better see, that for the first time in history we are facing the prospect of the complete secularization of the opinions, practises, and emotions of mankind. They confront a common enemy. They see their boys and girls, in whom they try to light a flame of spiritual life, going out into a world so pagan that only a few flames persist. They see their families, the very roots of a Christian culture, where the great names that Christianity uses—father, mother, son, daughter, sister, brother—get their native meaning, so played upon by the forces of secularity that even the sacredness of family life is on an ebb tide and in consequence state and church alike are shaken. And they are beginning to ask, as they had better ask, How important are our differences in the light of this common peril?

We have often been told that if there were an invasion of this planet from Mars, even the most hostile nations would make a pact of common resistance. So far as our Christianity is concerned, there is, as it were, an invasion from Mars, the complete secularization of human life. Let all who see that peril join the forces that would resist it.

This leads us to one further matter: this is a problem about which each of us can do something. It is immense, planetary in its scope, and yet concerning it each of us can do something. I have drawn rather a stark picture of the secular world, drained of spiritual meaning, but to leave it so would not be fair. For here in this secular life are all the makings of the kingdom of God. We need no other materials than we have here in our secular world to build a home for man happy and fortunate beyond our dream. Indeed, so true is this that I could rebuke myself for some things I may have seemed to say.

Is science merely secular when it opens before our astonished eyes the endless vistas of this universe, where, as Carlyle said, our sun is but a porch-lamp, until our minds are filled with wonder and our souls with awe? Is medicine merely secular when, as the psalmist sang about God, it healeth all our diseases? Since when for a man with eyes to see has love of physical nature been merely secular—trees, as Joyce Kilmer said, that only God could make, or a sea gull poised against a stormy wind above the whitecaps of a spray-blown sea. I know love-music that never thinks of God but is so beautiful that if it be true that "God is love; and he that abideth in love abideth in God, and God abideth in him," it must have come from him; and poetry like Shelley's, who called himself an atheist and yet described life as "a dome of many-coloured glass" that "stains the white radiance of Eternity" and so talked of God even when he denied him. Is a public park or a public library or a children's playground or a sound business run on friendly lines merely secular? No, to the eye that can see there is at the heart of this secular life such sacredness, such possibilities that the makings of the kingdom of God are there. And sometimes people come—they are the benediction of our days—with religion so real that they blend the sacred and the secular in a home, in a school, in a business, in a community, and the kingdom of God does come. I had a mother who did that in a home. I had a father who did that in a school. As George Herbert says,

> Who sweeps a room as for thy laws,
> Makes that, and the action, fine.

Lift up the slogan that this generation so critically needs: Make your secular sacred!

Joseph Jefferson said about his fellow actor, Edwin Booth, that behind the scenes he ran his theatre as though it were a church. Once a cowardly clergyman with parishioners who thought it wrong to attend the theatre, wrote to Booth asking whether there wasn't a back door or a side door in his theatre where he could slip in unperceived, to which Booth answered, "There is no door in my theatre through which God cannot see." No door in my theatre, my business, my recreation, my home, through which God cannot see—that is real religion.

At any rate, for my part, I made up my mind long ago that I never would be minister of one of those churches that open their doors two or three days a week so that some one can make a speech about religion and for the rest serve no better purpose than to be decorative backgrounds for undertakers' signs. That is not Christianity, not the Christianity of Christ, who said, "Inasmuch as ye did it—not talked about it, did it—unto one of these my brethren, even these least, ye did it unto me."

When one looks out on the community, the test of our religion is not so much what happens inside the churches as what happens to the total life of the neighborhood. Ah, Jeremiah, greatest of all ancient prophets, speak to us again: "Seest thou not what they do in the cities of Judah and in the streets of Jerusalem?" That is the ultimate test of religion.

Indeed, if a man is to have a religion that so redeems the secular, it must be *very* real. No man can lift the world until he stands above it. No man can have a religion that elevates the secular unless within him there is a sanctuary pure and undefiled. No one can follow Paul's admonition, "Whatsoever ye do, do all to the glory of God," unless he first says with Jesus, "For their sakes I sanctify myself."

BILLY GRAHAM

The Prodigal Son

Now tonight, let's turn to the 15th chapter of Luke. I'm not going to read the passage because it's too long, but it is a familiar story that all of us have read and heard since childhood. It is called "The Story of the Prodigal Son." That's what we call it. There are many ways we could term this passage from Luke's Gospel. It could be called "The Story of the Loving Father." It could be called "The Story of the Church Member Without Christ," because that is exactly what the elder brother was.

But tonight I want to dwell on the story of this boy because he was a rebel. He rebelled against his father. And you know what I read the other day? That over two thousand young people who run away from home come to New York every month seeking fame and fortune. They become prey to all the thugs and con-men and drug merchants and sex perverts and all the others. Two thousand a month are lured away from their parents to New York City.

This is also a city where young people do a lot of damage. Do you know last year how many school windows were broken in New York? Over 200,000. Do you know how many telephone booths were wrecked in the city of New York last year? Over 300,000. And did you know that these crimes are largely among young people? Now I grant you the older people tell them how to do it, and it is the older people who print the pornography, and it is the older people who produce the motion pictures, and it is the older people who think up all the violence on television, and it is the older people who have handed this world and the mess we're in to our young people.

But young people are striking out at society in every kind of way today. Some of it is violent, some is destructive, some of it is just plain rebellion, and some of it is justified.

This is the story of a young fellow who ran away from home. Now in this passage Jesus tells three little stories. Jesus always used stories to illustrate spiritual truths. They are called parables in the Bible. He told a story of a lost sheep. He told a story of a lost coin. He told a story of this lost son, and in all three stories he is picturing a loving father searching for that which is lost, and that Father is God. You see God is searching for you tonight. God loves you. He is searching for you, and the search takes Him all the way to the Cross where He gives His Son for you. That is how much God loves you.

But it is also a story of how we are lost from God. The Bible teaches that we are like the lost sheep or the lost coin or the lost boy. We are away from God. We have rebelled against God. We have run away from God, but God loves us. He wants us back, and He is willing to go to any length to get us back. He won't compromise in telling us how to get back. Some people try to come other ways. He said, "There is only one way back and that's through my Son, Jesus Christ. If you are willing to come that way I will receive you and I will forgive you." And that's the story of this boy. One day he goes to his father and says: "Dad, you know I am tired of living out here in the country—all the discipline and the hard work—and I am eighteen years of age. I would like to have my inheritance now and I want to go out to 'New York,' because I am going to make it big up there." He had read about "Broadway" and he had heard all about the bright lights. He had heard about all the different things that happened there, and he decided he would like to go.

And his father said, "Son, I don't advise it, but if you are determined to go, go ahead." So he starts out for the big city.

You know this weekend one of the people who made the news all across the country was a brilliant young member of the senior class at Wellesley. She expressed how young people are feeling lost today. She described how young people are exploring a world that none of us understand, and are searching for more immediate and ecstatic and penetrating modes of living. And what she was saying was this: young people are lost, confused and frustrated and are searching for a way back.

And this is what Jesus Himself said. He said, "The Son of Man is come to seek and save that which is lost."

Well, this young fellow came from an affluent home. They had a great deal of love in the home, a great deal of discipline in the home, and there was faith in God. I imagine his father gathered the family together every day for prayer and Bible reading, and the boy said, "Oh, I don't want to talk about God. I don't want religion. I can't wait to get away from home."

How many young people are like that here tonight?

Or, maybe he had to go to church. And he said, "I don't want to go to church. I can't wait until I can get away and get to the university and get to college, and go to town—get somewhere so I don't have to go to church."

So he rebelled against his father, and rebellion became a way of life for him.

Now it is perfectly normal for a young fellow to pull away from his father. The Bible says, "Therefore shall a man leave his father and mother and cleave unto his wife and they shall be one flesh." After you are married you are in for trouble if you start living with your parents and depending on your parents. Live with your wife; be on your own; establish your own friends. But here was a young man in his teens, not married, and the reason he was leaving home was because he didn't like the discipline at home. He wanted to go out and have a good time. Now if he wanted to go out and work and get a job, that was one thing, but that wasn't what he wanted. He wanted to "goof off." He didn't want to go to school any more. He didn't want to get up and milk the cows on the farm any more. He wanted to go out and have a good time. It was to please self.

You know down here on Times Square—I've walked down there a couple of times, and one of those theaters down there has a big marquee that says, "Unsatisfied." And then you know the pop song that the Rolling Stones made so famous, "I Can't Get No Satisfaction"?

Well, this young fellow was going out trying to find fulfillment and satisfaction and happiness, and he thought it lay where all the bright lights and the music and the night clubs and all the rest were. He said, "I am going to have a real ball."

I heard about a girl the other day. She was wooed by a boy with promises of marriage. She became pregnant. He left her alone. Her father, mother and family suffered shame and disgrace because of a boy's selfishness, and that is the very essence of sin—selfishness. That is what sin is all about—self. I want to satisfy self.

I was interviewed on television by a group of students this past week, and one of them said, "What is wrong with being aroused sexually?" He said, "I go out and buy my sex. What's wrong with that?" Well, the thing that is wrong with it is that the ingredient that sex was made for is not there—love within marriage. Some go out and buy it like shopping in a supermarket—like a steak, like a lunch—with no love, no relationship.

The Bible goes further. It says it is wrong outside of marriage.

But you see this boy was already wandering away from home even while he was at home. He was thinking about it. We don't wander away all at once. Like sheep, we wander gradually. The Bible says, "All we like sheep have gone astray." And so this young fellow went, and when he got to town he was like the fellow I read about in London, England, in one of the British newspapers, who had a home in the country and a home in town. He said, "When I am in the country, I want to be in the city, and when I am in the city, I want to be in the country." The problem was not where he was; the problem was his own heart. Going to town is not going to meet your needs. Going to the country is not going to meet your needs.

I talked to a young person day before yesterday, and he said, "Boy, I'd like to get out of this rat race in this city and get out to the country and listen to the birds and see the grass." Well, he'd be out there about three days and he'd be wanting to hear the honking of the taxicabs and hear all the screaming of the sirens.

You see it is a heart problem we have. We want fulfillment in our lives. We want a peace and a joy and a happiness that we don't find anywhere in life. It is just not found apart from God. You can't find it just anywhere.

And during this past week I have been very interested in reading some of the addresses being given by valedictorians and professors and famous people at the various universities and colleges. Nearly all of them were pessimistic. Everyone of them said that young people were looking for something they can't find, and the youth themselves, I thought, brought the greatest message. They said, "We are living in a lousy, messed up world. We feel lousy ourselves. We don't know the answer." And it was very pessimistic, this commencement season across the country. And one young fellow got up and told them. He said, "This university is standing now, but we're going to be back. We're going to be back this fall and we're going to burn it down." That's how he felt.

I talked to a fellow the other day right here in New York City.

He said, "Yes, we're going to burn the town down." I said, "What are you going to build in its place?" He said, "Oh, we don't have any plans for that, but anything is better than what we've got now. We are going to tear it down."

Well, I agree there are a lot of things wrong. A lot of things need straightening out, but I don't believe the way to do it is to tear it down and burn it up. Let's try to use the democratic processes and straighten it out because I'm not so sure that some of the people I've seen marching around saying they are going to change it all would do any better than the people who are running it now. They don't seem to have any ideas—any constructive ideas.

But you see, this fellow went off to town, and when he got there he had his pockets full of money. Well, anyone who has any money has a crowd around him. You can make friends quickly if you've got money. I would hate to be a wealthy man because I would never know who my friends were. Everybody is after your money. When your money is gone your friends are gone. Some friends are free loaders. His friends were. He had a lot of friends around him.

Did you read the other day in the paper that in the Detroit Zoo they lost their prize ostrich? I think her name was Susie, and they performed an autopsy on Susie and found $3.85 in pennies, dimes and quarters inside that beautiful bird. That bird was killed by money.

This fellow had a lot of money—went off to town, and got a lot of friends around him. The Bible says there is pleasure in sin. He started doing the things that he learned from his city cousins. He learned a little bit about dope. He took some "trips." At first it was just a lot of fun, a lot of kicks. It wasn't long until he began to be hooked. He started taking a few sips of alcohol and it wasn't long before he had to have it before lunch. He began to fool around with a girl. It wasn't long before he was in trouble—had to move to the other side of town. All kinds of trouble plagued him.

You see the devil is fishing with bait. He comes along and whispers in your ear and tells you that it is greener on the other side of the fence. Everything is better over there. You just rebel against your parents, rebel against God, rebel against religion, and go out here on your own and you think it's going to be better. But the devil doesn't tell you that he's got a hook in you. Fools make a mockery of sin. The Bible says, "Be sure your sin will find you out." The Bible says, "There is pleasure in sin for a season." You see, for a short time you can have a good time, but it is very short. It disappears. It becomes empty. You become disillusioned! Disenchanted!

I was in a European country last summer, and one of the top young people told me—he said, "You know, we've had this permissive society now for a generation." And he said, "Anything goes and we are filled up to here with it. We are sick of it. Let's take a walk down through the streets of Stockholm." He said, "Do you see much laughter, much joy, much happiness?" There were throngs of young people, but there was something missing. They looked bored. They had one of the highest suicide rates among young people in the world. Why? Because all of this permissiveness without discipline doesn't bring happiness. Happiness and peace and joy are found in God, in a relationship with Jesus Christ, and in a disciplined life.

The Bible says, "Sin when it is finished bringeth forth death."

And the Bible says that this young fellow began to be in want. It wasn't long before his money was gone; he spent it all. And when his money left him, his friends left him.

I read the other day in the *Daily News*—I think they called it "The Prodigal Daughter." She was nineteen years of age, she had a steady boyfriend to whom she was engaged until one day she stepped out on him. She was unfaithful to him, and listen to what she says as quoted:

"I got into trouble with a guy I don't even like because I went to a drug and booze party. I completely lost control of myself, and I didn't even know what happened except that the guy whose baby I am going to have disappeared after he heard of my condition. I brought shame to my family and friends, and now I cry myself to sleep at night. I feel like I am falling apart. I haven't gone out of the house since it happened."

She began to be in want. She went to a party to have a big time, but there came a moment when sin paid its wages. And it always does. You see you can't commit a single sin without paying for it. You may not pay for it immediately. You may not pay for it as quickly as this girl, but you're going to pay for it.

The Bible says, "Whatsoever a man soweth that shall he also reap."

This young man began to be in want.

There is a film in New York for "Adults Only," and it is entitled, "I Want."

The Bible says, "The Lord is my shepherd, I shall not want." But you see, the Lord was not the shepherd of this boy. He began to be in want. His body began to be in want. Is your body in want tonight for bigger kicks, more high-powered drugs, more sex deviation to satisfy—trying to stay awake at night thinking up things you can do for kicks? Is your mind in want? The Bible says our minds have been affected by sin and the more we learn, the less truth we know many times—"ever learning but never able to come to a knowledge of truth," because, you see, God is Truth, Christ is Truth, and if you don't know Christ, you don't have the foundation of truth.

And, so many of our scientists today—see how many breakthroughs we have. They are beginning to see new areas of knowledge they didn't know existed a few years ago. Knowledge is now doubling every ten years so that no scientist can know it all. They can only specialize in one small field, and a scientist feels frustrated and hemmed in.

Dr. Elmer Engstrom, who spoke to you a moment ago, Chairman of this Crusade, is a great scientist, and he would tell you that scientists feel frustrated because they have to specialize now in little fields, and they cannot have the whole range of knowledge they once had.

And you see, the spirit began to be in want. He rebelled against God. The human soul is so large the world cannot satisfy it. "What shall it profit a man if he gain the whole world and lose his own soul."

And then something interesting happened. He became a slave. He had to find employment, but a depression had come, and he couldn't get a job. Finally, the only job he could get was to go out and feed the hogs. And so Jesus said he went out and began to feed the swine. And then he became so hungry that he began to eat with the hogs. It wasn't long before he looked like a hog. He smelled like a hog. He grunted like a hog. Down in the pigpen with the hogs—a boy who had come from a fine home—gone to have a big time in the big city. How many in New York are like that tonight? Or any of the other great cities of America? In rebellion, going into all kinds of sin, but becoming slaves of sin. Jesus said, "Whoever committeth sin is the slave of sin."

He had walked out on his father and the love and the discipline of his father, to come under the bondage of a stranger. What an exchange! "What shall a man give in exchange for his soul?"

You know Prince Philip was speaking a few days ago at Edinburgh, and he said something I like. He got pretty tough with some students. He said, "Shut up and grow up." He said, "Freedom is not license. You can destroy freedom as successfully by making a mockery of it as you can by retraction." Hurray for Prince Philip! Maybe he will become an evangelist yet.

The Bible says we cannot be neutral. Lots of people try to be neutral. They say, "Well, I'm not for God, I'm not against Him. I just don't take a stand." But God says you have to take a stand. You have to choose—you have to choose which road of life you are going to go—a broad road or a narrow road. The narrow Road leads to heaven, the broad road leads to hell, and you must make the choice.

And so this young fellow got to thinking one day, and it's a good thing when you start to think about yourself. He began to think, and the Spirit of God began to speak to him, and he began to think about his father back there on the farm. He thought to himself, "What am I doing here in these rags, in this dirt, in this filth, eating with hogs when my father has a beautiful farm back there with many servants and many cattle, and I could go be there and be a servant of his. What a fool I've made of myself."

You know the Bible teaches that sin is a form of insanity? The Bible says if our Gospel is hid or veiled, the veil must be in the minds of those who have spiritually died. The spirit of this world had blinded the minds of those who do not believe and who prevent the light of the glorious Gospel of Christ, the image of God, from shining in there. Notice, "The spirit of this world." There is an evil spirit in our world that blinds us to the reality of what God can do. It blinds us to our own condition. Then the Holy Spirit comes along and convinces us and disturbs us of our sins, and we sit and think about it and we are disturbed and unhappy about our condition. We don't know where to escape. We don't know which way to go. But this young fellow decided to do the right thing. He decided to get up and go back. He said, "I have sinned against heaven." He didn't just say, "I have sinned against my father." He said, "I have sinned against God." That's your problem. Your problem is not a family relationship. Your problem is not really a race problem. Your problem is a problem with God. You get the problem with God straightened out, and you will have a new perspective on how to straighten out some of the other problems. That's the real problem. The real hangup in your life is what to do about God, what to do about Christ. Let Him come and change and transform your life and see the fulfillment and the power and the strength you will have.

This young fellow reflected; then he made a resolution. He said, "I will arise and go to my father."

Sixteen thousand young people in Miami the other day arose and demonstrated for decency. Thousands of people followed an Olympic track star down the streets of Toronto the other day, to witness for Christ. They called it "A mile for morals march." When are we going to wake up? When are the young people in this country who believe in God finally going to start carrying their flag? Maybe we are going to see a great tide turned, but we will never turn unless we are willing to make Christ the very heart and the very center of our lives. There is nothing else in the arena of American philosophy and thought today except Christ. It is either Christ or it is chaos. Which is it going to be?

The Beatles' latest controversial record is called, "Oh, Christ, It Ain't Easy," and it's not easy to follow Christ. It is not easy to be a Christian. It's not easy to live in New York or any of our other great metropolitan areas and live the disciplined life for Jesus Christ. It's not easy for a young person to resist the temptations of this hour.

Jesus said, "Sit down and count the cost. If you want something easy, then go somewhere else. I'm not the man; I'm not the one." He said "Count the cost." He said, "It's going to mean death to your self—your own self-interests, your own self-pride." He said, "It's going to mean a cross. You may have to be crucified." He meant that not only figuratively; He also meant it literally. It is going to have to mean less of you and your desires and your ambitions, and Christ is going to have to be first, and He'll test you; He'll take you to many Crosses, and He will see if you are willing to go there without flinching. That is what it will cost to follow Christ.

This fellow said, "I will arise and go."

He started back home, and while he was a long way off, his father was watching for him. Now notice, this is a picture of God. Jesus is telling a story to illustrate a spiritual truth. Here is a picture of God watching for you all the time. He sees you coming down the road, and the son is filled with shame, and dirt, and filth, and sin, and rebellion. Was his father apathetic to his condition? Was his father indifferent? No. The Bible says that he was watching, waiting for his son to return, hoping and praying he would return. And when he saw him, he ran down the road and threw his arms around him and the son blurted out in tears, "Father, I have sinned against you. I am sorry. I have come home to be a servant."

But the father said, "Nothing doing." He said, "Bring the ring and put it on his finger, the ring of the authority of sonship. Give him a bath and put on the finest clothes, and then kill the fatted calf. We are going to have a barbecue, we're going to have a party that will be the greatest party we ever had. My son that was lost has been found. My son has returned." The Bible says, "There is rejoicing in heaven over one sinner that repents." That is why Madison Square Garden is worth all the expense and all the trouble and all the work if just one person comes to Christ. If you knew the value of one soul, if you knew it made heaven rejoice over one person returning to the Father, you would receive Christ. You would return to the Father. You say, "But Billy, you don't know my sins. You don't know how rebellious my heart has been. You don't know how many lies I've told, how many immoralities I've committed, how many drugs I've taken. You don't know all I've done. I couldn't possibly come."

You are the kind of person He is really looking for. He receives you tonight. Jesus receives sinful men. That's why He died. That's why He rose again—to receive you.

But then out in the field there was his brother. He hadn't seen his younger brother for years. He was working out in the fields and he heard all the shouting and all the commotion, and he said, "What's going on?" One of the servants said, "Your brother has returned." He said, "That scoundrel? You mean that reprobate, that sinner has returned and he expects us to welcome him?"

You see this fellow had been in his father's home all along, but his loyalty wasn't really to his father. His loyalty was to his own selfish interests. And it is possible to be in the church and be lost. It is possible to be in the church and be without a personal relationship with Jesus Christ. And there is many an elder brother here tonight. You are a member of the church, you haven't yet left home, but even while you are at home, in the church, your heart is not right with God. You need to repent of your sins and receive Christ as your Lord and as your Savior.

Lincoln—before he was killed—was asked how he would treat the rebellious Southerners, and he answered, "As if they had never been away." That is how God will treat you if you receive Christ tonight—as if you had never been away. He forgives all the past. He writes your name in His book. You have the assurance that you are going to heaven. Now it is complicated, and it is hard to live the Christian life. I don't want to fool you. I don't want you to come under false colors. It is not easy to be a Christian. It means reading your Bible daily, it means spending time in prayer, and it means persecution.

"All that will live godly in Christ Jesus shall suffer persecution," the Bible says.

We are to live disciplined lives, under the Lordship of Christ. That is not easy, but let me tell you something. The Holy Spirit comes to live in your heart to help you live the Christian life, and then He begins to live through you and in you. It is no longer you living. It is Christ living in you, and it becomes a life of joy. Problems? Yes. Difficulties? Yes. But a life of joy and peace and forgiveness. He can change your life tonight.

There is a man here in this audience whom I saw here a moment ago. Maybe you saw me put my arm around him when I came into the Garden. His name is Jim Vaus. Jim does one of the great social jobs here in New York City. Twenty years ago this year, Jim wandered into a tent where we were holding a meeting in Los Angeles. Jim—he wouldn't mind me saying this—was Mickey Cohen's wire tapper, had been written up as one of the great criminals of the West Coast. That night Jim found Christ. He and Alice with their children are here tonight, they love the Lord with all their heart, and Jim speaks all over the world. Thousands of people have found Christ under his ministry. What Christ has done for Jim Vaus He can do for you tonight if you put your faith and your confidence in Him. I am going to ask you to do it tonight. You ask, "What do I have to do, Billy?"

I am going to ask you to get up and come.

(Delivered June 16, 1969)

G. EARL GUINN

The Resurrection of Jesus

Romans 10:9-10

The Christian religion stands or falls with the resurrection of Jesus. Except for this the difference between the Jewish religion and the Christian religion is not as great as one might suppose. The empty tomb stands squarely in the path of Judaism and declares it to be inadequate. The trumpet of destiny blown by Judaism has an uncertain sound. Those who would delete from the faith the resurrection event and reduce Christianity to a philosophical or ethical system have no part with the apostle Paul. No one was more aware of the centrality of the resurrection than he. Apart from this he could see no unique value in the Christian religion. What he could see, assuming that Christ was not raised, was himself a false witness of God, a man without any basis for hope.

Jesus either came from the grave or he did not. If he did not, we are not sure that many things in life really matter. If he did, the future has hope, existence has meaning, and his teachings have significance as criteria for value judgments. Of the resurrection Paul had no doubts, nor should we. Faith here is crucial.

I

The resurrection of Jesus is indisputable history. Our religion is not a nebulous theosophy, an ethereal mysticism that was born of the distorted mind of an epileptic nomad. Our religion rests on historical fact. While it leads to heaven, its headwaters rise from earth. Once in time, within the framework of human history, the great God of heaven revealed himself to man in the person of a Son. This Son was rejected by men and hanged on a tree. His body was placed in a tomb. On the third day after burial God raised him from the dead. These are declarations of history. The empty tomb, the existence of the church, the testimony of credible witnesses, and personal experience speak eloquently of the historicity of the resurrection of Jesus. Other facts not nearly so well documented are accepted without question. DeWette was entirely correct in his declaration that we have no more cause, on purely historical grounds, to question the resurrection of Jesus than we have to doubt the assassination of Julius Caesar.

Ever since the crude lie was told about the theft of the Lord's body by his disciples, the resurrection has been the focal point of attacks against Christianity. It was once suggested that Jesus never really died on the cross. In the dampness of the grave he revived and managed to escape. Others have suggested that the disciples never really saw Jesus alive after death. They experienced hallucinations and thought they saw Him. This primitive view is seldom heard today. It is highly improbable that five hundred people would experience identical hallucinations simultaneously. The record has it that Jesus was seen by five hundred brethren at once.

During more recent years the "explanations" have been of a more sophisticated type. For instance, we are asked to believe that what was actually raised was not Christ's body but the level of interest in his teachings. The apostles got over their fright and disappointment upon seeing their leader slain and discovered the eternal value of His view. They reorganized around his idealism and sought to spread it to other parts of the world. The Gospel took the form of the resurrection story, but the oriental mind never intended for the vehicle to obscure the truth it contained. Succeeding generations of Christians prized the vessel above the life-giving water!

Even more recently we have been told that expediency was the reason for the invention of the resurrection story by the early Christians. As they made their way in the Mediterranean world they encountered many strange religions that made lavish claims for their deities. The Christians saw that if their cause were to progress against competition so formidable, claims even more lavish would have to be made for the founder of their religion. The resurrection story was the result.

Underneath all these "explanations" of the resurrection accounts there is more than disbelief in the resurrection itself.

There is disbelief in the authenticity of the Gospel records. Basically, the problem is one of the trustworthiness of the Scriptures. While there is no denying the large place given to faith in the Christian religion, this does not mean faith in a movement without regard to its historical roots. Any attempt to explain the early spread of Christianity apart from a frank recognition that the disciples believed they had seen Jesus alive from the dead is inadequate. Men would hardly die rather than renounce what they knew to be only fabrication. The resurrection of Jesus is indisputable history.

II

The resurrection of Jesus provides inspiring philosophy. Here we find ample proof of the indestructibility of goodness and the ultimate doom of wickedness. What further evidence do we need that the great God of heaven will never "suffer his holy one to see corruption"? History has known many dark hours, but none blacker than that hour when the Son of God was on the cross. The powers of evil converged upon Golgotha and there they released their fury. This is what evil left to itself will attempt to do. God in His wisdom has a way of taking evil, once it is set in motion, and making it serve a constructive purpose. Evil's terrible worst God made His wonderful best.

The realization of this truth has given assurance to God's people through the centuries that their "labor is not in vain in the Lord." This faith in the ultimate victory of good over evil is vastly different from the nineteenth century doctrine of the inevitability of progress. The philosophy of the true Christian is not that of Pollyanna. Everything will not turn out all right because of the nature of things or the inherent goodness of people. Neither have we here a confidence in social redemption through clashes between blind dialectical forces. The Christian's confidence rests upon the knowledge that God has identified himself with man in history and that, while he transcends history, he is active within it, guiding and shaping human destiny. He has taken captivity captive and stripped evil of any hope of victory.

God has never been without a purpose, the making of man after his moral image. Evil has made repeated attempts to defeat that purpose, but in the resurrection God defeated the would-be victor. The task of the Christian is not to defeat evil with the Gospel. The Gospel is the declaration that God has already defeated evil in Christ. By the resurrection, sentence has been passed on the evil that nailed Christ to the cross and which shackles man in his efforts to conform to the Divine image in personal life and social structure.

Several years ago while spading in my yard, I inadvertently disturbed a snake that had hibernated for the winter months. He came racing out to do battle with the intruder. Stepping aside, I took aim with the shovel point and severed the snake's head from his body. Even though the body was headless, the serpent writhed on the ground for some time before becoming still in death. The world in rebellion is like the snake in convulsion. The head of evil was crushed on Calvary and at the garden tomb. It is a matter of time until God will bring all things under his feet, whether within or beyond history.

The man who dedicates himself to an evil cause is on the losing side. The stars in their courses fight against him. The outcome of the struggle is not in doubt. The decisive battle is over. The task that remains is to consolidate the gains of God's redemptive act.

It is difficult to understand why so many professing Christians have a negative attitude toward life and a spirit of defeatism. To them the night is without a star. The forces of evil are so many and so mighty. The forces of righteousness have so compromised themselves and are so outnumbered as to be without hope of victory. This is the attitude the disciples had before the news of resurrection reached them. They locked themselves up because of their fear of the violent forces that had just destroyed their leader. Their hopes were dashed and their plans for a kingdom were shattered. There was complete triumph for Caesar. Then it happened. News came of the resurrection. The forces that sought to destroy were themselves defeated. God spoke and the earth stood still. The change that came over the disciples cannot be explained except in terms of victory for Christ over the powers that opposed Him. Night turned to day, sorrow to joy, and defeat to victory.

James Stewart reminds us that too many people are still living on the other side of Christ's resurrection. They are still locked in the upper room, terrified and hopeless. They need to be told that Christ lives, that evil has been defeated, that victory belongs to God.

The Christian is not whistling in the dark when he places

complete confidence in God's ultimate triumph. Nor is he attempting to escape social and missionary responsibility through theological determinism. His desire is to be an instrument in the hand of God to be used in consummating the gains of victory.

The Christian will have his dark hours when victory for truth seems impossible. A lie appears to travel so much faster than truth. Many seem more willing to embrace error than fact. Evil is not always unattractive. There is a certain fascination about destruction at work. But above it all stands the risen Christ with the keys of hell and death swinging from His girdle. His comforting word is: "I am He that liveth, and was dead; and, behold, I am alive forevermore." The cause of the Lord is not a losing cause. This assurance gives our lives a glow and zest for the task before us.

III

The resurrection of Jesus gives invincible hope. This does not mean only the hope of victory of goodness over evil, as significant as that is. What is meant here is the hope of resurrection and immortality for every believer.

Man has always longed for and dreamed of immortality, but he has interpreted immortality in many ways. For some immortality has been too much to hope for. Even the Christian sees "through a glass darkly."

To the ancient Hebrew immortality meant primarily to live in posterity. About the worst thing that could happen to a Hebrew was to be cut off without children. The Psalmist described the blessed man as the one about whose table children "sit like olive plants." To be cut off without children was to cease to exist. To be blessed with children was to survive the grave through them. A few of the Hebrews like Job and Daniel had glimpses or intimations of immortality. Daniel seems even to have had a vision of a limited resurrection, but, generally speaking, immortality in early Hebrew thought was very different from the immortality of Hellenism and Christianity.

Certain Greek thinkers were nearer to the Christian understanding of immortality than Hebrew thinkers. Some have concluded that just as the moral law was bequeathed to Christianity by the Hebrews, belief in immortality made its way into Christianity by way of Greek philosophy.

For most Greeks, however, death was an experience full of terror. They likened death to a river of darkness. They gave to this river a name that means to hate or to loathe. In horror they shrank from death as a mysterious land from which no traveller ever returned.

The Christian need have no fear of death. The Son of God has crossed the river of darkness and prepared resting places for his people on the other side. He has stripped death of its victory and removed its sting.

Certain of the Romans apparently cared little about immortality. Their civilization was sensual and their gods were pleasure and power. Archaeologists, while digging in Roman ruins, discovered an ancient cemetery. They were especially impressed with the marking NFFNSNC on some of the graves. They were even more impressed when they found the interpretation to be: "I was not, I was, I am not, I do not care." The marking itself seems to be a betrayal of a deep-seated hunger for immortality. Perhaps they sought to conceal it behind a cloak of sensual excesses and philosophical pessimism.

The Christian cares and readily admits it. But there is an answer to his care. Because Christ lives, the Christian shall live also.

Admittedly, mystery surrounds the Christian doctrine of immortality and resurrection. Paul was hard pressed to explain the body with which the Christian shall come forth. The term that he hit upon was "spiritual body." It has been suggested that this term was used to satisfy both the Jewish and Grecian elements in the Corinthian church. The Hebrews could not think of immortality except in terms of a body. The Greeks could think of immortality only in terms of spirit. Paul therefore attempted to satisfy both groups by his use of the term "spiritual body." To speak of spiritual body is like speaking of dry water or trying to measure distance with a thermometer. The concepts are mutually exclusive.

Admitting mysteries as to the *how* and *what* of resurrection and immortality, the Christian is confident of eternal life by reason of the victory of Christ over death. This was the conclusion of Paul as expressed to the Roman Christians: "If thou shalt confess with thy mouth Jesus as Lord and shalt believe in thine heart that God hath raised him from the dead, thou shalt be saved."

The Christian must not separate belief in Christ's resurrection from the confession of him as Lord. We are saved by the living Lord whom we confess and not simply by our faith in his resurrection. By reason of his resurrection and because he is alive from the grave, he is mighty to save us from sin and to give us an invincible hope of our personal victory over death. Our relationship is to a Person and not to a historical event. The event is our assurance that the Person can save.

Christ has built his church upon a rock. This church of redeemed persons has been given a quality that death cannot stop. When the believer in Christ comes to his death, the gates of death will not be able to turn him back. He possesses the kind of life that will push through into the "land that is fairer than day." God's child goes not to death as a slave to the quarry or as a prisoner to the dungeon. Rather, he goes through death into the presence of a victorious Saviour. This is not wishful thinking, a craven sublimation of life's chief frustration. This is the assurance of One whose victory over death has been attested to by history and experienced by every believing heart.

J. WALLACE HAMILTON

Ride the Wild Horses!

*When we put bits into horses' mouths to make
them obey us, we control the rest of their
bodies also.*
—James 3:3 (Twentieth Century Version)

The wild horses we have to deal with are our instincts—the
untamed impulses of human nature.

The Apostle James had never heard of the psychologist
William James, but he knew something of the problems of the
human heart. He had never heard of Freud, but he knew the
turbulence of desire. He had never read a book by Carl Jung,
but he knew about the conflicts in the soul. "What is the cause of
the fighting and quarreling that goes on among you? Is it not to
be found in the passions which struggle for the mastery in your
bodies?" (Twentieth Century Version).

It has never been said better. Wild horses there inside you!
That's your problem—and the whole human problem in a
nutshell: *What to do with the wild horses of human instinct?*

While we Christians do not accept the animal philosophy of
life, we are obliged to acknowledge our physical kinship with
the earth stuff of which animals are made, and in our natures too
there is a strong resemblance. Carl Sandburg thought he had a
whole menagerie under his ribs, and he felt in his nature the
stirring of many animals. "I am a pal of the earth," he said, "I am
come from the wilderness"—which is another way of saying
what the Genesis story tells us, namely, that we, like the
animals, are made of dust. We all have a bit of that wild stuff
within us. Often, in common speech, we say of one another,
"He's as sly as a fox"—"He eats like a pig"—"He's as brave as a
lion"—or "as stubborn as a mule"—or "as proud as a peacock."

The resemblance is there all right; sometimes, we suspect, it is a bit unfair to the animals.

We come into the world with a powerful set of impulses, which, though back of all our sins, are nevertheless the great driving force of life. They are not of our manufacture. We didn't create them. They were wrought in our nature by the hand of Him who made man in His own image.

Now, I would like, for clarity's sake, to call them *instincts,* though I am well aware that most scholars are wary of that word. Nobody seems to be able to tell us what an instinct is, except to say that it is a "natural impulse prior to experience and instruction." But we know that the name of a thing doesn't matter. Call it impulse, urge, or anything you wish, the reality is still the same. Psychological research of the past fifty years confirms what the Bible has always taught us—that not only in our bodies but in our nature, too, crouch these untamed animal forces which, like wild horses, sometimes run amuck; and that the great business of life is learning what to do with them. That is what all religions are about; all philosophies, all great systems of ethics and government are attempts to find an answer to the question of what we are to do with the wild horses of human instinct.

There are only three major answers, although there are many variations of the answers. The first answer is that of *self-assertion.* Let the wild horses run! Give free rein to your natural instincts. Nature itself endowed us with them; they are all natural—therefore self-justifying; whatever is natural is beautiful, and whatever is beautiful must be right! The only wrong, by the standards of this philosophy, is to inhibit or suppress a natural desire.

It is rather amusing to hear this view presented as "the new morality." It isn't new and it isn't morality; it is the oldest idolatry on earth. Dip down anywhere in ancient life and you will find men making gods. Often they worshiped animals—bulls, snakes, sacred cows. In some lands, they still do. More often, they worshiped the animals within themselves; they bowed down before the passions of their own natures, which they could not control or understand.

Ancient man deified his passions. Bacchus was the deification of his appetite; Venus and Aphrodite were the embodiment of his love passion; in Mars and Woden and Jupiter and countless other warring gods he incarnated his fighting spirit and his stormy impulse to conquer and kill. Men have always worshiped their own powers—powers which, stronger than themselves, control them and push them around.

Today man has outgrown the images of Bacchus, but he is still controlled by appetite. He has destroyed the temples of Venus, but he is still dominated by his passions. He has dismissed Mars as a creation of superstition, but the war gods still call him into battle, and the wild horses of carnal desire still drive roughshod over the earth.

So "the new morality" is nothing but a very old idolatry. A prominent modern writer, in a book which he called *Essay on Morals,* urged as our one great need the honesty to face the fact that we are what we are—animals. He called for courage to fling from us the hampering reins of artificial civilization and religious superstition, for which, he thinks, our nature is not fitted. We have had a deluge of books in recent years urging us to throw off the restraints of Puritan religion and "corset civilization," insisting that life was made for freedom and the sooner we start living by natural laws, the sooner we shall find the joyous exuberance of primitive life, "where wild in the woods the noble savage ran." What shall we do with the wild horses? The answer of self-assertion is, "Kill the riders and let the horses run. Obey your instincts!"

I suppose Nietzsche was the "number one" prophet of self-assertion. To him, civilization was the great corruptor, and Christianity was the great perverter of human instincts. Nietzsche seized upon that fascinating (Spencerian-Darwinian) phrase, "survival of the fittest," and came up with the solution, "Get rid of your pious priests and their weak-livered gospel of mercy. Purge out of your souls this disease, this devil of Christianity. Progress depends on the strong man and the strong peoples. Therefore be strong, and assert yourself; be a superman."

Nietzsche went on to paraphrase the Gospel: "Ye have heard how it was said in old times, 'Blessed are the meek: for they shall inherit the earth': but I say unto you, blessed are the valiant, for they shall make the earth their throne. And ye have heard men say, 'Blessed are the poor in spirit'; but I say unto you, blessed are the great in soul and the free in spirit, for they shall enter into Valhalla. And ye have heard men say, 'Blessed are the peacemakers': but I say unto you, blessed are the war-makers, for they shall be called, if not the children of

Yahweh, the children of Odin, who is greater than Yahweh."
The modern world is in part the product of that mad philosophy.

Along about the time of the American Revolution, Adam
Smith wrote his shorter bible for the industrialists; about a
century later, Karl Marx wrote his bible for the workers; both
contained essentially the same gospel—"Assert yourself—be
strong—follow self-interest or class interest and life will
balance itself." Then came the psychology of behaviorism,
which taught us emphatically that repressions are bad for
human nature, that instincts were made to be obeyed and that
life was made to be "untrammeled and free."

Thus the old idolatry got under way within our Christian
framework, until one sad day we woke up to discover that this
exuberant naturalism had some rather terrible consequences.
We saw flaming youth take avidly to the "new morality," raise a
generation to whom marriage was little more than a social
convenience, and come up at last with the Kinsey Report on
sex. We saw the Nazis take Nietzsche's self-assertion and put it
into government. The mastery of the strong man, the
super-race! Dachau and Buchenwald, where unrestrained
instinct piled human bodies like cord-wood and set them afire!
We saw Russia throw off "the slave morality." "There is no
God or heaven," they said; "we must make our own. We must
throw down our Bibles, take up our guns, level down the rich
and take their property for ourselves."

Out of that has been produced a vast underworld, fantastic,
revolting, unbelievable, a world without heart or conscience or
pity, in which men have the appearance of men while
underneath are fierce, cruel creatures scientifically extermin-
ating each other. Sometimes you wonder—What are we,
anyway? Savages?

None of us can afford to be smug about it, or to imagine that it
is all about other people made of different clay from ours. Long
ago Carl Jung warned us that the evils of primitive man are still
crouching in all of us, alive and ugly in the dark recesses of the
heart under the thin veneer of civilization; he said that only
Christianity is keeping them in check, and that if Christianity
be neglected the old horrors will sweep in again like a roaring
global flood.

"I tell you," wrote Paul, "the deeds of the flesh are quite
obvious, such as sexual vice, impurity, sensuality, idolatry,
dissension, . . . party-spirit, . . . drinking bouts, and the like

(Moffatt). If you live by the flesh, if you obey unredeemed, unrestrained instinct, you shall die—for that is the "Realm of Death." Sometimes it seems that the modern world is a commentary on Paul's text. Surely there are definite drawbacks to the answer of self-assertion.

The second answer is the extreme opposite of self-assertion: it is the answer of the way of *self-negation*. This answer holds that our primitive desires are so fierce that we must find a way to reduce them. The horses are wild, so we must tame them, take the fire and fight out of them, make them lie down and be still. If the way of self-assertion would eliminate the riders, the way of self-negation would eliminate the horses.

That is what Buddhism is, and Hinduism too: they are great religions dedicated to the elimination of desire. Buddha saw desire as the source of all evil and suffering and conflict. He said, "You must free your soul of desire. Cut out the roots of it. Denude your heart of every want, and in utterly passionless existence you will find peace of mind, contentment, and after much practice come at last to Nirvana, a state of nothingness." It is a good trick if you can do it: "Get rid of your headache by cutting off your head." Reduce the conflicts of personality by destroying the powers that make the person! At one time or another, one third of the human race was trying to do it on the Buddhist formula, praying three times a day, "Lord God of the Universe, heap worldly gifts on foolish men, but on my head only the sweet waters of serenity. Give me the gift of the untroubled heart."

Much of our Christianity in its historical expression has had in it this streak of Buddhist asceticism. The monastic life was often more Buddhist than Christian, monks, hermits and holy men withdrawing into the stillness of their souls to mortify the flesh, to kill the wild horses. The holiest man among them was the fellow who could sit, motionless and quiet as a gooseberry bush, contemplating God. He had elaborate methods of relaxing his body-mind, endless formulas to repeat over and over, until he had lost himself in the Infinite as a raindrop sinks into the sea. It has a certain fascination, and the appearance of deep spirituality.

The multiplicity of our modern peace-of-mind cults are not the products of Protestantism. They come out of the mystic soul of the East; they are the offspring of that ascetic strain in human nature which has plagued the Church from the beginning; it is a religion of escape taking over Christian labels and symbols and representing Christ as the spokesman of escape.

But you can be sure of this: *any religion whose goal is the destruction of desire has no kinship with the eternal Christ.*

Again, any religion whose sole aim is the mere *curbing* of desire is not Christian. A little boy was playing so quietly with his father's tools in the garage that his mother just knew he must be up to some mischief. She called from the kitchen, "Tommy, whatever you're doing, stop it!" Whole systems of religion, philosophy and government have been built upon just such negative restraint. Historically, it is represented in the Stoics, in Confucius, in the great endurance religions which seek to solve life's conflicts not by the elimination of desire but by the severe and systematic suppression of it. Curb the wild horses! Control your desires! You can't help but admire it, but it is still too negative an answer to be a Christian answer. You can hardly make a dynamic religion out of a coerced, negative morality.

So we come to it: the third answer, the way of Christ—not self-assertion, nor self-negation, but *self-fulfillment.* "I am come not to destroy but to fulfill." The answer of Jesus is that these strong passions in our human nature must not be destroyed nor suppressed, but be put to use, pulled together in a supreme master-passion and consecrated to the Kingdom of God. The transcendent difference in Christ from all who came before Him is summed up in this magic word, *fulfillment.* This poor world has always tried to alternate between two fruitless extremes: between a kind of Nietzscheanism that leaves man an untamed though sometimes educated savage, and that form of Buddhism which breaks the spirit of man, takes the fight out of him and leaves him a dried-up cabbage. Jesus is come not to destroy our powers but to bring them to fulfillment.

Jesus is not at war with our human nature. He does not say that our instincts were born of evil or that our only hope is to cast them out, or to beat them down. He understood perfectly, in the realm of human nature, what Luther Burbank discovered in the realm of plant nature: that every weed is a potential flower, and that the very qualities which make it a weed could make it a flower. Great sinners and great saints contain much the same stuff. The same instincts that made Napoleon could have made a Paul. What to do with the wild horses? Harness them! Put them to work! Ride them, rejoicing in their strength. That's His answer.

The religion of Jesus is no opiate, putting the soul to sleep and taking the fight out of men. Look at the record. Look at the men He picked to follow Him. It was a public scandal that He spent so much of His time with rough men and profane—with the sinners and the disinherited, the earthy, half-heathen fellows, and that He chose His followers from among them. Jesus was genuinely attracted to the irreligious. Because they were so loaded with earthy vitamins, they made good prospects for Christian discipleship. They were the weeds, the black sheep whom Marguerite Wilkinson describes as different from pious folks in that they had such amazing vigor:

> The white sheep are placid, and feed in quiet places;
> Their fleece are like silver that the moon has known.
> But the black sheep have vigor in their ugly faces.
> The best of all the shepherds wants them for His own.

They were stormy men, most of them, with turbulent passions that were often misdirected. One was a Zealot, a member of the Communist party of the day, a sworn brother in the rebels' battalion of death. But Jesus did not fear enthusiasm, or even fanaticism. He knew that torrents in men, like torrents in rivers and waterfalls, could be converted and harnessed, and their power made to serve and save. Bishop Arthur Moore says, "I would rather restrain a fanatic than try to resurrect a corpse."

Would you have chosen Matthew? He was a cheat, a gambler, a tax-gatherer for Rome. But Jesus knew that every weed is a potential flower, and that even a cheater is bound to have talents too valuable to waste on small issues. "Come," He said to Matthew, "follow me." He *chose* Matthew.

They were ambitious men. They wanted to get ahead in the world, even ahead of each other. "Grant us," said James and John, "to sit on the right hand and the left." Jesus never feared their consuming ambition; He laid His hand upon that powerful human impulse, as He found it in James and John, and guided them into a worthy use of that impulse. In one immortal sentence He lifted ambition from selfish jostling for place and position to the high level of spiritual devotion: "Let him that would be great among you be the servant of all."

Again there was the fighting instinct, which was very strong in them. Peter was no shrinking violet. The big fisherman could take care of himself on the waterfront. James and John were nicknamed "Sons of thunder." Does Jesus take the fight out of men? No, He redeems and redirects it in what Canon Streeter calls "creative strife."

You say you have a temper. You would like to be rid of that temper, so you could be a Christian. You will be of little use to God without your temper; He already has too many disciples who won't get mad at anything—not even the liquor traffic. Asking God to make you "a better Christian" by taking away your temper is like trying to make a better watch by leaving out its works. God *wants* men of temper. He chose such men. Saul of Tarsus was a man of temper. He was a born fighter. After he met Christ on the Damascus Road he was still a fighter—but now for truth and the Kingdom of God. When he reached the end of his missionary road he said proudly, "I have fought a good fight . . ." In the army of the Lord, he was still a warrior with his temper harnessed. He didn't tame his horses. He rode them, rejoicing in their strength.

There are many ways of describing or defining conversion. I like to put it like this: conversion is that process, through which the redeeming power of God brings all the powers of your being into perfect focus and co-ordination—by which He harnesses the wild horses of your nature to His majestic purposes and makes them the servants of the new life in Christ.

CLARENCE JORDAN

The Adventures of
Three Students
in a Fiery Furnace

The adventures of three students in a fiery furnace is told in the
Book of Daniel. This book, in point of time, was written perhaps
closer to the New Testament than any other of the Old
Testament books. Most scholars agree that it was written about
167 B.C. If this is true, it was written at a time of great
persecution. On the throne was an emperor who called himself
Antiochus Epiphanes. The Greek word *epiphanes* means
"illustrious"—Antiochus the Illustrious. But so terrible were
his persecutions, so bloodthirsty was this king that his subjects
did not call him Epiphanes; they called him Epimines, which is
Greek for "a man who's gone berserk," a fellow who is cuckoo.
So this was written during the reign of an emperor who had
gone cuckoo and it was written primarily to young people who
were being forced against their will to obey government edicts
to which they could not conscientiously agree.

The book, then, purports to be a treatise—at least the first
six chapters of it—on what happens to a spiritually sensitive
person when his government and his God are on a collision
course. Now, since we today are facing more and more of this in
the world, where governments are prone to assume the
prerogatives of God, this book might become the most relevant
of all the Old Testament books. It is not a historical narrative.
While the setting is in about 587 B.C. in the court of
Nebuchadnezzar, everyone who read the book would know that
the writer was not talking about King Nebuchadnezzar. He's
talking about King Epiphanes. And everyone would know that
Shadrach, Meshach, and Abednego, and Daniel are really not
actual historical figures. They are people as real as Rhett
Butler and Scarlett O'Hara in *Gone With the Wind*. This might

From *The Substance of Faith and Other Cotton Patch Sermons* by
Clarence Jordan, ed. Dallas Lee (New York: Association Press, 1972).

be considered a historical parable in which the writer has concealed a truth; and the truth is that in the time of testing, when God and government are on collision course, God calls his people to be faithful to him even though it means disobedience to the government.

Now, let's take just one episode of the many in this book. The king had brought these three students over as foreign students, as international students, to go to school at Babylon. They were taken from south Geor—uh, Judea and brought over into Babylon to be trained in all the wisdom of the Babylonians. And then, at the end of the three-year course, they were to be sent before the king. They already had their undergraduate work and they were now in the divinity school. And when they got through, they were to appear before the king to see whether they had the proper ministerial tone and etiquette. They had completed their ministerial training and, unfortunately, they had had some good teachers who had helped them to catch on to what God is all about. I think one of the worst things that a teacher can do in the seminary is to help his students understand what Christianity's all about. It gets them into all kinds of trouble. I think one of the worst things about Jesus' sermons was that you could understand them.

These three fellows had caught on to the fact that God was still alive and kicking around in the world and that he was the Lord of human history and that he was not to be tinkered and tampered with and that no professor, even though he had a Ph.D. and was teaching at a university, could bury God. Now, I want to take one episode that's in the third chapter of the Book of Daniel. This writer sets the stage. He says:

Nebuchadnezzar the king made an image of gold, whose height was threescore cubits and the breadth thereof was six cubits.

It's sixty by six. Now, we're not Hebrews, but the Hebrews would get a real bang out of this because numbers symbolized certain things to them. The number thirteen to us symbolizes unluckiness. Many hotels don't have a thirteenth floor. Airplanes sometimes don't have Number Thirteen seats. To the Jews, the six meant incomplete, imperfect. Here's an image now that's sixty cubits high and six cubits wide, and to the Hebrew students this would mean that this is a blasphemous image. It's the acme of imperfection. The government had made a great mistake in ever embarking upon it.

He set it up in the plain of Dura, in the province of Babylon.
Now, the plain was out where the peasants work, where they
toil in the fields and grow the corn, the cotton, the peanuts, and
the tobacco, and all that kind of stuff. In other words, the king
was setting up this golden image out there on the plains where
he had extracted the taxes from these farmers. He had ground
their faces to the earth and squeezed the blood out of them so
that he could erect a mighty image of gold and he had the
audacity to put it up out in front of the very people he had
exploited. It would be about like levying a heavy tax on
Negroes and then putting up a gold monument to Abraham
Lincoln and locating it in Harlem. It would be blasphemy.
I think in all fairness we ought to say that this great golden
image was not financed by the C.I.A. through an aid to the
Babylonian Ministry of Worship. This was the real stuff. This
guy had gotten it out of the people and he hadn't gotten it from
any foreign aid. It was an image of gold. Now, I'm not sure who
built it; he might have let the contract out to some of his allies. It
could be that he might have let the contract out to some big
American firms to build the head, the body, the legs, and maybe
the local people got to contract for building the little finger on
the left hand.
Now, Nebuchadnezzar was proud of this thing, and so he
wanted to have a big dedication. The writer says:
*Then Nebuchadnezzar the king sent to gather together the
satraps, the deputies, the governors, the judges, the treasurers,
the counsellors, the sheriffs, and all the rulers of the provinces.*
I imagine the Imperial Lizard was invited and all the other
folks; this was just a big to-do and the emperor invited them all
to come to the dedication. Just prior to that, he might have had
a $100-a-plate dinner for fund-raising to help defray some of the
expenses of the image, and they were all going to have a big
time at this dedication. They even had the Marine Band out
there.
*The satraps, the deputies, the governors, the judges, the
treasurers, the counsellors, the sheriffs, and all the rulers of the
provinces were gathered together unto the dedication of the
image that Nebuchadnezzar the king had set up, and they stood
before the image. Then the herald cried aloud* (the herald—in
those days, that was the equivalent of the Baptist preacher who
opened the meeting with an invitation)—*the herald cried aloud,
"To you it is commanded, O people, nations, and languages,*

that at what time ye hear the sound of the cornet, the flute, the harp, the sackbut, the psaltery, the dulcimer, and all kinds of music, you fall down and worship the golden image that Nebuchadnezzar the king has set up."

Now, you would have thought that when the herald cried that everybody had to fall down on their face when they heard the first strain of "The Stars and Stripes Forever," that somebody would have objected. But all these bigwigs obediently bowed down and all fell on their face.

Because (Nebuchadnezzar says) *whoso falleth not down and worshippeth shall the same hour be cast into the midst of a burning fiery furnace.*

In those days, you didn't burn your draft card; you got burnt.

Therefore, at that time when all the people heard the sound of the cornet, the flute, the harp, the sackbut, the psaltery, and all kinds of music all the people and the nations and the languages fell down and worshipped the golden image that Nebuchadnezzar the king had set up.

I think in all fairness we ought also to say that the sackbut player had not infiltrated the royal orchestra to try to find out whether or not the dulcimer section was Communist. This was the real thing and they were there to pay homage to the king and they were to bow down in unison. The king had learned that to get real obedience out of the people, you had to have them marching to music, you had to have a big festive occasion, whip up the spirit of unity, and say, "We're not going to have any dissent." This seems to be a very pleasant occasion for the king. He's been elected by an overwhelming majority and it looks like his chances for re-election are pretty good, and he's quite happy that he's built this big image. Of course, he had to levy a 10 per cent surcharge, but other than that, he got by all right and everything looked fine and rosy.

But then, there's always a fly in the ointment. These young theologs have a way of getting out of hand and some of them are going to kick over the traces if you aren't careful—and, sure enough, this is what happened.

Wherefore at that time certain Chaldeans came near and brought accusation against the Jews.

Now, I don't know who these Chaldeans were. My guess is that they were the ancient "John Besmirch Society" and that they were noticing that these Hebrews weren't quite 100 per cent loyal. They had studied the history of these Hebrews and found that these aliens who had been brought over there to Babylon at one time had been sojourners in Egypt—their great-great-great-great-great-great-grandfather had been a servant under Phara-ho, and it might have been that they still carried over some of those doctrines, you know. And these John Besmirchers were watching them very, very carefully.

And here's what they said: *They answered and said to King Nebuchadnezzar, "O King, live forever!"* (That's the ancient counterpart of "Heil, Hitler!") *"O King, live forever! We got some news for you."* Now, you would have thought at least they would have waited until the dedication was over to spoil the king's day. But they didn't. Right in the middle of the dedication service, they come whispering up there: "Hey, Nebuchadnezzar, we got some news for you. There're some folks that are not bowing down. There're some folks that didn't fall on their faces when the band struck up." And Nebuchadnezzar is just furious.

In his rage and fury he commanded to bring Shadrach, Meshach, and Abednego. And they brought these men before the king. Nebuchadnezzar spoke and said to them, "Is it a-purpose, O Shadrach, Meshach, and Abednego, that ye serve not my gods nor worship the golden image which I have set up?"

That's a lot of royal jargon for saying, "Bubba, did you do this on purpose? Did you know what you were doing? Didn't you hear what I ordered?" Then Nebuchadnezzar softens up a little bit, gets rather paternalistic and says:

"Now if ye be ready at what time ye hear the sound of the cornet, the flute, the harp, the sackbut, the psaltery, and the dulcimer. (King Nebuchadnezzar knew how many pieces there were in his orchestra.) *If then ye be ready, ye fall down and worship the image which I have made. But if ye worship not, ye shall be cast the same hour into a burning fiery furnace and who is that God that shall deliver you out of my hands?"*

He's saying, "Now, fellow, I hope you didn't do this on purpose. But in case you did, I'm going to get the band to start over with the 'Star-Spangled Banner' and if you're ready to give the loyalty oath at that moment, then we'll forgive you. But if not"—and then Nebuchadnezzar pulls his trump card out of his deck—"into the fiery furnace!"

That fiery furnace was the central heating system of the whole empire. That's what heated up everybody. All this hot patriotism was really not so much love for the country but fear of the furnace. Nebuchadnezzar offers these kids the prospect of doing one of two things: 1) just simply falling down and worshipping before that image which would have been a relatively easy thing to do. They were already standing up there before it. All they had to do was fall down. Or 2) take a little trip to the fiery furnace. Well, these kids answer in a way that I think is really superb. Here's what they say. I want to read their words.

Shadrach, Meshach, and Abednego answered and said to the king, "O Nebuchadnezzar, we have no need to answer thee in this matter. If it be so, our God whom we serve is able to deliver us from the burning fiery furnace; and he will deliver us out of your hand. But if not, be it known unto thee, O king, that we will not serve thy gods nor worship the golden image which thou hast set up."

They said, "O king, this God we serve is no foreign God. We know him quite well. And we are convinced that he is greater than you are and that he can deliver us out of your hands. We might be ashes, but he'll blow us out of your hand. You don't have the power to hold us. But even if he doesn't, we want you to know, O king, that we still aren't going to bow down to your image." Now, this took some real dedication, saying they believe that God will deliver them but even if he doesn't, they still aren't going to bow down. These young fellows were saying, "You know, if we've got to take our choice between living in a country where men are slaves or dying in a furnace where men are free, we choose the furnace. We had rather be ashes than asses." That's rather straight talk that even a king can understand. And the king gives the order, "Fire up the furnace. We got some stuff to go in it."

Now, with normal criminals like car thieves and dope addicts and bootleggers, you can run the furnace at normal temperature. But when you've got a civil disobedient guy on your hand, you've got to heat it up, 'cause this is no normal crime. You can even handle such crimes as murder at normal temperature. But when you get up to challenging the authority of the king himself, then the king can't deal with that kind of violation with just the furnace running along as usual. So he says to them, "Heat that thing up seven times hotter than it's ever been before."

Here again, there's a little bit of symbology in the numbers. The number six indicated incompleteness. The number seven indicated completeness. The week had seven days in it; the whole number of seven meant completeness. What Nebuchadnezzar's saying here is, "Open up every burner, even the afterburner , and get it as hot as it can possibly be heated." He orders that they be bound and they are thrown in. The fire is so hot, it says, that the guys that threw them in got killed by it. That's a hot fire.

Well, the night passed and the furnace began to cool down a little bit. By the time it got to where you could get within reasonable distance of it, Nebuchadnezzar decided he would go see whether these three young civil disobedient guys were properly cremated. So he goes out and looks in. And, to his amazement, he sees four men in there. He calls his men and says, "Looky here. Didn't we sentence three men? How is it that now I see four men and one I see in here is like unto the Son of God?" Nebuchadnezzar cries out, "Shadrach! Meshach! Abednego! Come forth and come hither!"

That was no time for civil disobedience, and Shadrach, Meshach, and Abednego obeyed the king, and they came out— all three of them. Three? I thought there were four. Where is the fourth? The one like the Son of God—maybe he's still in there. Maybe he's waiting for more students named Shadrach, Meshach, and Abednego, so he can walk around with them in the fiery furnace; for he knows what a fiery furnace is like.

What then is this book saying to us? I think it says four things. First, that human institutions, whether they be political, ecclesiastical, or otherwise, are capable of gross error. The error is usually in proportion to the power and pride of the institution, whether it be ecclesiastical or political. Secondly, this book is saying that extreme attempts are made to produce total conformity to the error. We see this in the Roman empire when it was about to fall apart at the seams the emperor deified himself and set up emperor worship and commanded that there be no dissent. Thirdly, it is saying that God's call to obedience can be heard above the tumult, above the bands, and above the flag-waving. This means that his call may be costly and extremely dangerous. Anyone who embarks on a course of obedience to God when his government is on collision course with God must be prepared for the fiery furnace. And fourthly, it says that God alone is ultimately the Lord of history, that he is greater than kings and their furnaces, as well as their gas chambers.

Are there any Shadrachs today? Are there any young students in the fiery furnace? Yes, I know of one. His name isn't Shadrach, his name is Tom Rodd. Tom Rodd is a young man nineteen years of age. He was eighteen a year ago when he felt that he could not conscientiously go into the draft system. He refused to register. He was brought up before a judge in Philadelphia and sentenced to four years. The judge probated the sentence on the grounds that Tom Rodd would not engage in any peace demonstrations of any kind. Tom began to serve his probated sentence; but then as the war in Vietnam became to Tom an increasingly immoral affair, he felt that he had to violate his terms of probation and participate in a peace demonstration. He was brought again before the judge, and I want to read you Tom's statement just prior to his resentencing. It's one of the most eloquent statements that I have heard from any man of any age in America. How a young fellow could make this kind of statement, I don't know. It must have been that he had been with Jesus.

Tom said, "Your Honor, one year and four months ago, you and I met each other in this building. What brought us together then was my conscientious refusal to co-operate with our government's draft system. You came as representative of the government with the authority and the responsibility which that office implies. Now we are together again, and again you are here as a representative of the United States Government, this time because I have openly violated the special terms of probation that you set down the last time we met. I'm sorry that I have only known you in your official capacity. You and I are human beings; we are together, as brothers, wrapped up in this joyful confusion called life. It is presumptuous of me to say so, but I sense—and I say this in all humility—that you are a good man. I hope that you will not deny me the right to affirm our brotherhood, for in that brotherhood with all people I find the only basis for living. You, sir, are a representative of this government, and often unwillingly I too am a representative. With a profound feeling of inadequacy and unreadiness, I am forced by my conscience to stand as a representative of the suffering millions of Vietnam. I am forced to stand for the girl-child burned to death in Bin Hoa, for the refugee cold and hungry in a camp on the outskirts of Saigon, for the weary guerrilla fighter, for the Buddhist monk who is now a handful of ashes, for the thousands with no legs, thousands more with no eyes. Yes, Your Honor, I am representative even for the U. S. Marine now slowly dying in a Philadelphia hospital. These people, sir, are my constituency. I stand for them; and my word from them to this government, to this country, to both countries, is this: stop your war; your dominoes, your escalation, your computer theories. Your phony negotiations are at best human madness and at worst insidious, deliberate lies. Your war—all wars—are immoral and insane. Stop it.

"So here is Tom Rodd. I have tried, sir. Lord knows I have tried to obey this probation. I wanted to go to Selma and walk to Montgomery, but I didn't; I wanted to go to Washington and confront the President, but I didn't. I wanted to picket Girard College in Philadelphia, I wanted to help picket a nonunion store on Lancaster Avenue in West Philadelphia, but I didn't. But this war is too immediate, too pressing, too terrible, for me to say later, 'but I didn't.' What about the prison term I face? It's real, Your Honor; it scares me. But while I face isolation, my constituency faces death. My risk is minuscule compared to their reality. So, if prison comes, I will accept it and make the most of it. Now, let me reiterate what anybody who knows me should know: that I am an incorrigible optimist, that I love life. I play the banjo and daily toss my head and tap my feet to the romping stomping all-pervading beat of human existence. That's all I wanted to say, Your Honor, and I wish you and everybody a happy New Year."

GERALD KENNEDY

Always in Debt

I am under obligation both to Greeks and to barbarians, both to the wise and to the foolish: so I am eager to preach the gospel to you also who are in Rome.
—Romans 1:14-15 RSV

One of the bishop's privileges in The Methodist Church is to welcome young men into the ministry. After a boy has been on trial with us for three or four years, the time comes when he stands before an annual conference and answers questions read by the bishop. The questions have come down to us from John Wesley, and they have been little changed throughout the years. One of them is: "Are you in debt so as to embarrass you in your work?" I never heard a young man answer "yes," and I do not know what I would do if he did. I have found out later that some of them had pretty heavy financial obligations, and I have come to the conclusion that they are hard to embarrass. Maybe they should be asked if they are in debt so as to embarass anyone else.

Some time ago I was reading St. Paul's letter to the Romans and these words captured my attention: "I am under obligation both to Greeks and to barbarians, both to the wise and to the foolish." Supposing, I thought, that Paul were seeking admission into one of our Conferences and this question about debt were put to him. He would answer, "Am I in debt so as to embarrass me? I sure am. I owe everybody from the cultured to the crude; from the wise to the foolish; from the good to the bad. Why," he might say, "if I lived a thousand years I could not pay back what I owe."

He was saying, of course, that a man is always in debt and that no one can ever say he owes no one. We are born owing so much that none of us ever gets clear of obligations. So far as debt is concerned, the affluent society is no different from the poorest society. This point of view presents us with a rather grim outlook. For the truth is, and this is the first thing I want to say,

We Fear Debt.

On this subject I speak with some authority. I cannot remember a time in my childhood when my family was clear of debt. Although it always seemed that we were just about to make it, we never did. My father would call a family conference and tell us why we could not do what we had set our hearts on. But, he would tell us, we only had so many more payments on this particular debt, and then we ought to have a little more money to give us more spending choices. It never worked out that way, and while it was pleasant to dream and plan, debts were a part of my youth. I hated them and I feared them.

When my wife and I were first married, we had a friend who was a retired manufacturer and very wealthy. He often said to me, "A young man should be willing to go into debt and have no fear of owing money." I believed him with my head but not with my heart, for the constant pressure of debts had been a continual worry all my childhood.

A few years ago in India a young missionary took us out through the country to visit some of the many small villages. He told us that these people were born into debt and they hardly ever escaped. Living always on the edge of starvation and want, the peasants had to borrow from time to time and always at outrageous interest rates. They spent their lives hoping to escape debt, but they never got free. So no matter what their legal status was, they actually lived in financial slavery until they died.

The sharecropper in this country went through the same experience. In hopes that a good year would get him even, he found always that he was not quite clear when the crop was harvested. There was nothing to do but go to the store where he could get credit to feed and clothe his family after a fashion, and sink deeper and deeper into debt every year. There comes to such people a deadening despair and hopelessness. They ask,

"What is the use?" In a moment of realism such people know that things will never be better and that they will never be free. It is against this kind of dull, hopeless struggle that we wage our war on poverty. Such people are never in a position to make the contributions we have a right to expect from our citizens. They never know the joy of playing a real part in the nation's life.

A friend of mine who has directed a social agency for young men and boys for forty years in the Elephant and Castle district of London, once told me of his family's fear of sickness when he was a boy. Sickness meant loss of work and going into debt. They were urged to "work it off" when they felt ill. Those of us who are more fortunate must not forget the burden of debt on the poor. It is a very real thing around the world, and it is of concern to all of us.

We are also afraid of being in debt intellectually. We want to be known as men of new ideas and originality, and consequently we are tempted to claim as our own what came from another. There was an American preacher whose wife published some of his sermons after he died. An English preacher read them and thought they sounded strangely familiar. When he checked them carefully, he found they had been appropriated with little change from one of his own books. It was such a flagrant case that the publisher settled in a hurry, but this did not appease the Englishman's anger. Of course if the American had lived, he would never have consented to the publishing of his material. Still, the theft was a shameful thing. No preacher should use another's material in such a way as to feel embarrassed if that other man appeared unexpectedly in the congregation while he was using the material. If it is uncomfortable to be in debt, it is even worse to be in debt and not to confess it.

Almost any writer is tempted constantly to minimize his obligations to other writers. Most of our material comes from somebody else, but we ought to think it through, give it the style of our personalities so that it has the stamp of our minds. While few of us will ever be regarded as original thinkers, all of us have something of our own to contribute. The man who thinks he is expressing an original idea will most likely find that a Greek said it better five or six hundred years before the birth of Christ. To confess our debts does not make us poor but rich, and plagiarism is the sin of a small mind.

A country boy was given some money by his father and told to see the circus. He rode into the town, tied up his horse, and followed the crowd. In a little while the band came down the street, followed by the wild animals in cages, the acrobats, and the clowns. The boy watched it to the end and then rode home again. His father was surprised to see him so soon, and he was even more surprised that he still had his money. "Didn't you see the circus?" he asked. "Sure," the boy answered, "it came down the street and it was free." The fear of having to pay and the desire to save money keeps many a man watching a parade but never seeing the show. Our fear of debt makes us settle for too little.

The second thing to notice is the opposite side of the coin:

We Seek Independence and Freedom.

The goal of life becomes the attainment of self-sufficiency.

There is a sense in which this is the legitimate process of growing up. The boy wants to arrive at the place where he can be independent of his father and be his own boss. He imagines a time when no one can tell him to be in at midnight or to mow the lawn. The girl thinks it will be wonderful when her mother cannot tell her to use less make-up and to wear her skirts longer. There is a time in life when parents are taskmasters whose chief function is to prevent their children from doing what they want to do and to make them do what they do not want to do. Then it is that to be free to do as one pleases seems like heaven. We learn one day that a man's real troubles begin when he can do as he pleases.

There is the slavery to money. The young couple begin bravely with a budget. It all makes sense on paper, and it is a new adventure to plan just how much can be spent for each need. Of course, it never quite works out that way, and the budget becomes increasingly a burden and an irritation. Someday, says the wife, may we have enough money to spend without having to worry about the budget! Happiness is a situation where an extra hundred dollars is not a matter of life and death. Madison Avenue spends most of its time and skill in persuading us that financial success is the true goal of life.

The lure of travel is an appeal to freedom from local responsibilities and obligations. The dream of many a man is to be free to wander at will and see strange sights in faraway places. Some of us whose work makes it necessary to travel a good deal have lost this spirit. When we have a holiday, we want to stay home. But to be free from daily obligations and roam the world at will seems the ideal situation to most people.

The boy longs for the day when he can talk to his father man to man. No longer will he be the inexperienced youth expected to take advice and be told what he can do. The time will come, he hopes, when he will be a man, able to express his opinions on equal terms with his father. Maybe he will have children and can do unto them as his father has been doing unto him. Freedom from parental authority lurks in the minds of young people as a state very much to be desired.

The student who sits gratefully at the feet of a fine teacher wishes for a day when he knows enough about the subject to be treated as an equal. It is not that he does not respect the teacher, and indeed he honors him and will be forever appreciative. But he is aiming at that time when the professor will ask his opinion and consult him as a colleague. A good many years ago I was invited to teach preaching at my old seminary. I shall not forget the high moment when a former professor addressed me in an assembly as "Professor Kennedy." I had arrived.

There is a sense in which independence is the Protestant promise in man's relation to God. We do not have to pray through the priest or by way of the saints. No professional or expert is necessary to represent us before God. Each man is a priest and every man is confronted by God directly. The hierarchy may be necessary for the housekeeping duties connected with the institution, but it is not necessary to get me introduced to God. We sometimes forget that this means terrifying responsibilities for the individual. But the ability of every Christian man to enter directly into fellowship with God is a precious heritage.

There was once a boy who found a dime in the road. He was so impressed with getting something for nothing that for the rest of his life, he walked with his eyes on the road. After forty years he had picked up nearly thirty-five thousand buttons, more than fifty thousand pins, about four dollars in loose change, a bent back, and a terrible disposition. This is the reward facing the man who makes a career out of being independent. Unless he is careful, he will miss the richest things in life.

Let us, therefore, look at a third proposition which will sound like bad news. It is simply that

We Can Never Be Out of Debt.

The whole dream is false and the goal is unattainable. From the day we are born until the day we die, we owe more than we can pay, no matter how long we live or how rich we get. My parents died before I could do much to repay them what I owed. My father was not alive when The Methodist Church, in a weak moment, no doubt, elected me a bishop. If he had been present when that happened, he would have thought it a greater honor than to have a son President of the United States. My mother, who gave so much that I am just now beginning to realize it, never received any proper recognition of my debt to her. This troubles me many times, and if there were a way to make plain to my parents how much I owe them, it would be joy. One thing is perfectly clear, and that is that I could never come near being clear of my obligations to them. Let any man or woman think two minutes of the love and sacrifice invested in them, and they will not talk any more about being self-sufficient.

I remember my teachers, especially a young man who taught my Sunday school class when I was about eight years old. We were an ornery bunch, and if anybody has trouble believing the theological doctrine of original sin, let him teach a class of eight-year-old boys. Yet that young fellow was patient and faithful, and now and again took us to the river on a Saturday. I have thought since how many things he must have preferred doing on those occasions and how often he must have been tempted to push us in. I wish there were some way to tell him what he has meant to me through the years and how many things he said I still remember. And when I think of all the other fine teachers who have enriched my life with their example and wisdom, the debt is so staggering that I am in despair.

Consider your neighbors. We do not seem to find time to be very neighborly with the people who live near us. But their good will is shown in a hundred little ways, and it lifts up my heart to know they are there. If I needed help, they would respond, and if anything happened to me, my wife would find them ready to help her. We live in a big city, but there is genuine friendship and concern all about us which we are aware of when we stop to think about it for a moment. Every once in a while a stranger does something for me so unexpected and so wonderful that a man wants to shout.

During the 1964 presidential election, there appeared on a few bumpers: "Please, Uncle Sam. I would rather do it myself." The first time I saw it I was speechless. Did the fellow know what he was saying? Did he ever count up the things he received from society and the extent to which he was dependent on his brethren for his life? Consider those who came before us and built the cities, the transportation systems, the schools. I would like to have such a man build these things himself for twenty-four hours and see how he comes out. His sentiment is nonsense, and only thoughtless people ever believe that they do not need the help of government in maintaining themselves.

The man who began with nothing and achieved success is tempted to speak of himself as a self-made man. All this does is relieve the Almighty from a mighty embarrassing responsibility. No man is able to claim that he is a self-made man. Every one of us had friends who strengthened us by believing in us and giving us encouragement. Let us not minimize our own efforts with false humility, but let us not forget how much we owe to other people. When a football player makes a long run, there was a key block which sprung him loose. There are always key blocks when we break away for a big gain, and only small men will forget it.

Many years ago a wealthy student at Williams College was accused of defacing college property and was sent to see President Mark Hopkins. He came in arrogantly, took out his purse, and asked how much were the damages. This was too much for President Hopkins, who commanded the young man to sit down. "No man," said the president, "can pay for what he receives here. Can you pay for the sacrifice of Colonel Williams who founded the college? Can you pay for the half-paid professors who have remained here to teach when they could have gone elsewhere? Every student here is a charity case." So are we all.

The last thing to say is that

Acknowledging Our Debts Brings Us a Strange Joy.

This process is paradoxical. We learn as we grow older how often a seeming contradiction leads us to a higher logic. We follow a hard path and come to a magnificent view which reveals the meaning of the journey. Strange it is that giving up means receiving, and that humility is victory.

You see, the acceptance of our status as debtors destroys our pride, and that is good. It brings us to the end of a vain search, and finally we accept the truth that we are loved. We are filled with such thankfulness that our hearts overflow with joy. It is the discovery that all our giving is merely a drop in the bucket when it comes to settling our accounts. While it is true that giving is more blessed than receiving, being the object of loving concern brings a blessedness all its own.

The Good Samaritan is a case in point. But do you suppose he might have been a man who realized how often he had received? Could he possibly have fallen among thieves himself at one time and found unexpected help from a stranger? Was he a man aware of how much other people had done for him? Nobody can know about these matters, but it is interesting to speculate, for men with no sense of owing are less likely to be generous or helpful in a crisis. May the good Lord save us from the hard hearts which are formed in those who consider themselves beyond obligation.

One of the amazing things is that people who do the most seem to be least aware of it. There is never the slightest tendency to let others do the difficult work or to regard themselves as excused from the hard jobs. Those whose lives have been models of service never seem to realize they have been making sacrifices. Rather, at the root of their characters is a sense of something owing which is sheer joy to acknowledge.

God has brought us the spirit of joyous obligation through Christ. The Gospel is glad announcement that God loves the world and gave His son for it. We are the ones for whom Christ died. We discover that before we sought him, he sought us. Christianity is a proclamation that we are always in debt and service to our brethren is our privilege. All of the great Church Festivals have this as their basic theme. For our debt is not one that makes us unhappy and worried, but one that sets us free from arrogance.

When Abraham Lincoln was killed, his body was taken to Springfield by way of the large cities in the East. Usually the funeral procession went from the railroad station to the city hall, where the body would lay in state and the people would come to express their sorrow and respect. As the hearse was moving slowly through the streets of New York City which were lined with thousands of people, a big, husky woodsman pressed forward through the crowd to see it. He jostled a few people and stepped on the feet of a man who cried out angrily, "Don't walk on my feet!" The big fellow was instantly apologetic and said, "Excuse me, sir, but I must see the coffin." "Why must you?" asked the man. "Two of my brothers died in the same cause he did," replied the woodsman sadly. "Besides," he said proudly, "he was one of my craft and I could never go back to the woods without seeing and blessing his coffin." The crowd parted and let him through.

That man was expressing what is in the heart of all men when they see life clearly. We are forever in debt and we must express our thanks. All that we have is little enough to give, and so the Christian finds joy in his giving. For no matter how long we live or how much we are able to give, it is never enough. Let us remember that and rejoice in it. For to be aware that we are debtors is one of Christ's gifts to his disciples.

JOHN KILLINGER

There Is Still God

The God who created the world and everything
in it, and who is Lord of heaven and earth,
does not live in shrines made by men. It is not
because he lacks anything that he accepts
service at men's hands, for he is himself the
universal giver of life and breath and all else..
.. Indeed he is not far from each one of us, for
in him we live and move, in him we exist.
—Acts 17:24-28 NEB

One day our oldest son, who was twelve at the time, startled us at the dinner table by announcing that he was an atheist. You can imagine the sudden consternation his mother and I felt. "I've been thinking about it a lot," he said. He could tell that we were stunned, and he was rushing on to explain. "You see, there are two principal theories about the origin of the universe, the 'big bang' theory and the evolution theory." And he proceeded to state in very precise language what the leading cosmologists are saying about the creation of the solar system. At the end he said somewhat hopefully, "So you see, I can't really believe all that stuff about God anymore—it's not scientific."

All that stuff about God! The boy will never know the mixture of pain and pride that shot through our hearts that day. Pain for his own growing up, for the sense of separation that comes as a child reaches adulthood. And pride too. Pride that he was thinking so seriously about the matter all on his own, and pride that he had the courage to confront us with his conclusions the way he did. It took some guts.

You know what I thought of, what kept running through my head as he talked? It was a line from Lorraine Hansberry's play

A Raisin in the Sun. You remember the play, about a black family in the Southside of Chicago during the years of depression. Beneatha, the proud young daughter, says she is going to become a doctor, and Mama, the wonderful glue that holds the family together, Mama says, " 'Course you going to be a doctor, honey, God willing." Beneatha flares up and says, "God hasn't got a thing to do with it." "Beneatha!" says Mama. An argument ensues. Finally Beneatha draws it all together in the biggest speech she's got. "Mama," she says, "you don't understand. It's all a matter of ideas, and God is just one idea I don't accept. It's not important. I am not going out and be immoral or commit crimes because I don't believe in God. I don't even think about it. It's just that I get tired of Him getting the credit for all the things the human race achieves through its own stubborn effort. There simply is no blasted God—there is only man and it is he who makes miracles!" Mama sits quietly for a moment as it all soaks in. She studies the face of this daughter she has raised. Then she rises, crosses the room, and slaps Beneatha firmly on the face. The daughter's eyes drop, and Mama stands supreme in the room. "Now," says Mama, "you say after me, in my mother's house there is still God." There is a pause, and Beneatha says, "In my mother's house there is still God."

Mama's words came to my mind like a reflex action in the face of my own son's announcement. I wanted to speak them, to shout them out loudly and clearly, to spit them like hot rivets into the table top, "THERE IS STILL GOD IN THIS HOUSE!"

But I didn't. It was not time to stop the conversation. It was time to probe and listen—and I did. My wife and I both did. No matter how much we each wanted to shout out something, we bit our tongues and didn't. Our son had to do his own growing up. Since he was born, we had preached our daily sermons in the love we gave him. But now—now he had to learn for himself.

I remembered my own first doubts of God. I had been much older than my son was now. I had had several years of rather intense religious experience. Once I even thought I had come face to face with an angel of God. I was a young Ph.D. candidate in literature, immersed in the writings of numerous 19th and 20th century agnostics. I was even writing my thesis on Ernest Hemingway, who said that our age was different from all previous ages, and who made a character in *For Whom the Bell Tolls* lament, "We do not have God here anymore, neither His Son nor the Holy Ghost." Until that particular moment I had resisted the logic of their agnosticism, had rejected it as shortsighted and erratic. But suddenly, as I walked along between the campus and my apartment, it hit me: What if there *were* no God?! What if I was wrong? What if it was all auto-suggestion or something? The thought was like a shudder passing over me, like a sudden cloud coming between me and the sun, casting a chill over the landscape. I felt guilty for having had it. I wanted to dismiss it, to forget I'd ever had it, to bury it in the instant it had been conceived. But it remained, hard and tactile, like a crystallized stone in the passage of my mind. And I can still feel it there. It has never gone away. Not completely. If I rub those passages I can always detect its presence. What if I am wrong?

It is easy for us to suspect today that we were wrong. There seems to be so little room for God anymore. Once there was a lot of room. People were so ignorant about the universe that they explained most of its phenomena in terms of gods and devils. If the lightning struck, they said it was God, and bowed down in fear. If a plague broke out, they said it was God, and cried to heaven. If a tree withered up, they said it was God, and did penance. If a child went mad, they said it was God, and treated the child as a holy person.

But not any more. Now there is physics to explain the lightning, and antibiotics to quell the plague, and fertilizer for the withered tree, and chemotherapy for the disturbed child. Now there is travel to the moon and satellite weather forecasting and farming in the ocean and water in the desert. Now there is instantaneous freezing and microwave heating and printed electrical circuitry and computerized economics and open-heart surgery. Who needs God anymore?! God is passé. God is out of place in this kind of world. He has not survived the transition from rural to urban culture, from naïve to scientific existence. He was, as somebody called him, a "god of the gaps," a deity who presided over the mysteries in our daily lives—mysteries like flooding rivers and pneumonia and childbirth and falling stars. But now there are no more mysteries. The gaps are all closed up, and there isn't any room for God. So shove off, God, this space is occupied. There's no more room for you.

Or isn't there?

You see, what I would have liked to say to my son, and tried to say, though he was not yet old enough and had not lived enough to understand it, is that the neat little world we have managed to fabricate out of our scientific knowledge is not the real world at all. Oh, it is part of it, to be sure. But it isn't all of it, not by any means. In the comfort of our suppositions about it, in the warm glow of our thinking we have decoded the major messages of the universe, and given more time, will eventually solve all its problems, we delude ourselves into believing that the antiseptic little space we have cleared of brush and brambles is the world, is the only space there is. We forget that there is another, that as Paul Tillich once talked about a "God beyond God," in order to speak of the wildness, the uncontrollable wildness of the *real* God, there is also a world beyond the world, a world that is real and mysterious and beyond our ever finding it all out.

We are like those people who sailed with Thor Heyerdahl on his little raft the Kon-Tiki. During the great storms, when the sea would heave and pitch like a great liquid serpent, they would huddle together in the small cabin and sing and talk until they had forgotten where they were, and felt as comfortable as if they had been at home in their own living rooms. We too know how to shut out the wildness.

But then something happens to counter our illusion, and we see that the neatness was deceptive, that we were building a little world like a soap bubble on the face of the infinite deep.

The son of the finest surgeon I know has become ill with leukemia of the bone marrow. They give him transfusions and new chemicals and wait and pray. There is nothing his father's talented hands can do to save him.

The wife of a colleague was about to take a trip to the Caribbean, and all her friends envied her. But for weeks before she left, she dreamed over and over the same frightful dream: she saw her monogrammed suitcase floating alone in the ocean.

A popular television star confided to me one day in the privacy of his office that he is so bored with his work that he can barely make it through the day. Sometimes, he says, he has an almost uncontrollable urge to hurl something at the camera and run away, never to return.

One morning as we were having breakfast, the telephone rang. The voice on the other end of the line was choked with emotion. "John, pray for me," it said. I asked who it was. It was a rising young businessman in our city with whom I had had some dealings several years earlier. "What's wrong?" I asked. "My son," he said. "My son took his life." The son was a handsome, mannerly young man, a senior in high school, winner of a merit scholarship to college. He had never given his parents a moment's trouble. He had been a thoughtful, dutiful son. And then, that fatal night, he had taken a pistol, put it to his head, and pulled the trigger.

God of the gaps? No room for him? Sometimes all life is a gap. Sometimes the whole universe is a gap. At least man's heart is a gap, the way Augustine said it is, and the universe seems to be one, until it is filled by the presence of God.

And the gaps aren't only in the horrors. They are also in the hopes. Sometimes it is as hard to explain the joys of life without God as it is to meet the tragedies without him.

For example, how else can I explain the simple radiance of my surgeon friend as he goes about his work of healing day by day, knowing that his son languishes at home? By rights, he could be angry or resentful or dispirited. But he isn't. He greets his patients as if there were no hurt at all in his heart.

And what of the air force veteran I met who took his retirement in the Orient in order to run a nursery for orphans and disabled children in a country where he had once been "the enemy"?

And what of the woman I met who had lost her son a few months before at the age of seventeen? He had been born retarded, and she had had a special room constructed for him so that she could see him at play at all times, even when she was working in the kitchen. His heart had been very weak, and she had slept with a hand upon him every night those seventeen years, so that she could tell if he were having trouble breathing and could administer artificial respiration. The day he died, she had gone to the hospital with a little neighbor girl who had fallen from a tree and hurt her arm. While she was at the hospital, her husband had come in bearing the body of the boy. She tried to stimulate his heart but couldn't. Then, standing there with the boy's body between them, she and her husband wept and gave thanks to God for the gift of the boy's presence those seventeen years. "He had taught us to love," she said, "more than we had ever known how in our lives."

How do you explain that kind of strength and devotion without God?

And what of my own son, sitting there announcing he was an atheist? I remembered the hour of his birth, and how the doctor squeezed on his head so misshapen by a hard birth and said, "It'll shape up." I remembered the times we had surrendered him to the surgeon during his early years to have his eyes straightened. Once, when he was about five, he had told the anesthetist that he was fond of Batman, and, when he awoke after the operation, there was a pack of Batman cards taped to his hand so he wouldn't lose them during unconsciousness. And I remembered when he was baptized at the age of ten. I had spent nearly the whole day Saturday searching for the right little cross to give him as a baptismal gift. And he knelt before the officiating minister and took the little cross in his hand and squeezed it, and afterwards he said, "Daddy, I wasn't afraid because I held on to the cross."

How do I explain the joy I feel in my son without God? I can't. I simply can't. It's like that passage in Theodore Dreiser's last novel, *The Bulwark.* Dreiser had been a life-long atheist and anti-churchman. Converted to scientism at an early age by reading Herbert Spencer, he was a mighty advocate of natural law and the survival of the fittest. Then, at the end of his life, he moved to California and began to look back over his experiences. Something happened to him, and he even went to church and took communion. And out of those last months came *The Bulwark.* Solon Barnes, the Quaker protagonist, has just died. His daughter Ella is weeping. Someone comes upon her and accuses her of thinking too much about herself. "Oh no," she says, "you don't understand. I am not weeping for myself, and I am not weeping for father. I am weeping for *life!*" That is what I feel sometimes. I want to weep for life. It is so beautiful, even with its problems, even with its suffering.

I can't explain it without God. Sometimes, when I am too busy, or when things are going too smoothly for me, I don't think about him. I don't bow my head and say "Thank you," or stop what I am doing and say "You," as if he had surprised me again. But when there is pain, I think of him, and when there is joy, I remember. Whenever I get off dead center of myself, I see him, and know that he sustains the world I live in, the real world, the world beyond the world of my comfort and forgetfulness.

Then I understand a remark which Tom Stoppard put into his play *Jumpers,* that atheism is only "a crutch for those who cannot bear the reality of God." And I remember why the medieval philosophers called him the *ens realissimum,* the "most real being there is." And I recall St. Paul's way of putting it, that "in him we live and move, in him we exist"—*esmen,* in the Greek—"In him we live and move and ARE."

And I say, THERE IS STILL GOD IN THIS HOUSE.

MARTIN LUTHER KING, JR.

The Answer
to a Perplexing Question

Why could not we cast him out?
—Matthew 17:19

Human life through the centuries has been characterized by man's persistent efforts to remove evil from the earth. Seldom has man thoroughly adjusted himself to evil, for in spite of his rationalizations, compromises, and alibis, he knows the "is" is not the "ought" and the actual is not the possible. Though the evils of sensuality, selfishness, and cruelty often rise aggressively in his soul, something within tells him that they are intruders and reminds him of his higher destiny and more noble allegiance. Man's hankering after the demonic is always disturbed by his longing for the divine. As he seeks to adjust to the demands of time, he knows that eternity is his ultimate habitat. When man comes to himself, he knows that evil is a foreign invader that must be driven from the native soils of his soul before he can achieve moral and spiritual dignity.

But the problem that has always hampered man has been his inability to conquer evil by his own power. In pathetic amazement, he asks, "Why can I not cast it out? Why can I not remove this evil from my life?"

This agonizing, perplexing question recalls an event that occurred immediately after Christ's transfiguration. Coming down from the mountain, Jesus found a small boy who was in wild convulsions. His disciples had tried desperately to cure the unhappy child, but the more they labored to heal him the more they realized their own inadequacies and the pathetic limitations of their power. When they were about to give up in despair, their Lord appeared on the scene. After the father of the child told Jesus of the failure of the disciples, Jesus "rebuked the devil; and he departed out of him: and the child was cured from that very hour." When the disciples were later alone with their Master, they asked, "Why could not we cast him out?" They wanted an explanation for their obvious limitations. Jesus said their failure was caused by their unbelief: "If ye have faith as a grain of mustard seed, ye shall say unto this mountain, Remove hence to yonder place; and it shall remove; and nothing shall be impossible unto you." They had tried to do by themselves what could be done only after they had so surrendered their natures to God that his strength flowed freely through them.

I

How can evil be cast out? Men have usually pursued two paths to eliminate evil and thereby save the world. The first calls upon man to remove evil through his own power and ingenuity in the strange conviction that by thinking, inventing, and governing, he will at last conquer the nagging forces of evil. Give people a fair chance and a decent education, and they will save themselves. This idea, sweeping across the modern world like a plague, has ushered God out and escorted man in and has substituted human ingenuity for divine guidance. Some people suggest that this concept was introduced during the Renaissance when reason dethroned religion, or later when Darwin's *Origin of Species* replaced belief in creation by the theory of evolution, or when the industrial revolution turned the hearts of men to material comforts and physical conveniences. At any rate, the idea of the adequacy of man to solve the evils of history captured the minds of people, giving rise to the easy optimism of the nineteenth century, the doctrine of inevitable progress, Rousseau's maxim of "the original goodness of human nature," and Condorcet's conviction that by reason alone the whole world would soon be cleansed of crime, poverty, and war.

Armed with this growing faith in the capability of reason and science, modern man set out to change the world. He turned his attention from God and the human soul to the outer world and its possibilities. He observed, analyzed, and explored. The laboratory became man's sanctuary and scientists his priests and prophets. A modern humanist confidently affirmed:

The future is not with the churches but with the laboratories, not with prophets but with scientists, not with piety but with efficiency. Man is at last becoming aware that he alone is responsible for the realization of the world of his dreams, that he has within himself the power for its achievement.

Man has subpoenaed nature to appear before the judgment seat of scientific investigation. None doubt that man's work in the scientific laboratories has brought unbelievable advances in power and comfort, producing machines that think and gadgets that soar majestically through the skies, stand impressively on the land, and move with stately dignity on the seas.

But in spite of these astounding new scientific developments, the old evils continue and the age of reason has been transformed into an age of terror. Selfishness and hatred have not vanished with an enlargement of our educational system and an extension of our legislative policies. A once optimistic generation now asks in utter bewilderment, "Why could not we cast it out?"

The answer is rather simple: Man by his own power can never cast evil from the world. The humanist's hope is an illusion, based on too great an optimism concerning the inherent goodness of human nature.

I would be the last to condemn the thousands of sincere and dedicated people outside the churches who have labored unselfishly through various humanitarian movements to cure the world of social evils, for I would rather a man be a committed humanist than an uncommitted Christian. But so many of these dedicated persons, seeking salvation within the human context, have become understandably pessimistic and disillusioned, because their efforts are based on a kind of self-delusion which ignores fundamental facts about our mortal nature.

Nor would I minimize the importance of science and the great contributions which have come in the wake of the Renaissance. These have lifted us from the stagnating valleys of superstition and half-truth to the sunlit mountains of creative analysis and objective appraisal. The unquestioned authority of the church in scientific matters needed to be freed from paralyzing obscurantism, antiquated notions, and shameful inquisitions. But the exalted Renaissance optimism, while attempting to free the mind of man, forgot about man's capacity for sin.

II

The second idea for removing evil from the world stipulates that if man waits submissively upon the Lord, in his own good time God alone will redeem the world. Rooted in a pessimistic doctrine of human nature, this idea, which eliminates completely the capability of sinful man to do anything, was prominent in the Reformation, that great spiritual movement which gave birth to the Protestant concern for moral and spiritual freedom and served as a necessary corrective for a corrupt and stagnant medieval church. The doctrines of justification by faith and the priesthood of all believers are towering principles which we as Protestants must forever affirm, but the Reformation doctrine of human nature overstressed the corruption of man. The Renaissance was too optimistic, and the Reformation too pessimistic. The former so concentrated on the goodness of man that it overlooked his capacity for evil; the latter so concentrated on the wickedness of man that it overlooked his capacity for goodness. While rightly affirming the sinfulness of human nature and man's incapacity to save himself, the Reformation wrongly affirmed that the image of God had been completely erased from man.

This led to the Calvinistic concept of the total depravity of man and to a resurrection of the terrible idea of infant damnation. So depraved is human nature, said the doctrinaire Calvinist, that if a baby dies without baptism he will burn forever in hell. Certainly this carries the idea of man's sinfulness too far.

This lopsided Reformation theology has often emphasized a purely otherworldly religion, which stresses the utter hopelessness of this world and calls upon the individual to concentrate on preparing his soul for the world to come. By ignoring the need for social reform, religion is divorced from the mainstream of human life. A pulpit committee listed as the first essential qualification for a new minister: "He must preach the true gospel and not talk about social issues." This is a blueprint for a dangerously irrelevant church where people assemble to hear only pious platitudes.

By disregarding the fact that the gospel deals with man's body as well as with his soul, such a one-sided emphasis creates a tragic dichotomy between the sacred and the secular. To be worthy of its New Testament origin, the church must seek to transform both individual lives and the social situation that brings to many people anguish of spirit and cruel bondage. The idea that man expects God to do everything leads inevitably to a callous misuse of prayer. For if God does everything, man then asks him for anything, and God becomes little more than a "cosmic bellhop" who is summoned for every trivial need. Or God is considered so omnipotent and man so powerless that prayer is a substitute for work and intelligence. A man said to me, "I believe in integration, but I know it will not come until God wants it to come. You Negroes should stop protesting and start praying." I am certain we need to pray for God's help and guidance in this integration struggle, but we are gravely misled if we think the struggle will be won only by prayer. God, who gave us minds for thinking and bodies for working, would defeat his own purpose if he permitted us to obtain through prayer what may come through work and intelligence. Prayer is a marvelous and necessary supplement of our feeble efforts, but it is a dangerous substitute. When Moses strove to lead the Israelites to the Promised Land, God made it clear that he would not do for them what they could do for themselves. "And the Lord said unto Moses, Wherefore criest thou unto me? speak unto the children of Israel, that they go forward."

We must pray earnestly for peace, but we must also work vigorously for disarmament and the suspension of weapon testing. We must use our minds as rigorously to plan for peace as we have used them to plan for war. We must pray with unceasing passion for racial justice, but we must also use our minds to develop a program, organize ourselves into mass nonviolent action, and employ every resource of our bodies and souls to bring an end to racial injustice. We must pray unrelentingly for economic justice, but we must also work diligently to bring into being those social changes that make for a better distribution of wealth within our nation and in the undeveloped countries of the world.

Does not all of this reveal the fallacy of thinking that God will cast evil from the earth, even if man does nothing except to sit complacently by the wayside? No prodigious thunderbolt from heaven will blast away evil. No mighty army of angels will descend to force men to do what their wills resist. The Bible portrays God, not as an omnipotent czar who makes all decisions for his subjects nor as a cosmic tyrant who with gestapolike methods invades the inner lives of men, but rather as a loving Father who gives to his children such abundant blessings as they may be willing to receive. Always man must do something. "Stand upon thy feet," says God to Ezekiel, "and I will speak unto you." Man is no helpless invalid left in a valley of total depravity until God pulls him out. Man is rather an upstanding human being whose vision has been impaired by the cataracts of sin and whose soul has been weakened by the virus of pride, but there is sufficient vision left for him to lift his eyes unto the hills, and there remains enough of God's image for him to turn his weak and sin-battered life toward the Great Physician, the curer of the ravages of sin.

The real weakness of the idea that God will do everything is its false conception of both God and man. It makes God so absolutely sovereign that man is absolutely helpless. It makes man so absolutely depraved that he can do nothing but wait on God. It sees the world as so contaminated with sin that God totally transcends it and touches it only here and there through a mighty invasion. This view ends up with a God who is a despot and not a Father. It ends up with such a pessimism concerning human nature that it leaves man little more than a helpless worm crawling through the morass of an evil world. But man is neither totally depraved, nor is God an almighty dictator. We must surely affirm the majesty and sovereignty of God, but this should not lead us to believe that God is an Almighty Monarch who will impose his will upon us and deprive us of the freedom to choose what is good or what is not good. He will not thrust himself upon us nor force us to stay home when our minds are bent on journeying to some degrading far country. But he follows us in love, and when we come to ourselves and turn our tired feet back to the Father's house, he stands waiting with outstretched arms of forgiveness.

Therefore we must never feel that God will, through some breathtaking miracle or a wave of the hand, cast evil out of the world. As long as we believe this we will pray unanswerable prayers and ask God to do things that he will never do. The belief that God will do everything for man is as untenable as the belief that man can do everything for himself. It, too, is based on a lack of faith. We must learn that to expect God to do everything while we do nothing is not faith, but superstition.

III

What, then, is the answer to life's perplexing question, "How can evil be cast out of our individual and collective lives?" If the world is not to be purified by God alone nor by man alone, who will do it?

The answer is found in an idea which is distinctly different from the two we have discussed, for neither God nor man will individually bring the world's salvation. Rather, both man and God, made one in a marvelous unity of purpose through an overflowing love as the free gift of himself on the part of God and by perfect obedience and receptivity on the part of man, can transform the old into the new and drive out the deadly cancer of sin.

The principle which opens the door for God to work through man is faith. This is what the disciples lacked when they desperately tried to remove the nagging evil from the body of the sick child. Jesus reminded them that they had been attempting to do by themselves what could be done only when their lives were open receptacles, as it were, into which God's strength could be freely poured.

Two types of faith in God are clearly set forth in the Scriptures. One may be called the mind's faith, wherein the intellect assents to a belief that God exists. The other may be referred to as the heart's faith, whereby the whole man is involved in a trusting act of self-surrender. To know God, a man must possess this latter type of faith, for the mind's faith is directed toward a theory, but the heart's faith is centered in a Person. Gabriel Marcel claims that faith is *believing in,* not *believing that.* It is "opening a credit; which puts me at the disposal of the one in whom I believe." When I believe, he says, "I rally to with that sort of interior gathering of oneself which the act of rallying implies." Faith is the opening of all sides and at every level of one's life to the divine inflow.

This is what the Apostle Paul emphasized in his doctrine of salvation by faith. For him, faith is man's capacity to accept God's willingness through Christ to rescue us from the bondage of sin. In his magnanimous love, God freely offers to do for us what we cannot do for ourselves. Our humble and openhearted acceptance is faith. So by faith we are saved. Man filled with God and God operating through man bring unbelievable changes in our individual and social lives.

Social evils have trapped multitudes of men in a dark and murky corridor where there is no exit sign and plunged others into a dark abyss of psychological fatalism. These deadly, paralyzing evils can be removed by a humanity perfectly united through obedience with God. Moral victory will come as God fills man and man opens his life by faith to God, even as the gulf opens to the overflowing waters of the river. Racial justice, a genuine possibility in our nation and in the world, will come neither by our frail and often misguided efforts nor by God imposing his will on wayward men, but when enough people open their lives to God and allow him to pour his triumphant, divine energy into their souls. Our age-old and noble dream of a world of peace may yet become a reality, but it will come neither by man working alone nor by God destroying the wicked schemes of men, but when men so open their lives to God that he may fill them with love, mutual respect, understanding, and goodwill. Social salvation will come only through man's willing acceptance of God's mighty gift.

Let me apply what I have been saying to our personal lives. Many of you know what it means to struggle with sin. Year by year you were aware that a terrible sin—slavery to drink, perhaps, or untruthfulness, impurity, selfishness—was taking possession of your life. As the years unfolded and the vice widened its landmarks on your soul, you knew that it was an unnatural intruder. You may have thought, "One day I shall drive this evil out. I know it is destroying my character and embarrassing my family." At last you determined to purge yourself of the evil by making a New Year's resolution. Do you remember your surprise and disappointment when you discovered, three hundred and sixty-five days later, that your most sincere efforts had not banished the old habit from your life? In complete amazement you asked, "Why could not I cast it out?"

In despair you decided to take your problem to God, but instead of asking him to work through you, you said, "God, you must solve this problem for me. I can't do anything about it." But days and months later the evil was still with you. God would not cast it out, for he never removes sin without the cordial co-operation of the sinner. No problem is solved when we idly wait for God to undertake full responsibility.

One cannot remove an evil habit by mere resolution nor by simply calling on God to do the job, but only as he surrenders himself and becomes an instrument of God. We shall be delivered from the accumulated weight of evil only when we permit the energy of God to come into our souls.

God has promised to co-operate with us when we seek to cast evil from our lives and become true children of his divine will. "If any one is in Christ," says Paul, "he is a new creation; the old has passed away, behold, the new has come." If any man is in Christ, he is a new person, his old self has gone, and he becomes a divinely transformed son of God.

One of the great glories of the gospel is that Christ has transformed nameless prodigals. He turned a Simon of sand into a Peter of rock. He changed a persecuting Saul into an Apostle Paul. He converted a lust-feasted Augustine into a St. Augustine. The measured words of Leo Tolstoi's confession in *My Religion* reflect an experience many have shared:

> Five years ago faith came to me; I believed in the doctrine of Jesus, and my whole life underwent a sudden transformation. What I had once wished for I wished for no longer, and I began to desire what I had never desired before. What had once appeared to me right now became wrong, and the wrong of the past I beheld as right. . . . My life and my desires were completely changed; good and evil interchanged meanings.

Herein we find the answer to a perplexing question. Evil can be cast out, not by man alone nor by a dictatorial God who invades our lives, but when we open the door and invite God through Christ to enter. "Behold, I stand at the door, and knock: if any man hear my voice, and open the door, I will come in to him, and will sup with him, and he with me." God is too courteous to break open the door, but when we open it in faith believing, a divine and human confrontation will transform our sin-ruined lives into radiant personalities.

RONALD A. KNOX

The Window in the Wall

*And now he is standing on the other side of this very
wall; now he is looking through each window in
turn, peering through every chink. I can hear my
true love calling to me, Rise up, rise up quickly,
dear heart, so gentle, so beautiful, rise up and come
with me.*

—Canticles 2:9

Set in the middle of the Old Testament, in striking contrast to
those collections of dry aphorisms which come before and after
it, the Canticle of Canticles occupies a position unique in sacred
literature. In form it is a drama, in literary inspiration it is a
love poem, such as might have graced any anthology in any
language; it has, in its literal acceptation, no connection with
theology from beginning to end. It is the story, apparently, of a
young bride carried away to the harem of King Solomon, yet
true to her lover, who comes and calls to her, rescues her from
her gilded bondage, and takes her back to freedom and to her
country home. And that book, as we all know, is a kind of
palimpsest, in which the saints of every age have read between
the lines, and found there the appropriate language in which to
express their love for God, God's love for them. No part of the
Old Testament gives rise more easily to outraged astonishment, to pharisaical scandal, when it comes into the hands of the
profane: that *this* should be reckoned as sacred literature! No
part of the Old Testament, I suppose, has more endeared itself
to the greatest friends of Christ; they would have spared all the
rest to save this.

In the passage from which I have taken my text, the voice of
the country lover makes itself heard, all of a sudden, amid the

From *The Pastoral Sermons of Ronald A. Knox* (London: Sheed & Ward,
1960). Used by permission of the Estate of Ronald Knox.

distractions of Solomon's court. He stands close to the wall of the harem, and whispers through the window. The voice of the beloved—everywhere, in the mystical interpretation of the poem, the voice of the beloved is understood of Christ speaking to the faithful soul. And that voice at the window brings to my own mind a fancy which I have often had, which I suppose many of us have had before now, in looking at the sacred Host enthroned in the monstrance. The fancy, I mean, that the glittering disc of whiteness which we see occupying that round opening is not reflecting the light of the candles in front of it, but is penetrated with a light of its own, a light not of this world, shining through it from behind, as if through a window, out-dazzling gold and candleflame with a more intense radiance. Such a visual impression you may have just for a moment, then you reflect that it is only an illusion; and then on further thought you question, Is it an illusion? Is it not rather the truth, but a truth hidden from our eyes, that the Host in the monstrance, or rather those accidents of it which make themselves known to our senses, are a kind of window through which a heavenly light streams into our world; a window giving access on a spiritual world outside our human experience?

Behold, he stands behind "our wall"; the wall of our corrupt nature, which shuts us off from breathing, as man breathed in the days of his innocency, the airs of heaven; the wall of sense, which cheats us when we try even to imagine eternity; the wall of immortified affection, which shuts us in with creatures and allows them to dominate our desires; the wall of pride, which makes us feel, except when death or tragedy is very close to us, so independent and self-sufficient. Our wall—we raised it against God, not he against us; we raised it, when Adam sinned, and when each of us took up again, by deliberate choice, that legacy of sinfulness in his own life. And through that wall the Incarnation and the Passion of Jesus Christ have made a great window; St. Paul tells us so; "he made both one, breaking down the wall that was a barrier between us," as the temple veil was torn in two on the day when he suffered. He "made both one"; made our world of sin and sight and sense one with the spiritual world; made a breach in our citadel, let light into our prison.

Not for a moment, amid the confusion of an historical situation; the window is there for all time, if we would only recognize it. He himself, in his risen and glorified body, is the window between the two worlds. As the window belongs both to the room inside and to the open air outside, so his glorified body belongs at once to time and to eternity; belongs to time, because he took it upon himself, when he was born in time of his blessed Mother, belongs to eternity, because it is now transfigured with the light of glory which is part of our future inheritance. That glory is something human eyes cannot bear to see; when Moses had talked with God on Mount Sinai, he came back with his face shining, so that he had to put a veil over it lest the people's eyes should dazzle when they beheld him; and if he, who was only God's ambassador, who had only spoken with God in the darkness, was so illuminated by it, what of him who is himself God, whose human nature has been caught up into the Abyss of all being? When he rose from the dead, and still for forty days walked about our earth, that glory was hidden from mortal eyes by a special dispensation. And now, now that he reigns in heaven, he will make himself manifest on earth still; but his glory will be veiled, more jealously than ever, as he confronts, now, the gaze of the sinner and the doubter, as he gives himself into the hands of the unworthy.

We all know what veil it is that covers him now; it is the mystery which occupies our thoughts this morning. In this mystery of transubstantiation, he has broken into the very heart of nature, and has separated from one another in reality two elements which we find it difficult to separate even in thought, the inner substance of things from those outward manifestations of it which make it known to our senses. Burn all the candles you will in front of it, call to your aid all the resources of science, and flood it with a light stronger than human eyes can bear to look upon, still that white disc will be nothing better than a dark veil, hiding the ineffable light of glory which shines in and through the substance of Christ's ascended body. A veil, that is what we look at, a curtain drawn over the window, as you may curtain the windows of a sick-room, because the patient's eyes are not strong enough to face the full glare of daylight. But behind that curtain, all the time, is the window which lets our world communicate with the world of the supernatural. As the angels ascended and descended on Jacob's ladder, so here our prayers go out into the unseen, so here grace comes flooding through, like a rushing mighty wind, into the stagnant air of our earthly experience.

And at the window, behind the wall of partition that is a wall of partition no longer, stands the Beloved himself, calling us out into the open; calling us away from the ointments and the spikenard of Solomon's court, that stupefy and enchain our senses, to the gardens and the vineyards, to the fields and the villages, to the pure airs of eternity. Arise (he says), make haste and come. Come away from the blind pursuit of creatures, from all the plans your busy brain evolves for your present and future pleasures, from the frivolous distractions it clings to. Come away from the pettiness and the meanness of your everyday life, from the grudges, the jealousies, the unhealed enmities that set your imagination throbbing. Come away from the cares and solicitudes about the morrow that seem so urgent, your heavy anxieties about the world's future and your own, so short either of them and so uncertain. Come away into the wilderness of prayer, where my love will follow you and my hand hold you; learn to live, with the innermost part of your soul, with all your secret aspirations, with all the centre of your hopes and cares, in that supernatural world which can be yours now, which must be yours hereafter.

Not that he calls us, yet, away from the body, from its claims and its necessities; that call will come in his own time. Nor yet that the occupations, and the amusements of this life, his creatures, given us for our use, are to be despised and set aside as something evil. Rather, as a beam of sunlight coming through the window lights up and makes visible the tiny motes of dust that fill the air, so those who live closest to him find, in the creatures round about them, a fresh charm and a fresh meaning, which the jaded palate of worldliness was too dull to detect. But he wants our hearts; *ut inter mundanas varietates ibi fixa sint corda ubi vera sunt gaudia*—our hearts must be there fixed, where are pure joys, before we can begin to see earth in its right perspective. We must be weaned away from earth first; and the means by which he does that is holy communion. That is the medicine which enables the enfeebled soul to look steadily at the divine light, to breathe deeply of the unfamiliar air.

I wonder, is that why some of us are so frightened of holy communion, because we still cling so to the world of sense? It is certain that Catholics are most apt to neglect communion just when they most need it; in the spring-time of youth, when the blood is hot, and the passions strong, and ambition dominates us. Why is that, unless that we are more wedded, when we are young, to the desires that perish? I wonder, is that why so many of us who go often to communion find that it makes, apparently, little difference to us; that we are still as full of bad habits as we were ten or fifteen years ago, that our lives, if anything, compare unfavourably with the lives of others, who have not our opportunities for going to communion frequently? Is it perhaps because, all the time, we are shrinking from the act of confidence which would throw the whole burden of our lives on our Lord; do not want holy communion to have its proper effect on us, which is to make the joys and distractions of this world have less meaning and less appeal for us? We must not expect him to work the marvels of his grace in us, if we oppose its action through the stubbornness of our own wills, still clinging to self and to sense.

DONALD MACLEOD

Something Happened in Church

*As for me, my feet were almost gone; my steps had
well nigh slipped. . . . until I went into the
sanctuary of God, then I understood.*

—Psalm 73:2, 17

One day at the seminary in a class discussion on worship, a
rather perceptive student made this remark, "Long ago when
you came home from church, people would ask 'Who was there?'
or 'What was the sermon about?' Today, however, they are
more apt to say, 'Well, you were in church this morning, what
happened?'"

Some years ago Henrik Kraemer of Geneva wrote as follows:
"Every Christian needs two conversions: the first to Christ; the
second to the world." Now in several ways Kraemer was
entirely right. Often you and I are surprised by the number of
people we meet who have been converted only to the
world—the busy people in the welfare agencies and the PTA or
on the political fronts and among the pressure groups—but who
have never been converted to Christ. On the other hand, we are
not so easily disturbed by the number of people who have been
converted to Christ, but never to the world: the priests and the
Levites on the Jericho Road or the clergy in John Milton's
seventeenth century England of whom he wrote, "The hungry
sheep look up, but are not fed." Kraemer was right also in using
the word *convert* rather than *reconcile,* because to reconcile
oneself to something or someone can mean merely to resign
oneself to it or to make the best of a situation or even to grin
and bear it. However, he was particularly right in putting
conversion to God (or Christ) and to the world together,
because they are parts of one event and because no devotion to

This sermon was first delivered on October 10, 1976, in The Riverside
Church, New York City.

God is worth much unless it includes also conversion to the claims of humanity.

Our text comes from Psalm 73. This psalm is the story of a religious Jew who had reconciled himself to the world in a negative sort of way and of how this affected his conception of God and of how God was running things. He was a good man in the conventional sense of the term, but his outlook upon the world and life drove him into a fit of doubt and skepticism; he was confused and all mixed up. He looked out upon his community, and what he saw shook his soul: wicked men, prospering and successful, striding arrogantly across the stage of life as if the world were theirs alone. Spineless "do-gooders" trying by flattery and flunky-ism to cash in upon gains they had never earned. On every hand, goodness was persecuted, inequality flaunted, fairness flouted, and with James R. Lowell, he might have said, "Truth forever on the scaffold, wrong forever on the throne"—Watergate, Chappaquiddick, nursing-home scandals, judgeships gained through bribes— and like an angry man he was about to jettison his faith. He doubted the integrity of God and was skeptical regarding the dependability of man; indeed before the bar of his own judgment, both seemed to be wanting. He felt his grip on God was breaking and in a sour, peevish bit of temper he was ready to write the world off as the victim of blind fate. There were no rewards for goodness and the prizes went inevitably to scoundrels. All this was too much for him. Seemingly he cried out, "Is there anyone at all in charge here?"

But then in something of a spur-of-the-moment decision, when his "feet were almost gone" and his "steps had well nigh slipped," he went into the sanctuary of God and there, once and for all, he understood. Now we have no knowledge of what actually occurred, but we do know the psalmist gained a new perspective upon things, and he began to see the world and life in God's context and not his own. In the sanctuary he put himself where God could get at him more effectively and have some chance with him. And from then and there on he could face Monday through Saturday a different person because he was straightened out spiritually, because his perspective went through a radical reorientation, and because he was converted to both God *and* the world. Life was no longer a moral chaos or a jumble of things going it blind, but something God-centered and God-controlled. "As for me my feet were almost gone; my steps had well nigh slipped. . . . until I went into the sanctuary of God, then I understood. . . ."

I

Something happened in church—and the first thing the psalmist learned was the simple, age-old principle that what a man is and not what he has is what counts.

Up to this point, however, the psalmist had had his doubts, because as he looked out upon the earth, it were as if God had abandoned it or rather as though there were no God at all. The wicked were the haves and the good the have-nots. Six days a week he saw life admired for, and equated with, those things men and women could see or flaunt or grab. And success was measured, not in terms of involvement or saintliness or service, but by the power of one's clout or by big wheels making big deals over big meals. And God seemed to stand idly by. Sounds familiar, doesn't it? Are we talking about 1976 B.C. or A.D. 1976?

Some years ago, Dr. E. Stanley Jones, the great Christian missionary to India, was speaking to a large audience of American young people, and he declared, "You have everything; you are a much better generation than mine, better trained and two inches taller; but you lack one thing—you lack a cause!" And a young man arose and interrupted him, saying, "But, Dr. Jones, we have a cause!" "What is it?" asked Jones. "To succeed," came the reply. A newspaper man, who was present, remarked to a colleague, "What a magnificent answer!" But he was wrong, dead wrong! It was a tragic answer, because that young boy meant only more power, more prosperity, more know-how, and more things. He was very much like a brash young man who turned to his future father-in-law on the eve of his engagement to his daughter and snapped, "I make three hundred bucks a week; what do you care whether or not I've got a character?"

But then you and I go to church and there we hear of the greatest person who ever lived, who cleft history in twain and left his stamp forever on human destiny; that this man—Jesus of Nazareth—led an amazing life, not measured in terms of investments and dividends, but in quality of spirit. He showed men and women the real things to live by, the prescription by which to become truly human, and his focus was consistently upon what a person is rather than upon what he or she has. His was a vision that claimed people's energies; a faith that gripped their imagination; a cause for them not only to live for, but also to die for, because neither is worthwhile without the other. This is what you and I find in church. A new dimension to life opens up before us, and we go out into the hurly-burly of the world, not saying, "This belongs to me" or "That belongs to me," but because of who I am in God's sight and of what I have from God's hand, I belong *to* this world and accept moral responsibility in it and for it. An old missionary shrank from the sight of the foreign field with its contradictions of everything he ever knew, yet in the sanctuary of his devotion he prayed, "There let me burn out for God." The psalmist declared at length: "Whom have I in heaven but thee? And there is none on earth I desire beside thee." This is not a matter of having or getting, but of being on the side of right as God gives us the ability to discern the right; and no man is greater than when he is possessed by God.

II

Something happened in church—and the second thing the psalmist learned was that the best way to handle wrong is to witness to what is true and right.

How very much the world of the psalmist resembles ours! People in those days were caught up in the world of fancy, of sham, and of make-believe; and somehow they liked it. It had something of a romantic flavor about it, although underneath lay the grim, dog-eat-dog way of life. Life as they lived it was paying off; therefore let us not rock the boat. We have never had it so good!

But the psalmist was disillusioned by what he saw. He witnessed the false crowding out the true, and the growing number of persons without any convictions who were ready to join any bandwagon as long as it was rolling. He wondered if God were asleep or whether he just did not care. So he was ready to quit. But then he went into the sanctuary of God, and there he saw reflections of real goodness, real purity, and real truth. Before him the hidden wrongs were exposed of what had become a popular and synthetic way of life, and there he saw, etched in clear outline, an image of the true and right.

Something happened in church—and is not this the risk all of us take every time we come here to worship? Often we wonder why many people today do not come to church. But have you and I ever thought that more people than we imagine are *frightened* to come to church? What do we mean? People who are satisfied with the slogan, "Anything goes," will avoid the church because it confronts them with facts that disturb and irritate them. They do not want to be reminded of the claims of truth, duty, love to God, and charity towards others. It is much easier to live by a philosophy of positive thinking that makes no demand beyond saying every morning before the mirror: "Every day and in every way I am getting better and better." It is much easier to talk about love of the synthetic kind which is paraded by the soap operas on the national television networks than it is to gaze on real love which dies on a cross. In church you and I come up against real virtues and God asks: "What is your personal relationship to these?" In church we encounter the eternal cleavage between right and wrong, love and hate, truth and falsehood.

It is just here that it is appropriate to say a word in defense of mass evangelism. Some people claim it has had its day and that the Grahams and Leighton Fords are as dated as the Model T. However, in an age in which the mass media has captured public opinion and popularized the shabby side of sex, the dividends of violence, and the notion that a certain brand of deodorant is the key to personal success, maybe it is for our nation's good that these religious mass rallies become symbols of human witness to the integrity of goodness and truth. Indeed, this church, as well as all other churches and chapels across the land today, is a sanctuary, like an oasis in our political and cultural deserts, testifying before men and women that above all truths there is THE TRUTH that saves and redeems.

III

Something happened in church—and this brings us to a final point: the psalmist saw himself as he had been, but particularly as what, by God's grace he could become.

One Sunday some months ago I preached at the fifteenth anniversary of the ordination of one of the alumni of Princeton Theological Seminary. I had given the sermon originally at his ordination on May 24, 1951. Few men I know have gone through greater tragedies and more sorry disappointments than he has;

yet he isn't bitter, nor defiant, nor complaining. Moreover, in the service of worship that morning he took a few moments to talk to his people about the goodness and loving-kindness of God. Nowhere else but in the sanctuary of God could he have talked in this way, and he understood; nowhere else is the knowledge and experience of the strong hand of God preserved and permitted to bring men and women to such splendid hours. "As for me," said the psalmist, "my feet were almost gone, my steps had well nigh slipped, until I went into the sanctuary of God, then I understood. . . ."

William Temple, the celebrated Archbishop of Canterbury in the 1940s said: "This world can be saved from political chaos and collapse by one thing only, that is worship. For to worship is to devote the will to the purpose of God."

As the psalmist left the sanctuary that day, he knew he was not alone, because he felt led by a hand and held by a power not his own. He was no longer against God or against the world, but he was converted to both. William M. Macgregor of Glasgow once said, "When a man comes to God, it were as if he looked from the other side of the sky, seeing the same things from another standpoint." That happened to the psalmist in church.

In the little village of Blantyre, Scotland, a common laborer by the name of David Hogg taught a small Sunday school class of young boys year after year with a devotion that was the wonder of all who knew him. Out from that class went a young man, David Livingstone, to the vast continent of Africa to wear out his life, going through the jungles from village to village, witnessing to the Christian faith. Some time later another missionary came to one of these same villages where Livingstone had been years before, and he told of the life and ministry of Jesus Christ. An old lady, however, interrupted him and said, "That man has been here!"

Think of it, men and women: a village church in far away Scotland; a little boy in the sanctuary; a consecrated Sunday school teacher; and you get the footprints of Christ in and out of the muddy villages of Africa.

Something happened in church!

May our prayer today be:

> *O God, do it again!*
> *And again! And again!*

CARLYLE MARNEY

A Come-and-Go Affair

Sometimes religious experience comes to a man with a shattering impact. The word of the Lord is like a hammer that breaks the rock. When this experience is later evaluated, the man wants to keep it safe forever. He wants a house to hold it. It was so with Moses, David, Solomon, Muhammad, Simon Peter, Joseph Smith. Then with his treasure safely housed, enshrined in an institution, others come to admire and remain to add rooms to the original building.

So it was that a House to the Lord arose in Shiloh. The tent of Moses to which they looked longingly, which they had dressed lovingly, was not enough. Hence, there arose a house for God at Shiloh, with a light for God to see by, day and night, where once he had been the light, and a taper to heighten the extraordinary darkness so that God could be seen there at the edge of the dark where he always seems to be. I wish he'd come out in the open someday.

Then—an horrendous discovery at the church in Shiloh—*some days God didn't come to church.* It was incredible how sloppy God's worship habits got to be. There were days when he was not there at all: not in his sandalwood box, not in the taper of light on the altar, not even in the name they dared not utter. What do you do with such a God? What's the point of a house to a God who may not come? Is God like quicksilver? He had told Moses he would come and go! This was the meaning of the tent. The tent had been better. Now they had real estate on their hands, but they had no God they could guarantee to inhabit it.

So the house fell down. For 900 years in a long, slow Shiloh way the waters of Shiloh trickled downhill until Samuel's early day when old Eli was really old, his sons defected, and the ancient holy man fell, broke his neck, and someone named the newborn baby Ichabod. The "glory of the Lord" had gone away, like your churches mostly. Or, as they put it, "The Lord came no more to Shiloh."

This is the way it is—a very human come and go. My religious experience, the kind I wish to keep, has a way of losing its bite and going away. All of us have had days when the glory of the Lord seemed closer. And every way we try to keep the primal day of our meeting with the Eternal becomes, in time, a furtherance of some externalism which smothers the primal glory. H. G. Wells tells it best about the turn of the century. He said that a young Sultan in a very wealthy province had a very beautiful bride whom he and all the people loved. She became sick, lingered, and died. In her memory he commissioned an exquisite memorial stone, over which he added in subsequent years, an altar, then a grotto over which he built a temple, then a great mosque, and finally a holy alabaster city. The original stone was now covered with layers of beauty, but the point of his beginning became a blot to mar the whole, and he ordered: "Remove that thing!" Thus we do.

Perhaps you know of E. Stanley Jones's story of the fort in India which used four thousand guards per shift of duty, but the city it was built to guard had moved a dozen miles away.

Must our appointment be a come and go affair? Is this the meaning of the tent? The tent does not mean that God is inconstant. Shiloh could have remained to this day for all of him. It is his people, I think, who come and go. The tent simply means that you never get him cornered. The tent means so much that you can't stay, for it means that God won't stay. Religious experience of a high order means that you have to keep coming back by it. Hence we could not yet abandon the Cross. We keep coming back by the Cross, the Kabal Stone, the Holy Land, and Easter. This is the meaning of the Sabbath, the Temple, and worship. One keeps coming by to be sure it is still there. This is the prophet's cry. "Turn, turn, return!" Keep coming by! God has been met with! And here you have an appointment—at the Tent of the Eternal—and it is a come and go affair. It is a constant reminder of what has gone by. One comes here in order to pass by again.

On the Sabbath he comes here to this tent. Here he expects and is expected. He has an appointment. Here he unchokes. Here he is reminded that once he was closer to the Eternal. Here he confesses, here the godliness rubs off from the neighbor, and here he quits going around unforgiven. Here the crosses in his own life deepen in meaning. Here he remembers what he must never throw away. And here, too, he may discover that the appointment which we have is not in a corner. It may well be on the road.

Sometimes a man comes and goes at his tent of meeting just because he ought, and sometimes he just sounds as if he gives and goes, even though he comes. But there is more than this at stake. Even God Almighty would have a hard time living off of the "free-will offerings of my mouth."

Coming to the Tent of the Eternal requires, said Moses, that one be of a "willing heart." You're supposed to bring what you've got, and this we have not done. We have brought what our neighbor on the budget committee convinced us we should give. I find at and around my tent an immense satisfaction in some people, as if God had been paid off, as if something big had been done here, as if there were proper reason for pride. Some of us had done our giving and could be finished with it.

There can be little doubt as to where the treasure of this particular culture lies. This culture features one kind of hero. He started from scratch and now owns the plow, or the plant, or the bank. Our treasure is money, and our hero is still that poor idiot, Horatio Alger, who usually married the daughter of the boss, after many temptations. Our treasure is money, and this is why we have to bring that, too. In fact, at whatever tent we go for worship, we cannot give God anything first when we have loved something else best.

This becomes a very great barrier. It is so difficult to teach, for how can you hear a man who is poorer than you are in money when money is what you respect? A voice like Moses' is from a world of fantasy, considering what you respect.

Hence, mostly, instead of doing-acting that is work and worship, we act out, and there is a difference. Even our discerning teenagers may spot many little dramas being acted out here. So they have quit the place. I do not mean a conscious "let's pretend" or even some hypocrisy. These we would confront. It is, rather, a deeper and subconsciously directed playing-out in a mythical setting of one's own making our existential splits, frustrations, and griefs. And this requires a great compassion.

It must require the great compassion of God to watch a man come to the Tent of the Eternal to act-out his fear of death with money, or to watch a man act-out his fear of love with money, or to see him act-out his hatred for his own beginnings with money. Sometimes he acts-out his fears of an old poverty with his children, or his misery at home with his office arrangements, or his adultery imposed by his wife with his loyalties to little notions and belongings which he polishes. But he nearly always, at the Tent, will telegraph his hurts with money. God must have a great compassion to watch a man suffering from an exhaustion he does not recognize acting-out all sorts of frustrations in a pulpit! We all do this.

It requires great compassion to live with this discerningly. And who can help us? This may be what you've missed about church, for whoever goes to church to be who he is? You go to church to be who you hope to God you look like you are. There is a difference. There must be a place where all the acting-out stops.

Ideally, the acting-out stops at the Tent of Meeting. And this is the Tent, we have been saying, where the Eternal, with whom you have an appointment, but whom you may not get in a corner, and who may be met with elsewhere, in a come and go affair— this is where he may be met.

Here you come on the Sabbath to long after godliness and to give God his due. That is to say, here the acting-out stops! This is where you are nobody; this is where you are somebody. Jesse Jackson in Chicago begins every service by saying: "You are somebody. You are God's child." Here "no-people" become "God-people." Here we are all "equally unqualified actors." Here we are as he first loved us, without anything to recommend us. Here we "take off our bloody dollars" while he decides whether he'll have us or not. The grace that hurts us is here, and we are left with nothing to do but to give this to God.

If all our humanisms run out at the edge of death and if all our moralisms run out in the face of our overwhelming evil, then all our acting-out of subterfuge runs out before Reality. Only here, at some Tent of Meeting, where death, evil, and fantasy must face Reality, do we outspan our oxen, throw off the journey's dusty gear, wash ourselves, come in to supper, and restore to what we were and are—in worship.

Here we come, called to come, anxious to come, rejoicing to come to unchoke, to be renewed, to accept our living. This we do by offering up what we have loved. Here all our dragged-in-things are offered up. Here the prices we have paid for nothing are atoned. The real issues in the form of our trampled and butchered relations are met with. You come here to pay your due to a Father, and it is really due.

Nothing is so devastating to love as a casual coming together when ardor is expected. It is an unforgivable sin! How casual we Protestants are about comings together. By and large, we live and meet as if nothing were at stake.

The Tent of Meeting was where Israel had waited to see if God would take them as his people, though they hardly knew his name. Then he acknowledged them by identifying himself: "I am the Lord your God who brought you up out of Egypt." Here for centuries they came to unchoke. But now, the wonder gone, Jeremiah recalls them to an old relation.

Is there ever a *casual* return to an old home? I think not. To go back home has its tremors. Jeremiah recalls them to the meeting of the meeting. Israel forgot it again and again, except that there was a Supper they had kept, a feast, "the day of the Lord's visitation . . . the day God Almighty came to see us . . . when he brought us up out of bondage."

Out of this Passover we keep a Supper, too, at our Tent of Meeting. Here you are invited, prepared for, expected to come to Table.

Look what they carry to the Table. In a few days Simon Peter will be the last great human hope for the church, the hope that a man will happen here. James will be slain by the club and pushed to his death from a wall. The publican, Matthew, will be skinned alive in Alexandria, they say. But what do they know of the meaning of the meeting as they dip in the dish? And Judas? He carries already the weight for all others of a consummate betrayal that's almost universal. And our Lord? No casual supper is possible. This is a great concern, if ours is a true Tent of Meeting. There can be no casual supper, no merely functional meeting. All the calendar-events of the church year ought to offer the prospect of a meeting somewhere—a chance to say a Yes or a No that matters.

No casual meeting means no casual *occasions* and no casual *persons*. Remember the classic opening phrase in *The Miracle of Dialogue:* "Every man you meet is a potential adversary." Who can be casual among his enemies? Conversely, who can be casual among his beloved? This can happen only where the meeting has been taken for granted.

So, here we are at Supper. What brought you here? Were you invited? Were you prepared for? Expected? What do you carry to Supper? Some consummate betrayal? Old regrets? Old age? Deep scars? Look, forgiveness and communion are here in the Tent, but they involve the one beside you.

I keep re-translating that passage where Esau and Jacob finally meet and Jacob says, "I see your face, you look like God." No casual greeting, offertory prayers, sermon, benediction, no scheduled, really scheduled "Amen." At my place they were always scheduled. Triple-layer, tutti-frutti, chocolate and vanilla amens, but never unscheduled ones. It would have broken up the meeting. At Highland Park Methodist in Dallas, a little girl in a choir once when I was preaching there forgot herself and said, "Amen!" It was so devastating I don't think she came back all week.

On the night in which he was betrayed, our Lord said, "Take, eat, this is my body." There is no casual response to that.

PETER MARSHALL

The Rock That Moved

There are not many cities in the heart of which you may
suddenly hear the crowing of a cock.
That is one sound that is not likely to arouse the guests in any of
Washington's downtown hotels.

One will never hear it in Times Square
    at Broad and Market
   at Five Points
  at Woodward and Michigan
 or along Michigan Boulevard.
Yet even to this day you may hear it in Jerusalem, for
Jerusalem is different.

One who was visiting the Holy City was enjoying the quiet of his
room when suddenly the silence was pierced by the shrill
crowing of a cock, and he immediately thought of a man named
Peter, for whom the trumpet of the dawn opened the floodgates
of memory.

What would it do for some lonely, homesick young woman in
Washington, if, before the city has yawned itself into action,
she were to hear the familiar bugle of the farmyard?

In a tide of sudden nostalgia she would be back home again
  on the plains of Kansas
    in the mountains of western North Carolina
      among the red barns of a farm in Ohio
        on the rolling green countryside of Pennsylvania
        or among the red clay hills of Georgia.

"The Rock That Moved" is from *Mr. Jones, Meet the Master.* Sermons and
Prayers of Peter Marshall. Copyright © 1949, 1950 by Fleming H. Revell
Company. (Some of the ideas in this sermon are attributed by Dr. Marshall
to Claude McKay, *Knowing Jesus Through His Friends,* Revell.)

There is many a young man in the city, bright in the nighttime like day, his pulses racing with the throb of jungle drums and the moan of the saxophone, intoxicated with the lure of the city and in strong temptation, who could be saved were he to hear once again on the heavy night air the lowing of homeward-driven cattle and the calls of the old farmyards.

It is in mysterious and different ways that God comes to the rescue.
He has a hundred ways of plucking at a man's sleeve.
He nudges some.
Others He taps on the shoulder.
To some it comes in music, to some in a picture, a story or a chance meeting on the street.
All these are used by God Who keeps watch over His own.

One St. Andrew's Day—a date all Scotsmen remember, I attended the annual banquet and had an emotional experience I shall not soon forget.

The Irish flaunt the shamrock in March, and the English remember Saint George and the dragon in June.
But to the Scot the 30th of November is one time when he throws aside his accustomed modesty and forgets he has always been outnumbered by the English eight to one, for this night is his own.
It is the night of the tartan and the haggis
    the night for thoughts of home . . . a night for memories.

The hotel was filled with bagpipe music.
The skirl of the pipes, indescribably thrilling to the Scot, came dancing into every conversation, and must have made them wonder who had no Scottish blood.
There was a full pipe band—and a good one it was.
There were the old Scottish songs, and the Doric—the broad Scots tongue, soft and kindly and warm.
There were the kilts and the glengaries, the Balmorals and the honest faces of the sons of the land of the mountain and the mist.

My, what memories came back, as the drumsticks twirled above the drum, and the kettledrums rolled . . .

and our feet tapped out the time to Cock o' the North
   The Forty-Second
   and Hieland Laddie.

In memory I saw a battalion of the Gordon Highlanders,
swinging down from Edinburgh Castle on to Princes Street
when I was last in Scotland—
   the pipes skirling
   and the kilts swinging
with the pride that only Scotsmen fully know.

I thought of the Fifty-first Division at El Alamein going
through the German mine-fields to the blood-tingling call of the
bagpipes.
I thought of home . . . and long ago . . . and choked back many a
lump in my throat.
We sang the old songs . . . the songs my mither sang . . . and
many an eye was misty.
We didn't say very much. Words were useless.
We just averted our eyes and blinked a bit and swallowed hard.

Memories . . . they come surging back into the heart to make it
clean again . . . or to accuse it.

Yes . . . to some it is music . . . or a song.
   To others it is a picture of the face of a friend
but to Simon Peter it was the crowing of a cock.

He had seen the last flickering torch disappear round the turn of
the path that wound down hill.
Only once in a while could the lights of the procession be seen
through the trees like giant fireflies.

The murmur of voices died away
   the crackling of twigs
   and the rustling of dislodged stones through the grass.
There swept over Peter the realization that his Master had at
last been captured and was marching away to die.

The icy fear that gripped his heart was a startling contrast to
the flaming courage with which he drew his short sword a few
minutes before, for this was a different Peter.

He realized that he had blundered, and that he had been rebuked.

Disappointed and puzzled, he could not understand the calm submission with which Christ permitted them to bind His hands and march Him off, as a butcher would lead an animal to the slaughter.

Realizing that he stood alone in the deserted garden, Peter stumbled blindly down the trail, heedless of the twigs that lashed his face and tore at his robes.

Stumbling on down hill, instinctively hurrying to catch up with the others, and yet not anxious to get too close, he followed down to the foot of the Mount of Olives, across the brook Kedron, and back up the hill to old Jerusalem, still asleep and quiet.

The procession made first for the house of Annas, into which they escorted Jesus. The heavy door creaked shut behind Him, and when Peter approached timidly, it was to find John standing there.

John persuaded the girl stationed at the door to let them in, and as they slipped past her, she scrutinized Peter and said to him:
"Art not thou also one of this man's disciples?"
He said: "I am not."

Perhaps she felt that she could speak to Peter.
Perhaps she felt sorry for him, seeing the hurt, wounded look in his eyes and the pain in his face.

Who knows what was in her mind?
Perhaps she had seen the Master as they led Him in, and felt the irresistible attraction of the Great Galilean.
Perhaps in that brief moment, as they had crowded past her, *He had looked at her.*
If He had—then something may have happened to her,
    within her own heart.
Her faith might have been born,
a fire kindled by the spark the winds of strange circumstance had blown from the altar fires in the heart of the Son of God.

Perhaps she wanted to ask Peter more about the Master.
Perhaps she would have said—had Peter acknowledged Him:

"Tell me the sound of His voice.
Is it low and sweet, vibrant?
Tell me of some of His miracles.
Tell me how you are sure He is the Messiah.
What is this salvation He speaks about?
How can we live forever?"

Maybe these questions would have come tumbling in a torrent
from her lips . . . who knows?

But whatever she meant, whatever her motive for asking the
question, "Art not thou also one of this man's disciples?" Peter
denied his Lord and said: "I am not."

We can only stand aghast at Peter and wonder if the strain and
the shock have destroyed his memory.

Simon, surely you remember the first day you saw Him.
Andrew and yourself floating the folded net . . . His shadow
falling across you as you worked.
Don't you remember His command, His beckoning finger,
the light in His eyes as He said: "Follow Me, and *I will make
you fishers of men?*"

Peter, don't you remember?

And that night when Nicodemus came into the garden looking
for the Master, don't you remember how he crept in with his
cloak pulled up over his face?

Don't you remember how he frightened you, and how the Lord
and Nicodemus talked for hours about the promises?
Don't you remember the wedding in Cana where He turned the
water into wine?
Do you remember the music of His laugh
and the Samaritan woman at Sychar?
Don't you remember these things, Simon?

And now, they brought the Lord from Annas to Caiaphas, and
the soldiers and the temple guards mingled with the servants in
the courtyard.

Because the night was cold, they had kindled a fire in the
brazier, and Peter joined himself to the group, and stretching
out his hands warmed himself at their fire.

Peter was glad to join the hangers-on huddled round the blaze,
for the morning air bit sharply,
    and he found himself shivering. . . .
It was a kindly glow of warmth.
Coarse laughter greeted every joke and they discussed the
things such people talk about:
    the coming cock-fight in Jerusalem
        the new dancing girl in the court of Herod
            the prowess of the garrison's drivers
                the gambling losses of their friends
                    the latest news from Rome.

Peter was not paying much attention to their conversation until
one of the soldiers nudged him and said:
    "Thou art also of them."
And Peter said, for the second time: "Man, *I am not.*"

Peter, you must remember . . . surely . . . it must be that you
are afraid.
Your brave heart must have turned to water.
Surely you cannot have forgotten . . .
many a time . . . crossing the lake in boats like your own,
    with its worn seats
        its patched sails, slanting in the sun
            and its high rudder?

Remember the night He came walking on the water, and you
tried it, and were walking, like the Master, until your courage
left you . . . your faith gave way?

Simon, has your courage left you again?
Have you forgotten the pool at Bethesda and how you laughed
when the impotent man rose up . . . rolled up his bed

threw it over his shoulder
and went away leaping in the air and shouting?

Ah, Simon, you spoke so bravely . . . and now here you are.

For the next hour or so they merely waited.
What was keeping them so long? They little knew the difficulty
of getting witnesses to agree.
They little knew that sleepless men, with tempers raw and
irritated, were trying to find some reason that they could
submit to Pilate that would justify their demands for the death
of Jesus.
After an hour had passed, there joined the group a soldier who
had come out of the palace.
As he greeted his friends in the circle, his eye fell on Peter. He
scrutinized him very carefully, and Peter, feeling the examination of the newcomer, looked round as the soldier asked: "Did
not I see thee in the garden with Him?"

One of his friends joined in:
    "Certainly—he's one of the Galileans.
    Just listen to his accent."
And the soldier stubbornly went on: "I am sure I saw him in the
garden, for my kinsman, Malchus, was wounded by one of
them—who drew a sword,
and if I am not mistaken—it was this fellow here."
Then Peter, beginning to curse and to swear, said:

"I know not the man."

He used language he had not used for years.
It was vile. . . . Even the soldiers were shocked.
They all looked at him in amazement.

They did not appear to notice the shuffling of feet, as soldiers
led Christ from Caiaphas to Pilate.
Perhaps they did not make much noise. They were tired
    Worn with argument and talk
    so they were very quiet.

The group standing round the fire was silent, shocked at the
vehemence and the profanity of Peter's denial.

It was a torrent of foulness, but it was his face that startled
them.
It was livid
      distorted
      eyes blazing
   mouth snarling like a cornered animal.
It was not a pleasant sight, and they kept silent.
It was a silence so intense that the crowing of a distant cock was
like a bugle call . . .

Immediately, Peter remembered the Lord's prophecy:
      "Before the cock crow twice, thou shalt deny Me thrice."
Like a wave there swept over him the realization of what he had
done.
All of a sudden he remembered what Jesus had said, and with
tears streaming down his face, he turned away from the fifire.
Through a mist of tears he saw ahead of him the stairway that
led to Pilate's palace . . .
and by a terrible Providence, it was just at that moment that
Christ was being led up the stairs to appear before Pilate.

The Lord had heard!
   The Lord had heard every hot searing word . . .
      The Lord had heard the blistering denial . . .
         the foul, fisherman's oaths . . .
He—He had heard it all!

Christ paused on the stair, and looked down over the
rail—looked right into the very soul of Peter.
The eyes of the two met . . . at that awful moment.

Through his tears all else was a blur to Peter,
but that one face shone through the tears . . .
   that lovely face
      that terrible face
         those eyes—sad
            reproachful
               tender . . . as if they understood and forgave.
Ah, how well he knew Him, and how much he loved Him.

The world seemed to stand still, as for that terrible moment,
Peter looked at the One he denied.

We shall never know what passed between them.
Christ seemed to say again:
  "But I have prayed for thee, Simon,
  Satan hath desired to have thee.
  But I have prayed for thee."

His tears now overflowed and ran down his cheeks—
    hot and scalding tears they were—
and with great sobs shaking his strong frame, Peter spun round
and rushed out to have the cool morning air fan his burning
cheeks.

He fled with his heart pounding in his breast, while the
Nazarene walked steadily to meet the Roman governor.

Something died within the heart of Peter that night.
Something was killed. That's why his heart was broken.

In fact, *the Simon in him was killed*
    the old arrogant boasting bravado of Simon
      the old cocksure confidence of the strong fisherman
        the impetuous stubbornness
          the impulsive thoughtlessness of Simon . . .
these all died in that moment.

Simon had ceased to be. Peter was being born.

Nothing more is heard of Peter for two days.
Christ has been crucified.

The hammer blows seem to be re-echoing still among the temple
domes, and in the very heart of Peter he feels the thud of the
hammer and hears the screaming of the impenitent thief.
But we must follow Peter further. It is not fair to leave him a
sinner, a swearing traitor, a fugitive from the heart of love.
This apprentice apostle is still in the making.
And he is running true to form.

Only last night the Master had spoken a personal word of
warning when He said:

"Simon, Simon, behold Satan hath desired to have thee that
he may sift you as wheat—"
and it had come true.

But he remembered that word of hope added by Jesus:
"But I have prayed for thee that thy faith fail not."

His Lord had prayed that somehow he should not fail.
That prayer must be—would be answered—but how?
Never again would his Master trust him.

And what of the other disciples? What would they think of him?
What could he do?

Ah, but Jesus had said even more:
"And when thou art converted"—that is, turned around—
when you have got new bearings
when you turn your face once more toward Me—
"strengthen thy brethren."
What did He mean?
"Black Saturday passed.
A new day dawned . . . a new week . . .
aye, indeed, a new age . . . though they knew it not."

There came the strange story gasped out by breathless women
who had come running from the tomb.
Then a race with John and the discovery of the empty grave . . .
Then the strange tale of the two disciples who came back from
Emmaus.

Something had happened.
Life could never be the same again.
The dead had come to life.

The Christ who had been crucified was alive, but still Simon
could only nurse his deep and bitter shame.
He was a changed man, still smarting with the searing of the
iron that had eaten into his very soul.

There came that night when, having gone back to their boats
and their nets, they had worked hard and in comparative
silence. Now as they came back, discouraged and sad, they saw

Someone standing on the beach in the early light of morning. The sea was calm—calm as a mill-pond—and the light, early morning mist still clung to the surface of the water.

They saw the flames leaping from a fire, and this mysterious figure waiting while their boat drew nearer to the shore.

"It is the Lord," said John, and that was enough for Simon. Here was the opportunity for which he had longed—to tell the Lord that he loved Him—to show how well he knew Him.

Without a moment's hesitation, he jumped overboard and waded ashore.
And then comes the loveliest record of God dealing with a penitent sinner . . .
Its tenderness and understanding come stealing into our own hearts like the perfume of crushed flowers.
For every denial, Jesus asked a pledge of love.
Three times the question: "Simon, . . . lovest thou Me?"
Three times the answer—and then the restoration,
"Feed my lambs. . . . Feed my sheep. . . . Feed my sheep."

And when he had spoken this, he saith unto him, "Follow me."

When next we see Simon, he is Simon no more—
but Peter—the Rock.

We see him fearless and eloquent
fire in his eyes
and his voice vibrant with conviction
melodious with good news.
His own will has gone; his Master's will has taken its place.
Peter stands up and preaches the gospel of his crucified and risen Lord.

Is this Simon preaching a sermon?
No, this is Peter.

Simon which was—the rock which had moved, but now is firmly established in the gospel.

The sinner-saint has become a witness
  a pillar of strength to the brethren
    an apostle to the ages.

The same Jesus, who called Simon, is calling you.
The same Jesus, who saved Simon, can save you.
The same mighty hand will hold you up.

The denials that you have made were made by Simon.
Yet he was restored; so may you be restored.

Christ changed Simon into Peter,
  the sinner into the saint.

He can change your life, if you are willing!

WAYNE E. OATES

The Revelation of God in Human Suffering

When the Son of man comes in his glory, and all the angels with him, then he will sit on his glorious throne. Before him will be gathered all the nations, and he will separate them from one another as a shepherd separates the sheep from the goats, and he will place the sheep at his right hand, but the goats at the left. Then the King will say to those at his right hand, "Come, O blessed of my Father, inherit the kingdom prepared for you from the foundation of the world; for I was hungry and you gave me food, I was thirsty and you gave me drink, I was a stranger and you welcomed me, I was naked and you clothed me, I was sick and you visited me, I was in prison and you came to me." Then the righteous will answer him, "Lord, when did we see thee hungry and feed thee, or thirsty and give thee drink? And when did we see thee a stranger and welcome thee, or naked and clothe thee? And when did we see thee sick or in prison and visit thee?" And the King will answer them, "Truly, I say to you, as you did it to one of the least of these my brethren, you did it to me."   —Matthew 25:31-40 RSV

The audience to whom Jesus spoke had been reared on phrases like these: "No one has ever seen God." "Man shall not see me and live." The hiddenness of God was the meat and bread of their spiritual diet. What an affront it must have been, therefore, for them to hear the Christian gospel, which boldly said, "The Word became flesh and dwelt among us, full of grace and truth; we have beheld his glory, glory as of the only Son

From *The Revelation of God in Human Suffering* by Wayne E. Oates, The Westminster Press. ©W. L. Jenkins MCMLIX. Used by permission.

from the Father" (John 1:14 [RSV])! This full revelation became the center of the Christian faith, and the writer of I John could say, "By this you know the Spirit of God: every spirit which confesses that Jesus Christ has come in the flesh is of God" (I John 4:2 [RSV]). He could also say with breath-taking firsthandedness of experience, "That which was from the beginning, which we have heard, which we have seen with our eyes, which we have looked upon and touched with our hands, concerning the word of life—the life was made manifest, and we saw it, and testify to it, and proclaim to you the eternal life which was with the Father and was made manifest to us—that which we have seen and heard we proclaim also to you, so that you may have fellowship with us; and our fellowship is with the Father and with his Son Jesus Christ" (I John 1:1-3 [RSV]).

But in the last days of the flesh of Jesus Christ, he was acutely aware that men would revert to speculation, "gazing into heaven," and to fearful anxiety in order to recover the luminous radiance of his continuing revelation of himself to them. Therefore he told them in plain words where and when he would reveal himself to them. This instruction he gave in the parable of the judging shepherd, who reveals himself daily in the suffering of needy people. The vision of the living Christ in the needs of the hungry, the thirsty, the stranger, the naked, the sick, and the imprisoned was to be henceforth his primary meeting place with his followers, and their awareness of the cries of his "little ones" would be the basis of judgment and separation, acceptance and fellowship, before God. In the sufferings of needy persons he comes upon us in fullest clarity. We do not always expect to see him most vividly here. Therefore we may be unaware of his presence. More often, in being callous to the distress of his "little ones," we may be insensitive and blind to his revelation of himself to us. But in either event, the vision of God in Christ is most vividly real in the sufferings of human personalities about us. Therefore, let us look more closely at the nature of Christ's revelation of himself to us, the character of our response to this revelation, and the ultimate meaning that this revelation has for us.

The Continuing Self-Disclosure of Christ

The Christ who holds the fate of the universe in his hands, both in his earthly and in his continuing disclosure of himself, has chosen to make himself known through the pangs of the hungry, the desperation of the sick, and exposure of the naked, the loneliness of the stranger, and the self-defeatedness of the prisoner. Christ continues to reveal himself anew in the extreme needs of "the least of these his brethren." In them we do not find the mere footprints and fingerprints of where he *has* been. Here we find his feet and hands themselves. Here we do not hear an echo of his voice, but the voice of the Christ himself. Here we find the Christ himself achingly involved in the destiny of human beings.

During his historic incarnation, Jesus pointed to his identity with human sufferers as evidence for the fact that the Messiah had come. John the Baptist and his followers, in true tradition with their contemporaries, needed evidence as to his Messiahship. Men for centuries had looked for the Messiah to come. They had many wild guesses as to how he would make himself known. They averred that he would come in a blinding Shekinah of light, a brilliant theophany that would cause every other light among men to cast a shadow. They also thought that he would come as a military ruler and crush by his power the oppressor under whose heel they themselves were being held in subjection. They, like many groups today, had all sorts of astrologies and date charts to determine when and how he would come, how long he would rule, and what would happen thereafter. They scanned sacred books and pitted this authority against that until students wound up in confusion or decided to take advantage of the confusion and get as much out of it for themselves as they could. Little wonder is it that when John the Baptist heard "about the deeds of the Christ, he sent word by his disciples and said to him, 'Are you he who is to come, or shall we look for another?'"

In Jesus' reply we hear no debate, no protesting too much, no extravagant arguments, no insecurity of rejection. We hear him saying, "Go and tell John what you hear and see: the blind receive their sight and the lame walk, lepers are cleansed and the deaf hear, and the dead are raised up, and the poor have good news preached to them." These words rose to the surface of the awareness of the disciples of both John and Jesus. Underneath them was the deep-running sense of mission of the Anointed One who, strengthened by the Holy Spirit after the struggle of decision in the wilderness, made the prophecy of Isaiah fact in flesh as he preached at Nazareth and said:

The Spirit of the Lord is upon me,
because he has anointed me to preach good news to the poor.
He has sent me to proclaim release to the captives
and recovering of sight to the blind,
to set at liberty those who are oppressed,
to proclaim the acceptable year of the Lord.
. . . And he began to say to them, "Today this scripture has
been fulfilled in your hearing." (Luke 4:18-19, 21 [RSV])

In his commission to his disciples, he transfused his revelation of the intention of the Father into the work of his disciples. He thrust them into active involvement with the sick, the spirit-possessed, and the deprived ones. They returned from their first assignment with their eyes glowing with the fresh vision of the reality of their Master and the strength of his compassion. They said with breathless excitement, joy, and exaltation, "Lord, even the demons are subject to us in your name!"

This triumphant ministry to the oppressed, this freeing of those bound by possessing spirits, was to Jesus an exultant revelation of the power of the Father released through him and his disciples as they gave themselves with abandon to "the least of these his brethren." He exclaimed at what he saw, "I saw Satan fall like lightning from heaven." Yet, he disciplined himself and his followers by saying to them that they were not to rejoice over the power that had coursed through their lives, subjecting demons unto them. Rather, they were to rejoice that through this ministry they were lastingly related to the Kingdom of Heaven. Then he gave thanks for the revelation of the Father to his disciples in the ministry to needy persons: "I thank thee, Father, Lord of heaven and earth, that thou hast hidden these things from the wise and understanding and revealed them to babes; yea, Father, for such was thy gracious will." (See Luke 10:17-22.)

Martin Luther caught the full thrust of Jesus' revelation of himself in the suffering of Frederick of Saxony, who fell desperately sick in September, 1519. Luther wrote a letter to his friend in the crisis of his illness and said:

When . . . I learned . . . that Your Lordship has been afflicted with a grave illness and that Christ has at the same time become ill in you . . . I cannot pretend that I do not hear the voice of Christ crying out to me from Your Lordship's body and flesh saying, "Behold, I am sick." This is so because such evils as illness . . . are not borne by us who are Christians but by Christ himself, our Lord and Savior, in whom we live, even as Christ plainly testifies . . . when he says, "Inasmuch as ye have done it unto one of the least of these my brethren, ye have done it unto me." (*Luther: Letters of Spiritual Counsel,* ed. by Theodore G. Tappert, p. 27. The Westminster Press, 1955.)

For those of us who are trained for the ministry of the gospel of Christ, one seriously sick person reminded us that we should not expect the revelation of God to be recorded in books and to be gathering dust upon library shelves before we sought it in earnest. Anton Boisen, out of the heated crucible of a severe mental disorder, discovered for himself and for succeeding generations of ministers that the real laboratory for discovering the clearest revelation of the meaning of God in Christ was among the sick, the outcast, the distressed failures of life. These "least ones" were, according to him, the "written, living human documents of flesh and blood" where God was most certainly making himself known.

Having had this man as a teacher, I can say as an eye-witness that he is right, because, as I have walked into hospital rooms under his supervision I have felt the living presence of the Christ and have had the meaning of his recorded words come alive to me. So much is this so that I am convinced that the shepherding ministry, to which every Christian is called and for which the pastor is specifically trained, is one of the headsprings of the ever-renewing water of life known as Christian theology. This shepherding ministry both vitalizes and purifies our knowledge of God.

Purity of Heart and the Self-Disclosure of Christ

Such a ministry to suffering people as we have been talking about does not *necessarily* imply that those who minister to the needy will automatically enter into a clear revelation of Christ. The clarity of their motives, the purity of their hearts, for performing this task has much to do with this discovery. In fact, the surprising element in the parable of the judging shepherd is that Christ's disclosure of himself came sometime later—after the acts of mercy and consideration had been performed. This leads us to believe that our motives for ministering to other people must be without a great deal of self-consciousness that we are doing something special, and certainly without a conscious campaign to "get a revelation" out of this ministry.

For example, those "blessed ones of the Father" of whom Jesus spoke were not aware of being on a "quest for revelation." They had not gone there looking for a revelation. So complete was their abandon and so unconditional was their love for those for whom they cared that their left hand was unaware of what their right hand was doing. They did not do their good works to be seen of men, to see Christ, or to increase their knowledge of theology. Surprisingly enough, the "blessed ones of the Father" asked the same question as did the accursed ones: "Lord, when did we see thee . . . ?" The unawareness of the one expressed the completeness of their abandon and love in serving; the unawareness of the other expressed the callousness of their neglect of the needy.

Those who inherited the Kingdom of Christ were rewarded on the basis of their ministry, but Jesus carefully revealed that they did not set out with this reward as their objective. Theirs was a ministry to "the least of these his brethren" because of an uncomplicated love for them in and of themselves. They were ends in themselves, worthy of love in their own right, and not means to the ends of those who did things for them. Those who ministered to them went to them with "clean hands and pure hearts," with no hidden motives, no attempt to minister to personal needs to be righteous, no attempt to get something out of them or to maneuver them toward previously self-chosen ends. They were not trying to make "rice" Christians of them, that is, giving them food to get professions of faith in the Christian religion. They were not trying to get a "confession" out of them, which would both be good for their souls and satisfy the curiosity of those who went to them. They did not have to have a reason other than their nonseeking kind of love and did not take time to become highly analytical about that. Theirs was religion that was "pure and undefiled before God," and their motives were "unstained from the world."

Today we are called upon to re-examine our motives for the service of needy people. We can very easily give and give and give to a needy family without ever taking the time to investigate the reasons for the family's plight or the motives for which we help. We may easily be undercutting the initiative of the family and failing to help them to help themselves. We may easily be doing our good deeds for them just to get them off our hands and to ease our consciences rather than to take the time to come to know them as persons, to minister to them totally rather than partially.

On the other hand, we may be exceptionally eager to turn our most recent ambitions to minister to needy people into grist for our public relations departments.

The laymen of the Committee on Institutions of the Louisville Council of Churches have steadily improved the condition of the inmates of prisons, hospitals, and childcare institutions through their co-operation with the administration and staff of these agencies. However, one of the key secrets to their effectiveness is that they have discreetly avoided publicity for their more important projects. Likewise, a negative example of this may be seen in the efforts of certain communities to set up church related counseling centers for the care of disturbed and unhappy individuals and families. One of the first mistakes such groups tend to make is to get wide newspaper publicity for their projects. By its very nature the counseling ministry is private, anonymous, confidential, and self-erasing. Such publicity contributes to the failure of such projects, because it is the antithesis of the ministry offered. Jesus in his ministry to disturbed people sent them away with instructions to "say nothing to any one." But we advertise ours in the papers. Little wonder is it that desperate people hesitate to entrust their heart's anguish to publicity-hungry churchmen!

The Bases of Christ's Judgment

The spiraling point of Jesus' parable of the judging shepherd reaches a dramatic climax as the Son of Man pronounces the separating judgment upon the "lived lives" of those before him! Jesus lived under the tension of the acute shortness of time. The words of this parable were apparently uttered under the very shadow of the cross that would end his own life. He was forced to thresh the issues of life down to the most urgent, pressing, and demanding ones and to deal with them in these fleeting moments. He breathed upon his disciples the shortness of the present age as well as the fact that his own personal hour was close at hand. He had said to them earlier, "There are some standing here who will not taste death before they see the Son of man coming in his kingdom" (Matt. 16:28). Now, in this parable, he described that coming, that event in eternity. He put his hands squarely upon the only issue that really mattered and held it up before them as the one issue that would balance the scales of his judgment: Hereby are we to be sure that we know him—if we keep his commandment to love our brother in the stresses of his life to the end that we will spend and be spent in his behalf without calling even our own attention to the fact.

My life and yours are being lived out under a promise of their appalling shortness. Many of the things to which we have given our lives are only peripheral to the central meaning of life. They are far afield from the core of Christ's continuing disclosure of himself. The issues over which we have been willing to bleed and let blood from others have been mere straw men compared to the poignancy of the hungry, the thirsty, the naked, the sick, and the imprisoned. We live our lives under the threat of world catastrophe and the impending cataclysmic end of the age. But when the clamor of the confusion of voices is overcome by the clarity of the voice of the Son of Man, we can say with Frank Mason North:

> Where cross the crowded ways of life,
>   Where sound the cries of race and clan,
> Above the noise of selfish strife,
>   We hear thy voice, O Son of Man!
>
> In haunts of wretchedness and need,
>   On shadowed thresholds dark with fears,
> From paths that hide the lures of greed,
>   We catch the vision of thy tears.
>
> The cup of water given for thee
>   Still holds the freshness of thy grace;
> Yet long these multitudes to see
>   The sweet compassion of thy face.
>
> O Master, from the mountainside
>   Make haste to heal those hearts of pain;
> Among these restless throngs abide,
>   O tread the city's streets again,
>
> Till sons of men shall learn thy love,
>   And follow where thy feet have trod;
> Till glorious, from thy heaven above,
>   Shall come the City of our God.

WOLFHART PANNENBERG

Religious Experience—
a Contemporary Possibility?

Exodus 3:1-12

There are many people today, to whom religious experience
appears to be something quite extraordinary. That may
explain, why—if they are interested in that kind of thing—they
look for it not in our domestic life and social context, not to
speak of the Christian church, but rather in the exotic world of
Eastern religions. The exotic seems more authentic, more
fascinating.

Now it may be correct that religious experience is in some
sense extraordinary. But it need not be supernatural. It need
not be separated from all other kinds of experience of reality.
Nor is religious experience obtained by special techniques,
techniques, e.g., of meditative praxis. Meditation, to my
understanding, leads to religious awareness rather than to
religious experience in the stricter sense of the word, referring
to a specific occurrence of Divine reality. Religious awareness
has not so much the character of a specific event, but of a
different attitude to everything real. It may be obtained by
meditation, but it can also be communicated by religious
education and tradition, by participation in the religious life of a
community, especially by participating in the celebration of its
worship. Religious awareness is awareness of the holy,
awareness of the awe inspiring mystery in the abyss and
process of our life and world. It goes together with some
appreciation of the precariousness of life so that nothing at all
can simply be taken for granted. Religious awareness changes
the familiar features of our world in a way similar to esthetic
awareness and to the vision of the artist. If you look at van

Dongen's painting of an old Dutch tavern in the Dutch countryside, on display in the Art Institute in Chicago, you recognize inevitably the transformation of the object in the vision of the artist: There is a circular movement in the wide fields as well as in the cloudy sky around the old tavern so that the decaying house itself is drawn into those dynamic circles. In a similar way, in religious awareness we perceive the familiar things of our world within a broader and unusual context; we see them—as Schleiermacher said—as a revelation of the universe, and thus their appearance is changed.

Religious experience in the proper sense is not all that different. After all, it is related to the same reality which what I called religious awareness is open to. The reality of God surrounds us; the dynamics of that deep mystery of our life and our world is at hand with every breeze and breath. It is true, we are not always aware of it, due to our propensity for looking on our own ways and being concerned for others and for the creatures and things of the world primarily insofar [as] they may be useful to our purposes. Isn't that largely what is called the secular aspect of life? In getting intrigued by utility and the profitable, we tend to suppress the awareness of mystery and the sense of wonder in our life. Thus we need being reminded. We need some messenger, some angel of God to remind us—just as it happened to Moses. The rumor of angels, to be sure, is resounding throughout the universe, but we usually don't listen. It takes an angel to be sent specifically to you, when your awareness has subsided or become dull.

The story about Moses' encounter with the angel of God in the thornbush offers, in the first place, an excellent example of what is true about religious experience in general. In the second place, it has also to do with Moses' particular mission.

Turning to the first point, we should realize that the story of the burning bush is a case of ordinary religious experience. There is nothing supernatural about it. The burning bush is just an ordinary thornbush. Certainly the appearance of the bush was transformed, as Moses perceived it, by the fire burning in it. Yet the bush was not consumed by the fire. It was a visionary experience, not a physical process. Nor was it only subjective: the burning bush was there! But what was going on need not be called supernatural in any way. Perhaps it was a sunset, the last red rays of the descending sun glimmering through the branches of the thornbush.

Similar occurrences can still happen today. At a midwinter sunset early in 1945, something happened to me, at the age of sixteen, that I never shall forget: there was not a thornbush, to be sure, but a flood of light suddenly all around me and penetrating my body in such a way that all gravity was forgotten. Nothing supernatural about that! Many people, in their years of adolescence at least, may have experiences like that. And yet it changed definitively my attitude toward reality for all my life, although at that time I did not yet know, as Moses did from his tradition, just what God it was, who was speaking to me.

We read in the text that Moses ran close to the bush in order to see what happened to it and why it was not burnt. I cannot believe that. In case of such an occurrence one is not so silly. Immediately you hear the voice: Get off your shoes, this place is holy. You may not hear precisely that, but something like that, don't worry! In the process of the telling and retelling of the story, somebody wanted to make sure that it was really God and not just the thornbush that appeared to Moses. Thus I assume the unbelievable extension of the story was inserted that Moses was first looking for a natural explanation of the bush. He had to have doubts for the benefit of a later audience. But nobody to whomsoever the angel of God occurs would react in such a way. It's a typical addition of a storyteller who wanted to pinpoint the event.

So much for religious experience as such. But then, unlike the continuous character of religious awareness in general, religious experience is always a particular event that happens to a particular individual. It therefore claims the individual in a quite specific way concerning his or her past and future; it transforms the meaning of the past and commits the individual for the rest of his or her future life. It sheds a light of promise and commitment not only on the private future of the individual, but also on his or her involvement with social life and with all mankind. However, what precisely that promise and commitment implies, is not always clear from the religious experience, we turn again to the story about Moses and listen more to the words of God spoken to him.

That Moses heard the voice of God, I take for certain. Of course he was struck by the event, and since he came from his religious tradition, he could recognize the God who gave himself to be known to him. By the way, we do not know for certain, whether to Moses it was indeed the God of Abraham, Isaac, and Jacob, or whether this is later interpretation. Anyway, he may have recognized in the event that occurred to him the God of *his* forefathers. So far I can follow the account of the story. But that God spoke such a long sermon to him on that occasion, I personally cannot believe. To me it seems rather striking that the commission entrusted to Moses by God in that long speech embraces all the essential development and content of his further life: his return to his Hebrew people, his attempts at persuading them to follow his lead into the desert, his formation of the people by the covenant and law to be received at Mount Horeb or Sinai. All that is contained in God's commission to him. Should Moses have known about all that beforehand? I doubt it. He certainly saw the burning bush, and he heard a voice that he recognized to be the voice of his fathers' God, and he trembled with awe and excitement. And he went to consider what it meant to him, and finally he identified the commission of God entrusted to him to the effect that he should liberate his people from Egypt and bring them out, and he returned to the mountain with them. It takes a long history in one's life to come to terms with such an occurrence as it happened to Moses. Only in retrospect it looks as if everything was spelled out in that very moment when it all began. It is no illusion, however. Of course God had assigned Moses in that very moment the commission that he devoted his entire life to. But it certainly took his entire life, also, to understand what he was called to by that voice that spoke to him through the burning bush. The word of God is not a miraculous entity that happens along a vertical line straight from above. God's word to us is spelled out through the course of our lives as much as it was spoken to us once in events that gave to our lives their direction and meaning. Therefore, it may be only in restrospect that we more fully understand the word of God spoken to us in the conspectus of all our life, issuing from the formative events of our personal history.

The case of Paul, admittedly, was different. There is not one single type of occurrence that would cover all religious experience. In Paul's case it seems that the event immediately was clear as to its significance. The voice which he recognized to be the voice of Jesus whom he persecuted was immediately speaking to him from heaven, and the core of its message did not emerge first from later experience and reflection, but must have been clear from the outset because that occurrence opposed the dominant intentions of the life Paul had lived up to that moment in persecuting the Christian community. That was all turned upside down by what occurred to him and convinced him of the living reality of Jesus the Christ. Only the further consequences of that basic occurrence could remain a matter of later reflection and consideration.

Religious experiences are not all alike. Ours may be more like that of Moses than like Paul's encounter with the living Christ. But always, I think, religious experience comes to us as an event that claims our entire life, by restructuring its meaning and committing us to the service of God in relation to our social world and to all mankind.

But perhaps some might complain that they never experienced such an event. Did you never see the burning bush? Perhaps you only forgot about it! Remember, and rethink your life from that event when you once felt the touch of eternity. You cannot remember? Well, then become aware of the mystery of life behind and beyond and then also within all the superficial business of everyday life. Start to consider what your personal life is all about. The answer may be modest and sobering, but the memory of those events that once promised meaning and personal identity to your life may still spell out what God wanted to tell you. And if you cannot see or hear anything at all, hold on in the dark, and God's angel will come to you, and your life itself will become a burning bush.

That happened to Jesus when his dead body was glorified, penetrated by the glory of God. Do we not believe that everything can be changed, even death can be overcome in the light of the burning bush? The same is promised to us, if we hold out—as Jesus did—in the dark and hope in the God whom he called his father and our father.

Moses also experienced that darkness. Think of his anxieties when the Egyptians almost destroyed his people at the sea of reeds. Think of his desperation when the people turned to the golden bull, when he surrendered his mission. And yet he looked forward to the promise of God.

Moses could not see the glory of Jesus, the light in his face of life everlasting, as Paul did. But he saw the burning bush and in that light he understood the promise and commitment of his life. No surprise that he only afterwards realized all that, since the fire in the bush was a flash of God's glory still to come. In the end, while looking across the Jordan River into the promised land, Moses saw his own laborious life—burning, but not being consumed by the glory of God. It was the same glory that irradiated the dead body of Jesus and brought it to life again. It was the same glory that became manifest to Paul as a dazzling light from heaven telling him that the one whom he pursued was his Lord. It is the glory of God that is about to transform this world, and when we become aware of it amidst the ordinary occupations of our lives, there our life is changed.

NORMAN VINCENT PEALE

Power Over All
Your Difficulties

*Wherefore take unto you the whole armor of God,
that ye may be able to withstand in the evil day, and
having done all, to stand.*
—Ephesians 6:13

You can have power over all your difficulties. It is quite easy, is
it not, to make such a statement. But think of the tremendous,
overwhelming implications of the words! Consider the difficulties to which human beings are prone, and then consider my
audacity in saying it. Yet I repeat, you can have power over all
your difficulties.

One of the kindliest, most understanding men in this country
is a gentleman whom I know, Angelo Patri. He has written for
years, in his newspaper column, wise and benign advice to his
fellow countrymen. "In you, before birth," Mr. Patri says, "was
stored all the power that you will ever need to meet all the
difficulties you will ever face. Draw on it, encourage it; for if
you do not use it, you will lose it." That represents one of the
greatest potential tragedies of human experience.

Now I, for one, would not want to rule out of the universe all
the troubles we have, though I have no more enthusiasm for
trouble than you have. But God knew what He was doing when
He allowed this kind of world to develop. The Bible says, "In
the world ye shall have tribulation:" and then it adds, "but be of
good cheer; I have overcome the world." Then what is God's
main purpose with us? To give us a soft and easy life? I think
not. His main purpose is to make men of us; to bring us back to
Himself, magnificent creatures who have fought the good fight,

and who have kept the faith. These difficulties of ours have a propulsive power.

Years ago I had a good friend, Channing Pollock, the playwright. He was a great human being and his passing was a sad loss to all of us. He said, once, "Men and motor cars go forward by a series of explosions. A beautiful motor car cannot fulfill its function until it has a series of internal explosions. Just so a human being with conflicts and difficulties to overcome gets somewhere and becomes someone."

You can never make anything out of yourself until you get a few explosions into the mixing-chamber of your life: crises, difficulties, hardships, pain, suffering, opposition. These test whether there is anything to you or not. If these explosions tear you to pieces, you are not drawing upon the power within you.

Well, how do we get power over our difficulties? I have a solution which may sound simple, but believe me, to the extent to which you use it, you will get real power over your difficulties. I am going to give you a text from the Bible, from the sixth chapter of Ephesians, the thirteenth verse. It might be well to commit this passage to memory, for it is one of the greatest statements ever made. "Wherefore take unto you the whole armor of God, that ye may be able to withstand in the evil day, and having done all, to stand."

You will notice that the text says to take the "whole armor of God." I suppose most of us have, at times, taken a little of the "armor" and so gotten only a little power. But this says we should go all out for God. And I know, as a result of long experience in dealing with human beings with indescribable difficulties to overcome that when they took the "whole armor" they were able to meet every difficulty.

The first essential in taking the whole armor of God is to practice His presence; practice it until you are absolutely convinced that God is with you, until you feel His presence. A woman came to me about her husband. She seemed so nervous as she told me of the state he was in that I thought she might be the cause of his disturbance. But when I met the husband I realized he was the cause, not only of his own state, but of hers, as well. He was a nervous, high-strung, sensitive, highly-organized person whereas she was the quiet, passive type—which has its advantages. He was so volatile, so filled with conflicts that he had brought her to the verge of nervous prostration.

"I love my wife," he told me, "but I drive her to distraction. She should never have married me. I suppose what I ought to do is to go off and die, so she can have a few years of peace."

"She doesn't want you to do that," I said. "She wants you to change, not to die."

"How can I change?" he asked.

I thought, myself, that it was quite a proposition. But I gave him an affirmation, the use of which I knew would help him. "If you say this a dozen times a day, it will do something for you," I promised. This was the affirmation: "God is the only power and presence in my life."

Just think of the power in a statement like that. If you say it until your conscious mind accepts it, until it drives down into your unconscious being, until you become aware that God is a presence in your life, then He will give you strength and renewal.

I haven't seen this man recently but I know he is nearly well. I know it because I met his wife and she looks twenty years younger.

"You are better," I said.

"Oh," she replied, "you wouldn't believe it! I can't describe to you what a wonderful thing has happened to my husband! He has risen above all the difficulties that used to overcome him. When I am with him I actually have a feeling of the presence of God." Quite a tribute to a husband, isn't it?

I know everyone academically believes in practicing the presence of God. But the secret is to believe it enough to practice it every day under every circumstance and difficulty. Practice the idea that God is with you. I have said this many times and it is hard to say it differently. But just once, won't you hear it as if you had never heard it before in your life? Listen. God can actually be with you, if you believe.

I was trained in a different religious conception from the one I am advocating today. And I had a hard time getting around to this simple idea of the presence of God. But it is the greatest idea I ever got hold of. It will see you through anything at anytime. And when people can become childlike enough to accept it, the most amazing things happen.

I have a letter on which is the great seal of the United States and the letterhead is that of the Foreign Service. This letter is from an American Embassy in a distant land and the writer is the Ambassador of the United States. He writes that the place where he is stationed is one of the worst posts anybody could get: dirty, filled with flies and bugs, hot, and a long way from home. He was angry when he received his assignment, felt he deserved a better appointment. He lingered in Miami, deferring going as long as possible.

In Miami, the letter says, he read something I had written about the idea of the presence of God. He had never taken much stock in religion before but he got a great deal of comfort from this idea of God going with him to his post. The result was a complete change of attitude. "Do you know why I am so happy and find so much beauty here?" he writes. "It is because God is here and I am in His presence. When I made my first call on the ruler of this country I prayed while I was waiting to be received. I could feel the Presence beside me and my joy is great because I know that God is with me at all times. I go to work and He, God, usually sits in a chair by my desk and at times He walks around behind me and puts His hand on my shoulder and I can feel His power flowing through me. This is usually when I have a difficult problem to solve or an important decision to make and of course I ask God's help. It is such a wonderful feeling to be in partnership with God. I don't worry any more and I am not unhappy because I know that God is with me."

Well, there is a man of intelligence and ability who found, through this very simple technique, that he could rise above many difficulties. Jesus has always appealed to real people, because real people are simple people. The simpler they are, the more real they are. You have to get simple enough and real enough to take the whole armor of God so that you can withstand in the evil day all your difficulties.

There is a second factor in this problem, one with which I have had great difficulty myself, but thank God it is no problem any more. We are told in the Bible that God will guide us in all the crises and difficulties of our lives. He will guide us by His counsel, it says, and afterwards receive us to glory.

Do you really seek God's guidance in your problems? I suppose you often offer a kind of prayer. But do you actually, whole-heartedly put your problems in God's hands? Are you simple enough, childlike enough, as Jesus says we should be, to put your problem up to Him, believing that He will actually give you a specific answer? This is what, I think, is meant by saying "take the whole armor of God." One of the most important elements in that armor of God against difficulties is to believe positively that God will guide you.

I have the privilege of knowing some great and beautiful souls who are childlike in their spiritual simplicity. One who comes to mind is Catherine Marshall, widow of the preacher, Peter Marshall, and author of one of the most inspiring books I have ever read, *A Man Called Peter.*

Catherine Marshall is a child of God. She believes that any problem, little or big, any difficulty, little or big, can be solved for her by God. She goes around telling people so.

Recently in an article written for *Guideposts* she tells of a friend who ran a summer hotel, a beautiful place. This friend tried to have there a gracious, Christian atmosphere. She usually opened the hotel on July 1st but one year she had so many guest-applicants that she opened on June 15th. But on the evening of June 14th she was lacking a pastry cook and dishwasher. Now, if you are running a hotel, you must have both a pastry cook and a dishwasher. She began praying and put the matter in God's hands. Her prayers were reverent, but very informal.

"I haven't the least idea where to find this help, Lord," she prayed. "This hotel is your business as well as mine. Will you please lead me to a dishwasher and a pastry cook."

She rose early the next morning and began dressing. Her business partner awakened enough to ask anxiously, "What are you going to do now? Where are you going so early?"

"I don't know," was the astonishing reply, "but somehow I know God will show me."

She got in her car and headed down the boulevard toward the business district. Half way to town she saw two colored men standing at a bus stop. On an impulse, she drew up to the curb beside them. "I run a little hotel down the beach," she said, "and need some extra help. You men wouldn't be needing jobs, would you?"

Big grins appeared on the two men's faces. "Yes ma'am, we do. We've been looking for jobs around here, and haven't found any. We were just starting back home to North Carolina."

"What can you do?" she asked.

"Sam here, he's a first-rate pastry cook. I'm a dishwasher."

"Climb in," said this friend.

The two men stayed the entire season and proved to be the best help the Inn had that year.

Coincidence, you say? But what is coincidence? Isn't coincidence subject to law? Does anything in this universe happen outside of law? Is there such a thing as happenstance in a well regulated universe? Somewhere, sometime, somebody is going to plot the scientific formula for coincidence. Certainly God works in coincidence.

Recently I met a man who told me that he was absolutely certain that God gives power over difficulties through His guidance, for he had experienced it. Once he went through a very hard period in his life when he was behind four hundred and fifty dollars on his rent, and the bank was calling him on a loan of seven hundred and fifty dollars. That meant debts of twelve hundred dollars and of course he was very troubled. He wakened in the middle of the night. He had never done much thinking about God but He seemed to come to him and ask, "Why don't you behave like a Christian?"

"What do you mean by that?" the man queried.

The Lord seemed to him to say, "Just put your troubles in My hands; then go to work and use your head." This seemed a very real message from God.

The man got up, knelt beside his bed and prayed: "All right, Lord. I owe four hundred and fifty dollars in rent and seven hundred and fifty dollars at the bank. If you will show me what to do, I will do it. I put the whole matter in Your hands."

Having done this, a feeling of calm came over him and he went back to sleep.

The next morning he found himself able to think clearly for the first time. He had been too agitated to do this before. God doesn't work in any foolish way, but through the processes of human nature. This man's mind suggested to him that he go to see two men to whom he had sold goods. He did this, telling these men that he had a money problem—but not telling them the amount he needed. They said they had done business with him for a long time and would be glad to help him if they could. They went into their private office to talk it over and he waited in the reception room. Finally they came out to say they had considered the matter and were able to help him up to a certain amount. Then came the amazing statement that if it would do him any good, they would be able to make him a loan for six months of twelve hundred dollars.

Of course the first thing a skeptic would say to this story is "thought transference." Granted. But who did the transferring? A psychological transference, you say? It could be. But I hear of so many just such happenings that I believe it is an application of the "whole armor of God."

Just to make sure you are convinced, I will give you another illustration. Years ago there graduated from the University of Illinois a super-sophisticated young man. After he got out of college, he went the pace and then began to run into difficulties. He lost one job after another. One day he went into a book store in Champlain, Illinois and saw there a book written by Dr. Blanton and myself called, *Faith Is the Answer*. He bought the book, read it, and wrote to me: "This is it. I have made a mistake." So he began following the idea that God would direct, God would guide. He became an advertising man and, at every step, he took his problems to God.

Not long ago he said to me, "You know, I ought to get married. I am thirty, I know a lot of girls, but I don't seem to fall in love. How do you do it?"

"Don't ask me," I said. "Just do it."

"I am never sure," he went on. "I get interested in a girl and then I ask myself, 'Are you really in love?' And I don't know. I have prayed about everything else. Do you think it is all right to pray about this?"

"You would live with the girl all the rest of your life, wouldn't you?" I said. "Certainly you ought to pray about it."

Later he wrote me that his secretary had left him and he had to get a new secretary. "I advertised, and then I prayed that the Lord would guide me in the selection of a good secretary. There were six or seven girls waiting for me at the office the next morning and, as soon as I looked at one of them I knew I had found, not a secretary, but the wife I was looking for. I had to see all the applicants, but I hired her."

I married this couple not so long ago and I was never more conscious of the sacramental quality of marriage. I have watched them grow together and work together into one of the most beautiful relationships of this life.

I have given a very simple dissertation and I have said only two things and there are many others which I ought to say. I should say that to overcome difficulties you must forget yourself in the service of other people. I should say that to overcome difficulties you should have a great Christian experience of the transforming power of God. But this must suffice. And I tell you from the bottom of my heart that on the basis of the Bible itself you can overcome every difficulty you now face by doing two things: practicing God as the great power and presence in your life; and taking every diffuculty you have, no matter how large or how small, to God—believing that He will guide you to a right answer and a happy outcome. "Wherefore take unto you the whole armor of God, that ye may be able to withstand in the evil day."

DAVID H. C. READ

The Gospel According to Mary

Luke 1:46-55

An ancient poem like the Magnificat is often regarded today as a
museum-piece—noble words to decorate a traditional service of
worship, a splendid background for musical compositions. Few
really believe that a religious song attributed to an obscure
Jewish girl from a peasant culture of two thousand years ago
can have anything of value to say to our generation.

It was natural for me to ponder this tension between Biblical
days and ours since this sermon was composed and written at
30,000 feet above the Atlantic between Paris and New York. It
didn't take me long to reflect that there is a very direct
connection between the religious impulse expressed in Mary's
Song and the jumbo-jet in which I was speeding through the
skies. We don't need to have the erudition of an Arnold Toynbee
to recognize that the dynamic of the civilization that produced
the jet and the exploration of the moon, the drive toward the
future and the sense of purpose, came from that unique
religious movement of which the Song of Mary is the perfect
expression—the Judeo-Christian belief in an active, living,
purposeful God. You have only to compare the Magnificat,
which celebrates a God who is active in human affairs—"he that
is mighty hath done to me great things"; "he hath shown
strength with his arm"; "he hath scattered the proud"; "he hath
put down the mighty"; "he hath holpen his servant Israel"—with the quiescent and static concepts of other great
religious traditions to realize why it is where the Biblical faith
took root that we find the dynamism of constant invention and
enquiry. Human beings have been most active and creative

where they have believed in an active and creative God. Thus it
was not difficult, poised in that symbolic jet, to celebrate
inwardly this dynamic and inspiring God.

So my thoughts went, but soon others took over. I couldn't
help some questions darting in. Does not the same inventive
power that is hurtling me in comfort across the Atlantic also
rain death and destruction on other members of the human
family? Has it not also produced the weapons that are poised to
wipe this Judeo-Christian civilization from the face of this
planet? Isn't there an awful arrogance and pretension, as well
as a religious impulse, behind this driving sense of purpose that
has been nourished by synagogue and church? Is it not
lamentably true that the peoples who have celebrated the
liberation of the Hebrews from bondage, and rejoiced in the
freedom that Christ has won for all mankind, have often been
the very ones who have been guilty of enslaving others in their
drive for power? And the further questions came: now that the
religious impulse behind this civilization has been waning, what
real purpose survives? The younger generation is not being
frivolous when they ask: progress toward *what?* Is the purpose
of mankind merely to produce more and more gadgets, to
amass more and more goods, to pollute the universe with our
devices, and to worship a growing Gross National Product
world without end?

At this point I found the Gospel according to Mary coming
alive with something both hopeful and shattering to say. It is
hopeful for it *is* a Gospel. The mother of our Lord is singing of
the Savior in her womb, the one in whom God has visited and
redeemed his human family. In the word "Savior" lies the hope
for 1974 as for Bethlehem when Herod was on the rampage.
"His mercy is on them that fear him from generation to
generation." The grace of God is still active in his world. But the
Magnificat is also shattering in its judgment on the Herods of
our world and on the Herod in your heart and mine.

This is what we miss when we think of the Magnificat as a
gentle cradle-song that ushered the Baby Jesus into the world.
It is nothing of the kind. Listen to these words of C. S. Lewis:
"The Magnificat is terrifying. If there are two things in the
Bible which should make our blood run cold, it is one; the other
is that phrase in Revelation, 'The wrath of the Lamb.' If there is
not mildness in the Virgin Mother, if even the lamb, the helpless
thing that bleats and has its throat cut, is not the symbol of the

harmless where shall we turn? There are no cursings here, no hatred, no self-righteousness. Instead there is mere statement. He has scattered the proud, cast down the mighty, sent the rich empty away. We have the treble voice, a girl's voice, announcing without sin that the sinful prayers of her ancestors do not remain entirely unheard, and doing this, not indeed with fierce exultation, yet a calm and terrible gladness."

"A calm and terrible gladness." He's right. The Gospel according to Mary speaks not only of the tremendous mercy of God but also of his rejection of every human pretension, his condemnation of our arrogance, our acquisitiveness, and our pride. Through this song we already hear the words of Jesus. He spoke about the man who boasted that he was "not as other men are, and prided himself on his religious virtues." "He hath scattered the proud in the imagination of their hearts," says Mary. He stood helpless before Pilate who boasted of his power to have him crucified and said, "Thou couldest have no power at all against me, except it were given thee from above." "He hath put down the mighty from their seats," said Mary (and what a putdown!). He told the story of the man who concentrated on the accumulation of material and planned to retire and enjoy it. "But God said, Thou fool, this night thy soul shall be required of thee; then whose shall these things be, which thou hast provided?" "The rich he hath sent empty away," said Mary.

The Gospel of Mary is the Gospel of her Child, which means that it is the good news of God's grace for all whom come to him in the rags of the Prodigal Son. "His mercy is on them that fear him from generation to generation." "He hath filled the hungry with good things." "He hath holpen his servant Israel in remembrance of his mercy." Like the words of Jesus this Song sends a lurid light across these real sins that keep people and nations from the kingdom of God—arrogance, domination, pride, love of power and possessions. The Magnificat, whether it was composed by this girl whose immortal words, "Lord, be it unto me according to thy word,'" signalled the response of simple human faith to the supreme gift of God's grace or whether she had already learned this song from the groups of God's revolutionaries who were looking for the divine act of liberation—the Magnificat forecasts the plain language of Jesus about the dangers that beset the rich, the powerful, and the oppressors. And it echoes his blessings on the poor, the meek, the oppressed, the workers for justice, and the pure in heart.

This Song is thus a manifesto of the kingdom of God which Jesus announced in his sermon at Nazareth with the words: "The Spirit of God is upon me because he hath anointed me to preach the Gospel to the poor; he hath sent me to heal the broken-hearted; to preach deliverance to the captives, and recovery of sight to the blind; to set at liberty them that are bruised." Cradle-song!

We see now why this Gospel according to Mary, which adumbrates the words and actions of her Son, is something more than a decorative appendage to a comforting Christmas story. It speaks to those same questions of power and arrogance, oppression and acquisitiveness, that plague us today. It accounts for the brighter side in the record of the Christian church—the care for the poor and helpless, the founding of hospitals, the sharing of wealth, the support of the oppressed, the defiance of demonic powers. At its best the church has translated the inward liberation and satisfaction that Jesus brings to each one who trusts in his cleansing and nourishing love into an outgoing concern for the rescue of the oppressed, the defense of the weak, and the feeding of the hungry.

Since all these matters are high on the agenda of the modern world, the Song of Mary is seen to be anything but a sentimental lullaby from a distant age that knows nothing of our problems. It is, among other things, a challenge to so-called Christian countries to reflect upon the dangers of their wealth and power and to see Lazarus at their gates. It is a warning that all the skills of technology lead nowhere except to destruction unless they are at the service of those values revealed in the kingdom of God—freedom, justice, compassion, and the expansion of the spirit of man. This Song is also a signal that the God who saves us in Christ is on the side of the poor, the weak, and the dispossessed.

I want us to all feel the impact of this Gospel according to Mary for it is the Gospel of her Son. What she is saying here is what he and his saints have done. They have turned the values of the secular world upside down. To respond to this gospel does not imply that Christians must espouse every revolutionary cause in our world today or that everyone who talks about "liberation" is on the side of the angels. I cannot see either Jesus or his mother as members of the party of the Zealots of that day with their program of revolutionary violence against the Romans. "My kingdom," said Jesus, "is not of this world; if my kingdom were of this world, then would my servants fight." Yet his disciples came to be called "those who turned the world upside down," for they were a disturbing and liberating force in that ancient world. One thing is clear. When Mary sang of the liberating power of God and rejoiced in the Savior she was about to bear, the world was being introduced to the revolution of love. There is no place for violence, for the fostering of hate, for the arrogance of the self-righteous in the Christian liberation movement. For the Gospel according to Mary extols the humble heart and leaves the judgment to Almighty God. But if you feel, as many do today, that the church is making grave mistakes on occasion in embracing very questionable movements that claim to stand for freedom and justice, you should remember that an even greater mistake would be to be found on the side of an oppressor.

"And Mary said . . ." Are we listening? She is telling of a gospel that offers to all who are humble enough to receive it, and all who are obedient enough to act upon it, a Savior who will free us from the burden of our sins, inspire us by his Spirit, and give to us and our world the meaning and sense of purpose that we desperately need. It is a gospel offered to all—at ground-level or at 30,000 feet—whatever our wealth, or status, or our job. It is offered to those who know they need what God alone can supply. This blessed girl who brought our Lord into the world had no pretensions. Nor did she place her hopes in any human deliverer. It is the mighty and merciful God alone whom she celebrates. From beginning to end her Song speaks of his revolutionary work in the fulfillment of the promise given "to our fathers, to Abraham, and to his seed for ever." If we can catch its confidence and respond to its challenge then we too may be able to say with her: "He that is mighty hath done to me great things, and holy is his name."

W. E. SANGSTER

Bearing His Reproach

*Let us go forth therefore unto him without the camp,
bearing his reproach.*

—Hebrews 13:13

Do you remember what a sin offering was as laid down in the
Old Testament? It says in the book of Leviticus that if the whole
assembly of the people shall sin, a young bullock must be
sacrificed, and, when the blood of the bullock has been
sprinkled in the holy place, its carcass shall be carried outside
the camp, lest it pollute the place where the people lived. The
Mosaic Law called it "a sin-offering for the assembly," and a sin
offering must not remain within the camp.

Reverent students of Scripture have long seen in Jesus the
consummation of all the ancient sacrifices of Israel, and it has
been noticed as something of minor but interesting significance
that he also suffered *without the camp.*

> There is a green hill far away,
> Without a city wall. . . .

"Without a city wall?"

That means, of course, *"outside the city wall"*—"without the
camp." *He* was the sin offering, and though the full inwardness
of what they were doing was hidden from his murderers at the
time (and is beyond our *full* understanding even yet), they bore
him to a hill *outside* the city and, "He hung and suffered there."
Cast out! Despised and rejected of men! Not permitted to
"pollute" the habitation of the people! And there, at the Place of
the Skull, with no encircling wall to give the gallows any
homeliness, he "yielded up the ghost."

So the author of this epistle says to the people of his day, "Let us therefore go forth unto him without the camp, bearing his reproach." He was writing to a suffering people, to people who had endured persecution and had still more persecution to endure, who knew what it was to be despised as followers of the Nazarene—covered with obloquy and soaked in shame. "Let us therefore go forth unto him without the camp, bearing his reproach."

Has this word significance for us today? We live in a country nominally Christian. What can this mean for us: "without the camp—bearing his reproach?" Do the words have meaning still?

I

The words *have* meaning still. Get this fact fixed firmly in your mind. *There is a reproach in this gospel*—even in a nominally Christian land. There is a shame at the heart of the cross, and it must be borne. You cannot have the hearty friendship of the world and the saving friendship of Christ. It cannot be "all this" (if by "all this," you mean things which your conscience condemns) "and heaven too." There is a choice to be made, and if you are going to be definite in discipleship, it must be faced: this or that, right or wrong, God or mammon. Let me prove that to you. Let me begin to prove it in little ways.

1. *There is a social ostracism which Christians often suffer:* a sense of being shut out, not in the camp, barred from the general fellowship.

I was visiting a Christian friend of mine recently in his lovely home, and, thinking of his generosity and hospitality, I said, "I suppose all your neighbors are your friends?"

His face puckered a little, and he hesitatingly answered, "Not really. We should *like* them to be, but all their social engagements are cocktail parties. When we went and kept to soft drinks, they lost what little taste they had for our company. They seem incapable of fellowship without drink. They think you positively queer not to join them. We are really rather lonely here."

And only a week or two ago I was talking to a lovely girl I know whose life is similarly lonely in a seaside resort because her husband is an officer in the army and on perilous service overseas. When I inquired what social life she had in the neighborhood, she replied, rather sadly, "Practically none. There are plenty of other officers' wives here, but the only thing they seem to care for is bridge—morning, noon, and night—and it's always for money. Because I won't join in, they all think I'm a frump. Life is rather lonely for me. . . ."

Can you understand both of those illustrations? I think you can. There is a social ostracism that Christians of the Puritan tradition (however gay in spirit they may be) must endure.

2. There is more than that.

Sometimes a man suffers in his professional advancement because he has identified himself with the Christian cause.

I could give many better instances, but perhaps you would forgive a simple personal reminiscence.

In my army days I had great ambitions—forgive my confessing so much—to get on the educational staff of my battalion. I was an auxiliary lecturer for a long time, and I had a comfortable understanding in my own mind (and other people had too) that when a vacancy fell due, I would get it. The vacancy fell due—I didn't get it. I will not deny that I was inwardly grieved and wondered why.

A friend of mine, already on the staff, enlightened me. He said, "The officer in charge wouldn't have you. You finished yourself off with him that night, months and months ago, when you came and borrowed the education tent for a weekly meeting of prayer and Christian fellowship.

"You should have heard what he said when you'd gone! He's the kind of man who carries picture post cards of nude women in his pocket. He has a mind like a cesspool. I've heard him say more than once, referring to you, 'Whatever happens here, we won't have that Holy Joe on the staff.' "

3. *Sometimes Christians are actually made a joke,* a butt, an object of common contumely, because they are in this way of life. I question whether zealous Christians have been accused of anything more often than they have been accused of madness. At Pentecost the apostles were thought to be silly through drunkenness, and when Paul pleaded his case before Agrippa, Festus, the Roman Procurator, said, "Paul, thou art beside thyself, much learning doth make thee mad."

I had in my hand recently the reminiscences of Sarah Bentley, one of the lovely early evangelicals of Yorkshire, who was, indeed, at the time of her conversion, a barmaid in the George Inn at York. When the great experience came to her, everybody said, "Sally's gone daft." She said herself, "They treated me like a mad woman who mustn't be left alone."

Not all Christians, of course, are suspected of madness, and it is no compliment that the dark suspicion doesn't fall. Often it means that their lives are so tepid, so lacking in challenge, so wanting in the penetrating power of holiness and the "arrestings" of grace that they are not conspicious in society and could pass for a pagan anywhere.

But where this life is vital, this consequence often goes with it. You are put outside on the mat. You are made to feel that you don't belong to the set. You suffer mild, or not so mild, ostracism; you may endure setbacks in your calling; you may be the subject of covert sneers. You are outside the camp.

II

Now, having established that, I want to hasten and say this: *Don't increase the reproach unnecessarily.*

What do I mean by that?

1. *Don't cultivate eccentricity.* There are some people who almost delight in being odd. I have known Christian men in this generation—though they are fortunately rare—who feel that the old vow of the Nazarite is obligatory today and who neither shave nor have their hair cut, regarding it as a sin to do so. You may never have met such people, but I have, and I say deliberately that the danger of that kind of oddity is this: it gives the impression to people outside that Evangelical Christians are queer. It gets them a name for being freaks when (as we know) they are among the most sweetly sane people on earth.

When Methodism first began to spread through this land, the Quaker people were already doing a fine work. John Wesley recognized that and gave God thanks for it, but the Quakers had certain oddities he couldn't approve. They wouldn't wear garments which had been dyed on the grounds that dyeing was a form of deceit. In common speech they used archaisms and addressed other people as "thee" where we would say "you," and they would say "thine" where we would say "yours." They would not use the normal names for the days of the week, Sunday, Monday, and so on, on the ground that they included pagan deities, and always said "First Day, Second Day."

I am sure John Wesley wouldn't have approved the schoolboy

howler, "A Quaker is two crotchets," because he thought, as we do, so very highly of the Society of Friends, but John Wesley *did* make this rule for his people: "We do not place our religion, or any part of it, in being attached to any peculiar mode of speaking, any quaint or uncommon set of expressions. . . ."

That rule still runs. Don't be eccentric in speech. Said Wesley (in effect), "When you quote the Scripture, quote them in their own words, but, apart from that, do not deviate from the most usual way of speaking."

I know Christians who never use their vote, not because, on one particular occasion, they were so confused on the issue that they didn't know what to do, but on every occasion and on principle because they say that they mean to keep themselves "unspotted from the world." If, therefore, a saint and a demon were rival candidates at an election (which pre-election publicity sometimes suggests!), these people would still not vote, contracting out, as it were, from the issues of our social life.

Avoid, I beg you, eccentricities. Don't cultivate peculiarities. Christ came to save and sanctify our humanity—not to make us quaint and queer.

2. In the second place, *don't be censorious.* A great deal of harm has been done in the world by the censoriousness of the good. You may have made a rule for yourself never to go to a place of entertainment. All right! You are at perfect liberty to abstain, but don't cast aspersions on people who enjoy a good film now and then. You may be a nonsmoker. I am myself. I bought my library out of the tobacco I never smoked, and I think my health has been better for my abstention. But you can be a nonsmoker without being an anti-smoker. It isn't proved that a pipe a day is a sin. If God wants a man to give up tobacco altogether, leave the Lord or the doctor to tell him so. Personal evangelism is not well begun by taking a man, as it were, by the lapel of his coat and saying, "No pint, no pipe, and no pools." If he comes into the fellowship of Christian people, he will learn why some Christians object to all three, but if you get a reputation for being a crank, people won't heed you when you are dealing with the most grave moral issues. When you speak out against adultery, they will say to one another: "You can't take any notice of *him!* He wouldn't let a man smoke a pipe if he could prevent it." Be quietly firm in your own way of living but only use the word "sin" as the New Testament uses it. There are

too many real sins in the world without our inventing any.
Censoriousness is a wretched sin. The admixture of pride in it
explains that. If there is a thing all men seem to resent it is that
"holier than thou" manner, and it has done more harm to good
religion than many other more obvious sins.

3. In the third place settle with yourself that, as a Christian,
*you will never sever fellowship with other people if you can
avoid it.*

Imagine a young fellow, a member of a set of gay sparks
whose whole idea of life in their twenties is to enjoy themselves,
and this young man is arrested by the Holy Spirit and drawn by
God into his way of life. Some Christians would tell him to sever
his fellowship with his old friends at once. "Forsake them," they
would say. "Cut them off! Finish with them!" I say quite the
contrary: "Don't forsake them. Hold on to Christ first, but hold
on to them too. You may be God's supreme opportunity in their
life. If the fellowship is to end, let *them* break it." If your
fellowship with them became a peril to your soul, God would
warn you and tell you what to do, but if Christians are always
going to withdraw themselves from the world, where will it get
us? There is a great deal of good in plain, ordinary people. There
is, indeed, a divine spark in them, and God might use you
to fan it to a flame. We shall be living little segregated lives,
with less and less influence on the modern world, if we are
continually "withdrawing" from all these social contacts. If we
believe in individual salvation but have no interest in society,
we shall be like men arriving at a great fire, willing to rescue a
person here and there from the holocaust but quite unwilling to
assist the authorities in putting out the blaze.

III

But what happens if, having avoided censoriousness and
eccentricity and remained, God helping us, sweetly human
—*what happens if they still exclude us from the camp,* still
thrust us out and treat us almost as if were pariahs?

Ah! *What then?*

Being sure that you are not a foolish eccentric, and not
proudly censorious and not yourselves quitting the fellowship,
but being thrust out, *exult in it!*

Say to yourself, "This is not *my* reproach. It is *his!* This is the shame of Jesus—crucified stark naked on a cross—and I am allowed to bear a bit of his shame. Hallelujah!"

Why is it that this reproach centers so often in the name of Jesus?

A fine Christian woman I know, who bears a witness for our Lord in an unsavory factory, brought that very problem to me some time ago. She said, "I can talk to the girls I work with about religion now and then, about moral standards, even about God, and they take it in silence, if not in acquiescence. But if I talk about Jesus, they will *not* take it; they seem to find his name offensive."

I knew what she meant.
Do you?

> Jesus is the Name we treasure,
>   Name beyond what words can tell;
> Name of gladness, Name of pleasure,
>   Ear and heart delighting well;
> Name of sweetness passing measure,
>   Saving us from sin and hell.

But it is a name others find offensive. They turn it into a swear word, a blasphemous oath. It is one of the bitterest experiences a Christian must endure to hear that holy name profanely used.

When that tide of reproach is rolling over you, when, for Christ's sake, you are made an object of reviling, "rejoice and be exceeding glad, for great is your reward in heaven; for so persecuted they the prophets which were before you."

In the late seventies of the last century there was a girl named Priscilla Livingstone Stewart. She was lovely to look upon: blue eyes, bright-colored golden hair, Irish gaiety. All the boys in the neighborhood thought she was grand. Her admirers lined up for a smile!

Then she met Christ. Having been heartily opposed to religion before, she became as ardent a disciple, and, soon after, the Salvation Army came to those parts. It was altogether characteristic of her that she could throw in her lot for a while with that despised people, and she chose to walk in their procession in days when they were pelted with old boots, stones, bad oranges, and worse eggs. Now, notice this! I give you the exact words of her reminiscences. She said, "None of my friends recognized me in the street, and all the young men who were fond of me walked on the other side."

I have no doubt that, being a normal girl, there was something of pain for her in that, but she felt that she had gained infinitely more than she had lost, and, truth to tell, God had other things in store for her. She went as a missionary to China and became the wife of that extraordinary missionary, C. T. Studd.

"None of my friends recognized me now"—"without the camp"—"bearing his reproach." What do you do when, without eccentricity and censoriousness and with no willing severance of old friendships on your part, they put you out?

You exult in it!

Don't miss the willing eagerness of the first phrase in my text: "Let us therefore go forth unto him. . . ." I am not going to be dragged. I am going willingly. Indeed, I am running. It is an honor of which I am all unworthy. I am going to thrust my shoulder underneath his cross and bear whatever I can of his reproach.

> I'm not ashamed to own my Lord,
> Or to defend His cause,
> Maintain the honour of His word,
> The glory of His Cross.

PAUL SCHERER

Creative Insecurity

*He is a chosen vessel unto me. . . . I will shew
him how great things he must suffer for my
name's sake.*

—Acts 9:15, 16

We are told that the new kind of person who is just now
making his appearance in history, post-Christian, post-individ-
ual, post-moral man, as he is called, finds it very hard to
believe that there is a God; though if one were to judge from the
plays and novels that he writes, with all their anguish of
rebellion, that bitter emptiness which comes of being utterly
without purpose when the mask is off and the chips are down,
he finds it even harder to believe that there isn't! Life for him,
as Christopher Morley once put it, turns into a kind of foreign language which everybody promptly begins to mispro-
nounce.

But none of that is really hard. What is really hard is to find
that every time you open the Bible, you have to reckon with
another kind of believing altogether: the kind that never will
allow you to manage your own life any more. There is the
picture of a pretty girl, with a lovely smile, on the cover of one of
the current magazines; under it is the caption, "I have earned
the right to live as I please." There are angels who rush in
where even fools are afraid!

You'll say a long farewell to that sort of thing when you come
face to face with the God of the Bible. It isn't then so much a
question of "believing" or "not believing": you run the risk of
finding out that he isn't at all the kind of God who will stay out

From the *Princeton Seminary Bulletin*, February, 1963. Published with
permission of the editors of the *Princeton Seminary Bulletin*.

there somewhere and let you look at him, or talk about him. He isn't as busy *being* as some people seem to think: he's busy *acting!* That's what shatters a man's peace. He's forever coming, and at his own convenience, not ours. He's forever choosing, and for some purpose he has in mind: it may not jibe with ours in the least!

Take the story of Paul's conversion, there on the road to Damascus. What God had in mind for him certainly didn't jibe with what he had in mind for himself. Something familiar, something which seemed solid and secure, was finished; he was snatched away from it. Something which looked like nothing at all that was solid, something which looked like the last word in insecurity, had begun; he was headed for it. That "from something"—"for something"—is our cue. That's how the lines run for us, these lines of God's direction.

I

From what comes first. Did it ever really strike across your mind with some little anxiety that Paul wasn't converted from an evil life, but from a good life; not from impiety, but from piety; not from irreligion, but from religion? Everything inside of him had been swept and garnished, not to say starched and ironed, for years. Every demand which his devotion to the God of his fathers had made on him he had done his best to meet.

Yet something was wrong. He doesn't seem to have had any overwhelming sense of sin. It wasn't his conscience that bothered him. It wasn't the boredom which comes of having nothing to do. He was doing a job, and it was the job he thought God had given him to do; he was going through with it. But from what he said later, he found it all very discouraging. You could breathe out threatenings against other people who didn't believe as you did, that was your plain duty; but you couldn't strike up a tune about it, or hoist a flag over it, or break out into any doxologies because of it!

And he tells us why. It's no secret. It was because all the way along he was trying to manufacture his own righteousness. I am not so sure that we ever get quite clear of it. That's why Christianity turns out so often to be so awfully dull. Have you noticed what a universal phenomenon student riots are all over our world? Part of the reason is that the culture of which they are a part has lost its enthusiasm, and youth can't stand that! Do

we at last have to say it as well of the Christian faith, that drama
which is far more exciting than any other the human mind has
ever conceived—unless indeed you think it's a fairy story: the
infinite and eternal God become man, to live as we are afraid to
live, and die as we are afraid to die? You may call Jesus
anything you like, writes Dorothy Sayers, but you cannot call
him dull. His enemies couldn't tame him; they had to crucify
him. It's his friends who have made a gentleman of him! Asking
of him only some sense of security, which in the end turns out to
be so false that even a bad cold can upset it!

Under such circumstances religion can do nothing more than
hand us over to the tyranny of that good which is always just out
of reach; and we have to go on clutching at it like a drowning
man to keep our heads above water, doomed always like Paul to
find ourselves desperately far away from the kingdom of God
precisely when we think we are safely and squarely in the
middle of it, and quite well, thank you; so well that we have no
need of a physician, grown used to the pride which we have
learned to call humility, content enough withal to mistake our
satisfaction for three hallelujahs and an amen.

It may even be that you are saying to yourself right now,
"Well, thank God, I am not like that!" In which case let me
thank you: you have helped me to make my point. It's what the
Pharisee said in the temple. And it's more than self-
righteousness; it's blasphemy. That's what frightens me. It's
the attempt to stake out a claim which is calculated to bind God's
freedom. You have some status with the divine bookkeeper,
haven't you? You aren't like that publican. Job said as much,
and said it out loud, shaking his fist at God: if he were any kind
of God at all, he would play the part, and quit pampering the
wicked—instead of the upright you-know-who! This way you
couldn't count on anything!

It all comes of looking around in our troubled world for
something safe—some thing to depend on; and "around" never
is the way to look. Nothing else so twists our judgments, or
sends us off on such weird tangents. Peter once looked
"around" at the other disciples. They had come a long, hard
road. And he said to Jesus, "We have forsaken all, and followed
thee; what shall we have therefore?" He was sure it would be
something special. If you couldn't spread out before God the
little decencies you had been able to bring off in your time, now
and then at any rate; if you couldn't count on his weighing them,

and entering them where they belonged—then for pity's sake what kind of world was it anyway? What was the use, if you couldn't set them up, and on occasion get in behind them for cover and say, "I told you so"? And Jesus told *him*—about the first who were last among the laborers in the vineyard, and the last who were first!

It simply means that there is no way at all of making a bargain with God and holding him to it. There was a tiny insert in *The New Yorker* some time ago: a picture of that huge machine in the Hayden Planetarium. A stepladder was planted against one of its great bulbous heads, and a little man on top with a screw driver was improving the universe—adding a few sputniks. Is this what we are after with our "righteousness" and our reform movements? Nobody should be so confident of himself as to be cynical about what we call the return to religion; but if it means no more than that we are afraid "for looking after those things which are coming on the earth," and so, not knowing what to do, are trying to get in under what the Bible tells us to do and think, arranging matters a shade more in our favor—then God pity us! I'm very doubtful that he'll have any way of showing it! I remember a cartoon in which a man passed a sign that read "Prepare to meet thy God"; in the next picture he had stopped before a mirror on a cigarette vendor, had taken off his hat, and was brushing his hair and straightening his tie! When we scuttle around for safety, we get nowhere. It isn't in the creed, it isn't in the liturgy, it isn't in the hymns, it isn't in the prayers. It just isn't "around." It may not even be up!

The truth of the matter is that the faith we talk so much about as if it meant believing something, or at least relying on somebody, means, before it means anything else at all, being back again with the Christ who gave himself to bring us back, in the company of a holy God who is also a kind of reckless pilgrim down the long reaches of his purpose. But he knows his way through. He hasn't faltered yet. The only trouble is that he is always in the dangerous vanguard of life, with nothing to clutter up his going but those of us who are forever digging our heels in the ground and holding back against the future that's on its way among the nations and among the races because we think we can be safe that way. It imperils all our lives!

We can't even sit still any longer on whatever it is we sit on and call it our faith—unless we want to be destroyed! Security at its peak is little more than sterility. It's only insecurity that has some chance of being creative; because it can never be overcome, it can only be resolved into some other brave chance for us to take. If your life is uninteresting, you have made it so; and you are not likely to help things much by acquiring a few added "interests" in the shape of luncheons and lectures and book clubs. Life doesn't want to absorb anything; it wants to create something, it wants to be gallant.

Have you ever seen that automatic Kodak advertised, with its electric eye? You don't have to gauge the light, you don't have to gauge the distance, you don't have to turn anything, and you don't have to set anything—and I say it's stupid! Let it jump up and take its own pictures! We used to sing "Blessed assurance, Jesus is mine." I've learned a little since then. You try to possess him, and put him in your vest pocket. I'm confronted now with the blessed disturbance that comes of being his! And I honestly think I prefer it. I hope so; because inside the disturbance there is something more than safety!

II

All right, then, what is it? It isn't just insecurity and nothing more. It's the insecurity of God's manifold and unreckoning grace!—which keeps giving us all we ask for when we're at our best, and keeps asking of us again all it gives. That's the "for what": clean away, as far as we can get away, from our safe and calculating lives, for the courage to be different, to make some incautious trial of compassion and of love every day we live, to find the good where we found only the fault before. You think it's tame? Try it!

I can't give you a blueprint of what needs doing—thank God! Paul didn't get one. He said, "Lord, what wilt thou have me to do?" And the Lord said, "It shall be told thee what thou must do." All you can count on is that it will be no craven thing: it will be a brave thing, something that will take more than you have in your own right, something that God wants to get done!

And he has it in mind, make no mistake about that. To say as much about him is to say no more than you have to say if you say anything about him at all. We are willing to concede that he has a purpose for everybody in general. That's a comfortable platitude. Or we say he had a purpose for Moses and the prophets, for the "saints" and for "all the glorious company of the apostles." And that's a comfortable alibi. There has to be some back door by which we can sneak out of our own unique and individual, our own personal and particular responsibility for the Christian faith and human history. Only there isn't. All through the Bible, from Adam to Abraham, from Egypt to Canaan, from Babylon back home again, every judgment and every mercy, every threat and every promise, comes hurtling straight at you, and you know it. You read it that way yourself!

Then why boggle? It's you that are chosen now for this thing God has in mind. Paul stands at the point where the transition is made from all the choosing God did in the Old Testament to all the choosing he continues to do in the New. When this violent little apostle talks of being hand picked, he isn't rationalizing some self interest. Read the story of his life. He isn't indulging any self righteousness. All that belonged to his false history, and he was done with it. He is simply saying something about himself which in his own way he insists holds true of everybody else: "Called to be saints . . . according to his purpose . . . in one hope of your calling."

He was aware of the absurdity of it; he was bewildered by it, baffled every time he tried to figure out the reason for it. Ananias said that day, "I have heard by many of this man, how much evil he hath done." Paul knew how much, and he knew it better than *all* the reporters. But he knew something more. He knew that this unreckoning grace which had beckoned to him wanted out, and it wanted out where he was. Nothing else mattered. He knew he couldn't manage by himself. Who can? But he knew enough, past and present, to know the way God works.

One is sometimes asked, "If salvation from one end to the other is the work of God, doesn't that let me out?" Nobody could ask it if he had the foggiest notion of what the love of God when it's experienced as law, and the law of God when it's experienced as love, can do when it gets hold of a man! Sinai turns into Calvary, and as surely as there is nothing you *can* do alone, so surely there is nothing now which at God's word you *won't* do!

And there was something else Paul knew. He wasn't going to be a man of "special privilege" any longer. That's what he had been as a Jew, he had thought so at any rate; and he had tried by strict obedience to hold on to it. For all his vaunted freedom after he became a Christian, he never let the obedience go; but it was a totally different thing now. Once, on that score, he had read all the others out, sinners and Gentiles alike. Now, on the same score, he had to read all the others in. The boundaries of God's kingdom were no longer his to tamper with. God could alter them, he couldn't. And God would alter them, that he knew, every time the elect began to figure that they were the elite!

One of the most touching incidents I have ever heard had to do with a Jewish scholar who had become a Christian; when he was asked why, with tender pathos, and with a profound understanding of his own history as a Jew, he answered, "I couldn't bear to leave Jesus alone among the Gentiles." And that's just where Jesus is—always! That's where he is bound to be—alone among the outsiders—until we go there too!

And we go not because we pity him, poor man, so far out of his element: that would be to look down the nose at those others, whoever they are. We go there, if we go at all, because we are that much like him! "Saving" the "lost" not so much because they are "lost"—better to let God fix the labels!—but because we are "saved," if indeed we are. We go there because that's what the grace of God has chosen us to do, and in the last reckoning nothing else! Why can't we get that straight? On the left hand of God in Jesus' picture of the final judgment were those who had no idea of why they were there, while on the right hand were those who couldn't make any sense of it either: "Inasmuch as ye did it not"—"Inasmuch as ye did it"—that was the secret! It's the "inasmuch" that upsets us where we are! If anything pleasant happens to us, like peace of mind, or heaven itself, it will have to happen along the way to "the least of these" his brethren!

But there is still more. And this Paul did not know. "He is a chosen vessel unto me . . . I will shew him how great things he must suffer." Are we somehow willing, in the shadow of a cross, to listen? C. S. Lewis, in *Till We Have Faces,* tells the story of Cupid and Psyche, and how bitterly Psyche's sister cries out, "Do you think we mortals will find you gods easier to bear if you're beautiful? I tell you . . . we'll find you a thousand times worse. For then you'll lure and entice. Those we love best—whoever's most worth loving—these are the very ones you'll pick out . . . I can see it happening, age after age, . . . growing worse and worse the more you reveal your beauty: the son turning his back on the mother . . . the bride on her groom, stolen away by his everlasting calling, calling, calling of the gods . . . We'd rather they were ours and dead than yours and made immortal."

But that's all changed now. Mr. Lewis knew it better than most. It was changed on a little hill outside the walls of Jerusalem. Ever since then we have been better able to understand that like the kings of old God can do us no higher honor, show us no greater hospitality, than to give us of his cup to drink. We may at times draw back a little and try to remain spectators. Matthew writes of what happened on Calvary: "sitting down they watched him there." Maybe we ought first to investigate some of his claims: couldn't he have spared himself the thorns and the reed and the nails and the spear, and at least looked a bit more like God? But the New Testament goes on taking it for granted that here is the very flaming center of life, and we'll be back, to flutter furiously, as someone has said, around the intensity of its burning!

I have more than just a twinge of conscience when I read this: "how great things he must suffer for my name's sake." Paul found out. It hasn't been given many of us. We have only to face the disciplines of life, and sometimes they are hard: its insecurities and uncertainties, the devotion that's without any safeguard; death, when it comes to us, or to someone we love. Shall we resent them? Can't we manage, with all we have, to bear redemptively what we shall have to bear in any case? The greatest joys the world has ever known have come that way out of its sorrows. It's the grace of God, that incredible, gallant thing, that wants out; and it wants out where we are!

You remember that painting where one of Sir Walter Raleigh's men—or was it Drakes's?—sitting on an old, upturned life-boat by the rocky shores of Devon is telling two lads about the wild hurricanes and the stinging spray—that's my guess!—how the ship would plunge nose down into the huge trough of the waves, and shudder up again with the water spouting from her scuppers, shaking her bow clear and rolling on into the next fearful dive. There is something in God like that! And unless there is something like it in us, what can he lay hold of? "Saul, Saul!" Something that will come at his signal, never mind what happens. We may ourselves perhaps have to pay more heavily than we thought, in a Father's house, for being that Father's child!

There was a youth who once sought eagerly for the court of King Arthur. When he came at last to the ancient gateway, there an old man stood. "Dare you?" the old man asked, glancing sharply at him. "Once past this arch, and our royal lord will lay vows on you which it were shame not to be bound by, yet the which no man can keep." What if we could answer, things being as they are, "Sir, write my name down!"

EDUARD SCHWEIZER
translated by James W. Cox

God's Inescapable Nearness

*Rejoice in the Lord always; again I will say,
Rejoice. Let all men know your forbearance.
The Lord is at hand. Have no anxiety about
anything, but in everything by prayer and
supplication with thanksgiving let your requests be made known to God. And the peace
of God, which passes all understanding, will
keep your hearts and your minds in Christ
Jesus. Finally, brethren, whatever is true,
whatever is honorable, whatever is just,
whatever is pure, whatever is lovely, whatever
is gracious, if there is any excellence, if there
is anything worthy of praise, think about
these things.*

—Philippians 4:4-8 RSV

"The Lord is at hand." Is that true? Or isn't it a fact that he is
far, far away from us?

We sit at the dinner table and talk about math tests,
yesterday's ball game, silly things we saw at the clearance sale,
or the story told by a businessman from America. After all of
this is over we might get around to thanking the Lord for our
meal. But even then it is difficult to pause and think about him
for just thirty seconds. The words so easily drift by us, and our
minds are still on the sale or on the man from abroad. No, as a
matter of fact the Lord is not at hand. He is far away. The
clearance sale and America are nearer.

Is it any wonder, then, that what goes on here in the worship
service right now is tremendously important? Paul tells us,
"The Lord *is* at hand." This is the way the Lord himself says to

From *God's Inescapable Nearness,* by Eduard Schweizer, trans. and ed.
by James W. Cox (Waco, Texas: Word Books, 1971).

us, "I am at hand." It is not because *we* live in his nearness, but
because he promises that to us. This fact has its source in him,
not in us. And why? Because the Lord has a name, the name
Jesus Christ. Nothing—neither devil nor clearance sale nor
businessman nor even my own unruly thoughts that go flitting
about everywhere but where they should be—nothing can undo
what has already happened.

How near is the Lord? As near as one born as I was born,
though probably under much more primitive circumstances; as
near as one who has a glass of wine with me under the
disapproving eyes of the onlookers; as near as one who passes
through the experience of death as I will have to do, but under
more horrible conditions. This is how the Lord is at hand.
Whether I think about it or not, whether I believe it or not
makes no difference. He *is* at hand for me anyhow.

Because that is true, because we live on the basis of what has
already happened, we therefore live also on the basis of what is
to come. We live from Jesus Christ, and we live toward Jesus
Christ. Timewise, Paul placed the Lord's coming not very far
ahead—no more than ten or twenty years from then. Of course,
he was mistaken about that detail. But what of his belief that
the goal of his life and the goal of all the world signifies Jesus
Christ? His mistake changes that very little. A person with
Paul's perspective lives not only in anticipation of the meeting
he will attend tomorrow evening, the book he will read this
afternoon, the examination he will stand in the spring, the trip
he will take next summer, his wedding this year, or the surgery
he will undergo next month. He lives toward the day when God
will be all in all, for then neither death nor "little-faith" nor sins
will be able to separate us from him any more. And he knows
that the entire world moves on toward that day.

But what does that mean? It means that God is always out
ahead of us. The totality of what is out there is neither the
wedding nor death nor meaninglessness, but God. However,
such an argument sounds completely different from what we
find in the Old Testament. In the Old Testament, when the
prophets speak about the nearness of the Lord they mean the
near wrath of God (see Zeph. 1:14–18). To be sure, the wrath of
God came. To be sure, what all of the prophets announced again
and again took place. To be sure, no one who has not come to
grips with the God of the prophets understands anything about
God.

However, this wrath fell upon the very one who is even now near us as the Lord. *He* passed through this day of wrath. God now wears the face of Jesus Christ. God lets us look into his own face and heart in Jesus. What, then, is awaiting us at the end? Not darkness, nothingness, or extinction, but God! *As an actual fact,* we come to be with him. Meetings, vexations, and vacations no longer stand between us and him. Nothing can insulate us from his nearness. This hope stands over all the world and over every event. So nothing about that has changed, even if Paul did die before the whole world achieved this goal. For this reason, the Lord *is* near.

We may have trouble believing what Paul says to us in our text. But we can practice it. And that is far more important. In four sentences, Paul tells us how to practice it today, tomorrow, and the next day, whether we can grasp its full significance yet or not.

Look at the first of Paul's four sentences: "Rejoice in the Lord always; again I will say, Rejoice." The most important thing for us to do is to rejoice. Paul is well aware that we need to be told to do it. Why? A person can, surprisingly, *will* to rejoice. One can work at the problem of seeing what our Lord who is near us gives us day by day.

Some time ago I went to visit a man who had been bedfast for literally decades. He told me about the pear tree that had stood until a short while before in front of the place where he lived. He spoke of how glorious it was, how it had survived the winter in spite of the snow that had weighted down its branches, how springtime had come to it with the first buds and then the blossoms, how summer had burst upon it with the full green leaves, and how autumn had been crowned by the fruit outside the window. This convinced me that one can practice joy. Obviously, all of us have much more to rejoice over than a mere pear tree. If we go at it in the right way, we will gradually get a better grasp of what is meant by the consummate joy prepared for us and our world. As we rejoice, a glimmer of that world where God sometime will be all in all will break through to us right here on this earth.

Consider Paul's second sentence: "Let all men know your forbearance!" Again, we can live by the nearness of the Lord if we take special pains to observe others and their needs and questions—even if it hurts us. We need very much to do that, at least until we can get free from ourselves at a few points and actually see other persons. The pear tree outside that invalid's window was old and unproductive and even shut out the sunlight. To get it to last a few years longer would have required fertilizing it and cultivating it with very tender care. The harvest it produced was scanty and worthless, I am sure. It was a wise decision of the owner of the house to cut it down. Doubtless every one of us would make the same decision. Even so, I believe that the tree would still be standing there if he could have seen it with the heart of the patient on the second floor.

Hundreds of other decisions, our decisions, decisions we have arrived at with wisdom and common sense, would have been different if we had made every effort to see their possible effect on other persons. As wise and sensible as they were, our decisions were wrong after all. How remarkable it is that God's love for us becomes real to an individual only when he himself begins actually to practice love and makes himself open his eyes and become aware of other persons. For the more serious and expensive that becomes for us, the more serious and precious becomes what God does for us. Nowhere does one learn so well how to have faith as in the chambers of those who have known adversity—the sick, the poor, and the burdened. If we succeed in letting a little bit of warmth and light go out from us, then that will be a foretaste of what awaits us all in God's kingdom.

Consider Paul's third sentence: "Have no anxiety about anything, but in everything by prayer and supplication with thanksgiving let your requests be made known to God." Once more we are summoned to practice something. If we refused to pray until prayer welled up spontaneously within us, we would never learn to pray at all. We have to practice even that. As to anxiety—of course, we do worry. And we do not help matters by pushing it down into the subconscious.

What did Paul have in mind? Certainly not precaution or provision, so that we would give no thought to having something to put on the table for breakfast! He had in mind solicitude, worry, dread. "What might happen next?" "What will happen if Anna Catherine does not pass the examination?" "How would we get along if suddenly I lost my health?" Paul had in mind the sort of calculating and scheming that so often shuts up our heart. It might be something that one would figure up as logically as the current cost of fertilizer for the old pear tree and how much more it might cost if a branch broke off.

He had an excellent solution to the problem: Pray! But pray in such a manner that thanksgiving is already in your prayer. Let us take Anna Catherine and her examination as an example. How utterly different the atmosphere at home would be if we could pray that she pass the examination, but while we pray be thankful that God will do exactly the right thing whether he allows her to pass the examination now or holds a different way in store for her. Then all of the nervous tension would be removed. Perhaps we might experience once again a little foretaste of how it will be sometime, when God is all in all.

Now consider the last of Paul's four sentences: "And the peace of God, which passes all understanding, will keep your hearts and your minds in Christ Jesus." Those words, dear friends, sum up, of course, all that we experience with the practice that we have been talking about. In brief, it is always God himself who becomes great and strong in us. We do not keep our own hearts fixed on Jesus Christ—his peace accomplishes that. We do not overcome the tumult and confusion and perplexity of our mind with our own peace—his peace does that again and again.

The nearness of the Lord consists in the fact that he takes a firm grip upon our heart and our mind a long while before we understand and grasp it. This is the nearness of the Lord: He awaits us with his kingdom, and his kingdom shines into this life of ours even if we are far from believing it. Here is the secret of every proper worship service: Perhaps in the singing, perhaps simply in sitting with the others, even if we can retain none of the sermon, we might see a tiny particle of this light and touch the near range of that coming world that is far more real and compelling than the host of things that are about to take us over and consume our days.

FULTON J. SHEEN

Easter

Friends:

As a soldier may return from war wearing the ribbons of victory, so Jesus rises from the dead wearing the scars of battle against sin!

Everywhere in the Easter scenes we meet a Great Soldier with His Scars! Mary Magdalen who had anointed His Feet for His burial just a few days before, and then once again knelt at His Feet on Calvary's Hill, now on Easter morn recognizes Him to be, not the Gardener but the Risen Savior, as clinging to His Feet she sees there the livid red memories of riven steel.

As the ten Apostles and their companions gathered around the evening lamp, in conversation with the travelers of Emmaus, suddenly, silently, without shadow, sound, without the lifting of a bolt, or the stirring of the latch, Jesus appears in the midst of them, saying: "Peace be upon you; it is myself, do not be afraid." Cowering in terror, He reassures them, saying: "Look at my hands and my feet, to be assured that it is myself; touch me, and look." And as He spoke thus, he showed them His Hands and His Feet (Luke 24:39, 40). Hands that had lifted up blind eyes to the sight of God's sunshine; Feet that climbed the mountain's stairs to a midnight holy of Holies to pray—but now Hands and Feet that show like luminous stars!

Later on Thomas, the individualist, who was not with the other Apostles when the Savior appeared—missing spiritual opportunities may cause doubt—when he was told by the disciples: "We have seen the Lord," answers: "Until I have seen the mark of the nails on his hands, until I have put my finger into the mark of the nails, and put my hand into his side, you will never make me *believe*" (John 20:25).

From *The Love That Waits for You,* a compilation of the Reverend Fulton J. Sheen's 1949 radio sermons published by the National Council of Catholic Men.

There are two kinds of unbelief: Those who say something is not true, *because* they *wish* it were not true; and those who say something is not true, because they wish that it was. This latter kind is curable. After eight days of the gloom that comes from doubt, the Savior appears to the Doubter and says: "Let me have thy finger; see, here are my hands. Let me have thy hand; put it into my side. Cease thy doubting and believe" (John 20:27). Thomas casts himself at His Feet, saying: "My Lord and My God" (John 20:28).

> O Captain of the wars!
> Why wear ye these scars?

First, to prove the law of Christian life that no one shall be crowned unless he has struggled; that no crowns of merit rest suspended on those who do not fight; that unless there is a Good Friday in our lives there will never be an Easter Sunday; that no one ever rises to a higher life without death to a lower one; that God hates peace in those who are destined for war.

Secondly, to prove His love. True love seeks not its own good, but the good of the other. As human love relieves the physical pains of others, so Divine Love relieves the moral evils of others. True love is proven not by words but by offering something to the one loved, and the greatest offering one can give is not what one *has,* but one's very life. Every scar tells the story: "Greater love than this no man hath."

Thirdly, to solicit our love; He rose not with wounds for those would betoken a weakness after battle, but with scars, glorious medals of victory on Hands and Feet and Side. As a little child may say to a wounded or scarred soldier: "How did that happen?," so Our Lord shows us His scars, that by our childish questioning, He might tell us: "I did this all for you!"

There are some who would have an unscarred Christ; they would have the Christ on the Mount of Beatitudes because they love beautiful sayings, but not the Christ on the Mount of Calvary because they deny they have ever sinned. They would have the Son of Man, but not the Son of God; the cowardly Christ Who shuns sacrifice; Who would have a victory without a battle, a glory without a struggle, a heaven without a hell; a broadminded Christ Who is indifferent to virtue and vice, Who knows no good sublime enough to die to espouse; and no evil wicked enough to condemn; the Tolerant Christ Who never made scourges to drive charlatans out of the Temple, Who never bade us cut off hands and feet and pluck out eyes rather than sin, Who never mentions hell or the devil or divorce.

Take your tawdry, cheap Christ Whom you call a moral teacher and ethical reformer, a social planner; Whom you put on the same plane as Buddha, Confucius, Lao-tzu and Whom you call a good man. He is not *just a* good man, for good men do not lie. If He is not what He claimed to be, the Son of the Living God, then He is the greatest liar, charlatan and deceiver the world has ever known! If He is not the Christ, the Son of the Living God, then He is anti-Christ, but He is not just a good man. A good man does not drive others to despair, but this is what He does, if the noblest life that ever the world has known can promise virtue no other reward than to hang on a gibbet to make a Roman holiday. If your weak, tolerant Christ be right, then wrong must be right; then what matter if we be saints or devils, if Christ on a tree or Judas on a halter must both taste eternal death!

Take your human Christ Who cannot save the Truth He preached, but drowns with Him for Whom He risked His life. Take your soft Christ, you polluters of Divinity, Who make Him just a man! Ye sculptors, writers, dramatists and poets, ye so-called men of God! Take your weak Christ Who could bless the seed that died to live again, but was not strong enough Who called Himself the Seed of Life once dead to rise again! Look to the flowers and grass and herbs that wake from winter's death! Will you deny that He Who made the blossoms break for April's sake, cannot Himself awake and move the stone from out of the tomb?

1) We need the Risen Jesus of the Scars for our times!

The only language we speak today is "blood, sweat and tears." A God without scars cannot understand our times: In this midnight hour of hopeless longing where even rivers run blood, and all the just of earth are a broken brood, when men are broken in heart, alone, and impotent, and where all men stand unmasked—to us no soft Christ can speak! Who can speak to those behind an Iron Curtain except a God on Whom it was once pulled down! Who can solace the Mindszentys, the Ordas, the Stepinacs, except Him Who alone has suffered under Pontius Pilate! Who can give courage to Poles, Lithuanians, Hungarians and the other dwellers in the catacombs of Eastern

Europe, except Him who was once in the underground to give to this earth its greatest wound—AN EMPTY TOMB!

Hold up your hands, ye people of Siberia; ye whose sides have been dug with a sickle and ye whose hands have been beaten with a hammer! Who can give you hope but Him Who can match your wounds with His Scars? Ye 194,000,000 good people of Russia, who are crucified by a minority of 6,000,000, where shall you find courage except in Him Whose life reveals that though the devil has his hour, it is God Who wins the day!

2) Only a Jesus of the Scars can speak to those who sorrow! Take your soft Christ; He is alien to our tears and broken hearts! What answer is there for the wounded, the sick and the dying; the unpitied, unheeded and alone; the veterans of wars, the children starved for lack of bread, for all who in their agony shout: "Does God know what it is to suffer? Did He ever go without bread for forty days? Was He ever betrayed? Was He ever abandoned? Was His Body ever racked with pain and what did He do?"

Jesus of the Scars knows what pain is. And if He Who is God took pain upon Himself it must be that somehow or other it fits into God's plans, therefore He could promise your sorrow shall be turned into joy.

Jesus of the Scars assured us that evil will never have an ultimate victory. The worst thing that evil can do is not to bomb cities, but to kill Goodness itself. But being defeated in its mightiest moment when evil used its strongest arms by His Resurrection from the dead, we may be sure that it will never be victorious again. Well, indeed, may the nail-torn Christ say: "I have overcome the world."

Jesus of the Scars knows what death is for He is the only one Who ever came to this world to die. Everyone else comes to live; death was a stumbling block to Socrates; it interrupted the teaching of Buddha. But to Christ, it was the goal of His Life, the gold that He was seeking. Breaking those bonds of the grave, by His Resurrection, He has taught us to say: "O death, where is thy victory? O grave, where is thy sting?" No longer can men say there are no tears in the eyes of the Eternal, no pain in the heart of God. Take then your Christ with lily-white Hands, with uncrimsoned robes and unpierced brows, and Eyes undimmed by sorrow! Take Him from our midst! He is too soft for these hard days!

Scarred men come for healing only to scarred Hands! Only a Risen Jesus with scars can understand our hearts. This is not an age of wars, but an age of scars! We all have scars! Everybody! Scars on bodies—the wounds of war; scars on souls—the wounds of godlessness. Scars of hate, fear, anxiety, melancholy, bitterness! Either scars fighting against Thee or scars fighting with Thee! Scars born of the offensive against Love; Scars born of the defense of Love!

Come Jesus of the Scars, I am not strong, until Thy pierced Hand clasps my own; I am not brave till I see the pledge of victory on Thy Heart; and I am not free, till Thou dost bind me to Thy Scars! Too long have we been hard on Thomas! He is now our spokesman—greater than all the rest! Since the world has scars, death surrounds and evil is strong, we too say: "Until I have seen the mark of the nails on his hands, until I have put my finger into the mark of the nails, and put my hand into his side, you will never make me believe" (John 20:25).

> If we have never sought, we
>   seek Thee now;
> Thine eyes burn through the
>   dark, our only stars;
> We must have sight of thorn-
>   pricks on Thy brow,
> We must have Thee, O Jesus of
>   the Scars.
>
> The other gods were strong;
>   but Thou wast weak;
> They rode, but Thou didst stum-
>   ble to a throne;
> But to our wounds only God's
>   wounds can speak,
> And not a god has wounds, but
>   Thou alone.
>   —Edward Shillito

DONALD SOPER

The Way of the Cross

There is a question that is becoming more and more urgent; more and more widespread, and I want to try to answer it tonight. In simple terms, it is a question of *priorities.* What is it that is so distinctive about the Christian faith? What is it that comes *first?* If you had, in fact, to put into a simple sentence or two the essence of the Christian Faith, what would you say?

When I was a student and a candidate for the ministry, I was arraigned before a spiritual court, where I was asked a number of questions. These I did my best to answer. But there was one question that was put to me that I have always remembered. An old and worthy member of the Methodist ministry asked me this. "Young man," he said, "suppose you were in a railway carriage, whose only other occupant was a man. You had just passed through one station, and you would arrive at the next station in five minutes. At this next station, the other man in your carriage would be leaving the train. You had till then to tell him what Christianity was about. What would you tell him?" It seemed to me that such a situation was not likely to arise; but I did my best to make some sort of answer—though I have forgotten what it was. But I have come to believe that this question was not so absurd or irrelevant as I then thought it to be.

There may be some of you (perhaps most of you) who are perplexed by the different opinions as to what is really the very essence of Christianity. It is not easy to be simple and concise. But I have been thinking over this problem, and of the question put to me so many years ago. I have been thinking, and trying to discover what answer I would give to that question now. And I know now—and I should have known it before—that there *is* an answer; and we have read that answer tonight in the New Testament, in St. John, Chapter 12, verses 20 to 28.

From *Aflame with Faith* by Donald Soper (London: Epworth Press, 1963).

You remember what happened? There were a number of Greeks who, we may take it, were somewhat contemptuous of the intellectual achievements of the Romans. They were equally contemptuous of the religious prejudices of the Jews. But they had heard about Jesus, and they wanted to know what He was saying, and they followed those who went up to worship at a feast. "We want to see Jesus;" they said, "will you introduce us to Him? We would like to hear what He has to say." They said this to Philip, and Philip told Andrew; and then Andrew and Philip told Jesus.

We know what Jesus said, for after He said it, John set it down; and so it has come down to us. First, Jesus said that if a grain of wheat dies, it bears much fruit. He then went on to say that he who loves his life shall lose it, and he who loses his life, in this world, shall keep it unto life eternal. And then He said, "If any man serve me, let him follow me; and where I am, there shall also my servant be; if any man serve me, him will the Father honour." But strangest of all were these words which follow: "Now is my soul troubled; and what shall I say? Father, save me from this hour?" No, not that, but "Father, glorify Thy name."

Now, these are three of the things that Jesus said in reply to the questions put to Him by those Greeks; and I want to talk to you about them tonight, because I think they are three cardinal factors in our Christian faith. And if we embed them in our minds, if we enthrone them in our hearts, then we shall be guided to see where Christianity is truly represented, and we shall be able to discriminate between that which is essential Christianity and that which is either a diversionary movement or just plain heterodoxy, or paganism.

Here were a number of Greeks who came to Jesus, and they said to Him something like this: "Master, what is this that you are talking about; what is this gospel you are proclaiming? What is this *faith* that you offer and where is this *kingdom,* and how do we get there?"

And when Jesus answered them, the first thing He said was this: "My kingdom is based on unselfishness of such a radical and fundamental nature that you have got to lose your life, if you are going to see it." His kingdom was based on a complete reversal of the Greek idea of prudence; it was based on a complete reversal of their idea of self-respect, or, as they would have put it, self-esteem. Now, whether we find that immediately and calamitously revolutionary, or not, I am sure that those Greeks did. Oh indeed, we do, too, for the whole of our life is rooted in selfishness; our world is centered upon ourselves.

I heard a man say the other day that, if the Communists came to this country, he would rather die than live under them. "Yes, that's right: freedom, glorious freedom! and if we can't have it, we'd rather die." These heroics are, in fact, the root of selfishness; a selfishness that is rampant in our everyday life. Pick up one of the glossy magazines and look at the advertisements; every one of them is based on an appeal to cupidity, to self-interest. Enlightened self-interest has, indeed, been invested in modern political thought with the stature of virtue, and even with the halo of goodness. Oh, I know that we Christian people say to ourselves, "I know I ought to be unselfish. I know that selfishness is the root of evil. I know that Jesus calls on me to be unselfish." We know all these things; but I do not think we have gone sufficiently deep down.

You see, here Jesus is going straight to the heart of the matter. He is saying that nothing in His gospel can mean anything to people unless they turn their very lives upside down. They have to see that the quest for personal self-satisfaction, or self-realization, or self-expression—this constant concern about themselves—is utterly wrong.

Let us face it; the Christian religion is not a religion of safety and comfort; its end is not to give us a comfortable release from our problems and an entry into that happy state when all will be glory for *me*. People who start off for such a goal will never reach Jesus Christ and His Kingdom. And that is why Jesus started off by saying to those Greeks—let me dare to paraphrase His words—

Now, my friends, if you are going to understand what I have to say to you, you must think of a grain of wheat that falls into the ground and dies, because it is only by its death that it will give new life. That is the law of nature; the grain of wheat loses itself, so that out of it may come something new and true.

And that is the beginning of the gospel.

I know that there are some who will say that the desire to be saved from the wrath to come is the beginning of the true Christian life; or that it is the consciousness of sin. But that is not so. The beginning of the Christian life is the crucifixion of selfishness.

We see a measure of that unselfishness—that selflessness—in the lives of the saints; in that of St. Francis of Assisi in the past, and in that of Albert Schweitzer today. We see it displayed in the heart and actions of a mother; in the natural way she gives to her children, without any bargaining, and without any assessment of her own interest. Occasionally, we come across an example of that quality of life, and it shines for us like a bright star. And Jesus said that this is what religion begins with.

I believe that Jesus sent those Greeks away to ponder on what He had said; and I believe He would send us away tonight to ask ourselves whether our own progress in Christianity is so poor, and almost unappreciable, because we have never really understood His words, "Except a grain of wheat fall into the ground and die, it abideth alone." It is only when the grain of wheat is completely forgetful of its own self-interest that it gives birth to new life.

And then Jesus said, "If any man (would) serve me, let him follow me." He said something else too. He said, "Where I am, there shall also my servant be: if any man (would) serve me, him will the Father honour." He said in effect that Christianity consists in discipleship, in serving Jesus, in obeying Him and in following Him. You may say that that was all right for the men and women who lived nineteen hundred years ago. They could see the footsteps of the Master. They could hear His voice. They could take meals with Him. They could even watch Him die. But it is different for us. Yes, it is different for us; but essentially it is the same.

The thing about Christianity that distinguishes it, differentiates it, from every other Faith the world has ever known is that it is the perpetual allegiance to the man Jesus. Let us not stay on a word for the moment: you can use the words *Savior,* or *God,* or *Lord,* if you wish, but it is in that allegiance that Christianity consists. Now that means that the first thing is not intellectual belief. It really is not; and I would ask you, in all sincerity, not to be side-tracked by those who would tell you that you cannot begin to be a Christian until you swallow, digest and accept a number of credal statements.

The beginning of the Christian life is getting up, as you are, with your doubts and with your sins, and following Jesus;

*looking to Him; praying to Him, and trying to imagine how He
would react to the circumstances in which you are troubled.
That is Christianity; that is where it begins.*

We know that that is true, because all sorts of people came to
Jesus and said, "Master, can I follow?" "Of course you can" He
said, "if you are prepared to walk with me; if you are prepared
not to turn back. If you are prepared to keep going, it does not
matter who you are, or what you are, or where you came from,
you can walk with me."

That is the way we must open our hearts; that is the way we
must open the doors of our churches and say to people, "We will
not keep you out because you cannot swallow the theological
propositions we agree to; we are not so sure about them
ourselves." And we are not so sure—it was a great convenience
when the Church spoke in Latin! It is much more tricky today,
when we have to put our dogma into basic English.

And the first thing about Christianity is not this *Book*. The
sooner we get away from this idolatry of The Book, the sooner
we shall see that Christianity is, first of all, following Jesus.
Those disciples had not got a Book—I do not suppose the
fishermen could read. They certainly had not got this Book. Did
Jesus say, "You cannot come with me till the Book has
appeared"? Of course not.

And supposing this Book were destroyed, and not one copy of
it remained. We could still walk with Jesus. I should know
enough about Him from the lives of those who have blest me by
their presentation and their example of His love. I should meet
Him in His Church, which is His body. Of course I treasure and
value this Book. But do not let anybody tell you that
Christianity consists first of all in a book. It does not.
Christianity begins in personal devotion to a Saviour, who, to
quote Dr. Schweitzer, comes to us as the Unknown; one who
does not say, "I am all these things attributed to me by prophet
and sage." No, He says, "Come unto me . . . for I am meek and
lowly in heart."

This leads me to the third thing that Jesus said to the Greeks.
He said, "Now is my soul troubled; and what shall I say?
Father, save me from this hour. But for this cause came I unto
this hour. Father, glorify Thy name." I wonder why Jesus said
that. I do not think I know entirely, but one thing I treasure is
that in those brief words he was not aloof, magistral or
self-contained. He did not say to those Greeks, "It is all mapped

out." It is reported that Hitler used to speak to his generals, even to the highest in his command, as if he had already solved all the problems that might vex them. How different was Jesus. He said to those Greeks, "Now is my soul troubled, and what shall I say? Father, save me from this hour." No, I cannot say that; I must not say that, for I was brought to this hour. "Father, glorify Thy name."

From this, we can take it that Jesus went on to tell the Greeks that he was going to face a crisis, and the challenge of everything He stood for. He was going to be crucified. He thought:

I know it in my bones that they will take me. I have heard that they are already laying a trap for me; I know that one of my followers will betray me if he gets a chance. I know what will happen. They will get rid of me. I shall be crucified.

"But," said Jesus to those Greeks, "it is a tremendous adventure. In that adventure I am troubled, and much is not clear. But I shall go on. Will you come with me?"

And, for me, the Jesus who is troubled in spirit, the Jesus who in the garden prays God that the cup may pass from Him, even the Jesus who cries out, "My God, why hast Thou forsaken me?", is the Jesus who is worthy to be followed in the seeking of a kingdom which is beyond our understanding; which is so complex and so wonderful that we can see it only a little at a time, so that we make our journey towards it step by step.

When Jesus had spoken to the Greeks about the utter unselfishness which was the new quality of the life that was His, He did not challenge them as one who sits upon a throne, with suppliants at His feet. He took them into His confidence, and offered them—as Garibaldi offered his warriors a hundred years ago—an adventure, much of which was yet unknown and shadowy, but an adventure in which He believed. He said: "And I, if I be lifted up from the earth, will draw all men unto myself."

I yearn for a return to that kind of Christianity: that Christianity which is first of all a searching of our hearts that we may discover His new way of life; a Christianity which today would set out to translate the words of Jesus for this twentieth century, so that we could see the footmarks of the Master along the streets of London and Moscow, and Peking and New

York—and, walking in those footmarks, could be content with the iron rations of adventure.

Now this could easily spill over into heroics, but it need not; and it never will, if we keep close to Jesus Christ. For there were no heroics in what He offered, or in what He exhibited. It was the way of a Cross, and He took it, whether anyone followed Him or not. Actually they did not. They fled.

But we need not flee. Last Wednesday we began, in memory, to walk that road which we call Lent, which leads to Good Friday and the Cross. I believe with all my heart that this world wants nothing so much as—in fact needs nothing at all but—a fellowship of Christian followers who, in unselfishness, will take up their Cross and follow their Master to His kingdom. I would like to think that you and I might be in that gallant company.

FREDERICK B. SPEAKMAN

What Pilate Said
One Midnight

I am glad you stayed after the others retired, Gaius. I want to
talk. I'm not at all certain what I want to say, but I want to talk.
It was a wretched dinner, wasn't it? No, don't rally your fine
patrician manners and protest that you enjoyed it. It's too late
in the night for even courteous lies. Lies use up so much
strength. Past midnight there's only enough strength left for
truth.

What? No, I'm all right. It's that word I used, that word
"truth." It slips up on me. I use it before I think. And then wince
always, as if I had jabbed that old spear scar on my thigh.

But full apologies for the dinner, Gaius. You've never heard
Pontius Pilate apologize before? Yes, I know the food was good.
This is the best resort in all Helvetia. And the air here in the
Alps should whet an appetite like a Damascene dagger. But you
didn't eat, nor did any of the other guests. And they excused
themselves noticeably early for holidaying Romans. Because of
me. Because I can no longer entertain. Because I poison the air
with both my silences and my remarks, with a restlessness of
eye, yet a vinegar of words that blisters even Roman hides. But
I want to know why, Gaius. Because I know you'll head back to
Rome when the summer heat subsides there. And you'll cover
its seven hills with your gossip within a week. There won't be a
cloistered, intimate salon along all the Appian Way in which you
won't have served up the rarebit of your news— that you saw
me, Pilate, at Lucerne this summer. That it's true that I've lost
my grip. That I've aged twenty years in the few that have sped
by since I lost my post in Judaea. That I spend my self-imposed
exile gnawing the bleeding knuckles of melancholy, while

Claudia looks on and pleads and weeps and babbles about the gods.

Oh, come, I can hear you, Gaius! How all the bleary eyes of your friends, and the jades they call their wives, will flock to you to hear a report that so suits their hopes. But whatever you tell them, I wanted you to know. Because—oh, because we once were close, before my failures isolated me. Or because, perhaps, confession needs no reason after midnight, since a burned-out heart must now and then blow its smoke in a different face. So here it is, Gaius. Let the slave fill your glass, and clutch it tight! I didn't just lose my post in Judaea. That in itself would have been release from prison. It was something else I did, and what maddens me is that I don't know what I did. But you might get an inkling if I say that I may have killed Caesar!

Oh, not our Caesar. No, I was serving him. The day I married Claudia, Gaius, Caesar said to me with that divine smirk, "Congratulations, Pontius. To marry a woman of royal blood is the best training for statesmanship that Rome can offer her sons." That's why I was so determined to rule well over the Jews. When the appointment came and the Senate sneered knowingly, "Family connections," I had to show them I was something other than a career soldier from the wrong side of the Tiber. And Claudia was with me. Imagine her going! What other provincial governor do you know whose wife shared his whole term of office? That isn't the pattern Caesar encourages. Wives stay in Rome, vegetating luxuriously and pretending to pine, while the husband is abroad squeezing enough tax and graft from the provinces to come home and retire on.

Don't squirm so, Gaius. Yes, the slaves can hear, but it isn't news to them that I mutter treason.

We were to be the royal pair, Claudia and I. But you don't rule the priests of Jewry. You bluff authority and they bluff humility, and each knows the other's lying. You scheme and plan and awaken one morning to find yourself a child at cunning. And you lose dignity, and you lose respect, and you fear for your job, and you hate.

Here's just one sample of how my record ran. I found no images of Caesar in Jerusalem. So I put them up. Placed them on the garrison of Antonia, overlooking the Jewish temple. The priests said nothing. But that night six thousand Jews surrounded the palace with a roar of prayer and chanting that went on night and day. I threatened a massacre and they bared their necks and chanted louder, six thousand of them, waiting for the sword. I removed Caesar's image, and back home the Emperor whined that he'd lost face!

That began it, and your busy ears have heard long since how it went. Every feast day a threat of revolt. Every revolt more blood. Every throat that was cut for Caesar bringing a sharper rebuke from Caesar. We built a summer place in their north country. We ate their sickening buttered quail. We conspired with their native rulers. But there was no avoiding trouble, and I grew sullen and Claudia had her dreams. Her dreams and her gods.

Suppose it helps, Gaius, to believe that there's more to the world than you can see there? Does it help to endure what you do see there? I'd always boasted in the Roman code—if you can't see it or touch it or use it or spend it or wear it, then it isn't real, it doesn't exist. But not Claudia. She had a Jewish hairdresser who talked to her of the Jewish God. One God, mind you! Which struck me as a sensible economy till I heard what He was like. An interfering God, one I'm afraid wouldn't leave room in His kind of world for Rome. And it was from this Jewish servant girl we first heard of this Nazarene. I don't know what He was. If I did— But I checked Him with spies. He seemed a harmless kind of traveling teacher such as thrive in that climate. And I couldn't understand why the Jews were so upset by Him. Claudia heard Him twice when He was in the city, convinced me that His quarrel was with the Jews, not with us.

Well, we had just arrived in Jerusalem this night. It was the time of the greatest feast, and the air reeked as thick of revolt as it did of pilgrims. And toward morning I was hauled from bed by their high priest, a certain Caiaphas, my nominee for the Prince of Rats. How our Roman Senate could have used him! He'd managed to get me heavily in debt to him. Temple funds he had loaned me that he knew I didn't intend to repay. And he had grown quite bold with his personal demands, and I was sick of it. Late this night he rouses me, all secrecy, all very much the sinister conspirator, to announce to me they had arrested this Nazarene. By night, mind you! Had tried Him at a hurried, trumped-up session of their Jewish court. Had convicted Him of blasphemy, a charge I just don't understand. Somehow, it's all tied up with their monopoly on God. But they were bringing

Him to me at dawn, to be condemned to death by Roman law for sedition.

The high priest's warnings were always well staged. Never spelled out, but plain as the knifelike nose of his holy face that either I convict this Man or there'd be trouble with the Jews at feast time, the brand of trouble I couldn't afford. I couldn't sleep after he left. I paced those hot corridors. I finally dressed, full an hour before the dawn. It had all tumbled in on me, the impact of how trapped I was. The proud arm of Rome, with all its boast of justice, was to be but a dirty dagger in the pudgy hand of priests!

I was waiting in the room I used for court, officially enthroned, with clerk and guards, when they led Him in. Well, Gaius, don't smile at this, as you value your jaw, but I've had no peace since He walked into my judgment hall that dawn! It has been years, man, but these scenes I'll read from the back of my eyelids every night. You've seen Caesar when he was young inspect the legions. His air of command was child play compared with the manner of this Nazarene! He didn't have to strut, you see. He walked toward my throne, arms bound, with a stride of mastery and control that by its very audacity silenced the room for an instant and left me trembling with an insane desire to stand and salute!

The clerk began reading the absurd list of charges, the priestly delegation punctuating these with the palm-rubbings and the beard-strokings and the eye-rollings and the pious gutturals I had learned to ignore. But I more felt it than heard it. I questioned Him mechanically. He answered very little. But what He said and the way He said it! It was as if His level gaze had pulled my naked soul right up into my eyes and was probing it there. And a voice kept singing in my ear, "Why, you're on trial, Pilate!" And the Man wasn't listening to the charges. You'd have sworn He had just come in out of friendly interest to see what was going to happen to me. And the very pressure of His standing there had grown unbearable, when a slave rushed in all atremble at interrupting court, bringing a message from Claudia. She had stabbed at the stylus in that childish way she has when she's distraught. "Don't judge this amazing Man," she wrote, "I was haunted in dreams by Him this night!"

Gaius, I tried to free Him. From that moment on I tried, and I'll always think He knew it. I declared Him out of my jurisdiction, being a Galilean. But the native King Herod discovered He was born in Judaea and sent Him back to me. I appealed to the crowd that had gathered in the streets, hoping they were His sympathizers. But Caiaphas had stationed agitators to whip up the beasts and cry for blood, and you know how any citizen loves, just after breakfast, to cry for another's blood. I had Him beaten, a thorough barracks-room beating. I'm not sure why. To appease the crowd, I guess. But do we Romans need a reason for beatings? That's the code, isn't it, for anything we don't understand?

Well, it didn't work. The crowd roared like some slavering beast when I brought Him back. If only you could have watched Him! They had thrown some rags of mock purple over His pulped and bleeding shoulders. They had jammed a chaplet of thorns down over His forehead. And it fitted! It all fitted! He stood there watching them from my balcony, swaying from weakness by now, but royal, I tell you! In the teeth of that mob, not just pain but pity shining from His eyes and seaming His face. And I kept thinking, somehow this is monstrous; somehow it's upside down. That purple is real! That crown is real! Somehow, these animal noises the crowd is shrieking should be praise! And then Caiaphas played his master-stroke on me. Announced there in public that his Jesus claimed a crown. That this was treason to Caesar. And the guards began to glance at one another. And that mob of spineless filth began to shout "Hail Caesar!" And I knew I was beaten. And I gave the order. And I couldn't look at Him. And I did that childish thing, I called for water and there on the balcony I washed my hands of the whole affair. But as they led Him away I did look up, and He turned and looked at me. No smile, no pity, just glanced at my hands, and I'll feel the weight of His eyes on them from now on.

But you're yawning, Gaius. I've kept you up. And as active a man as you are needs his rest on holidays. Claudia will be asleep by now. Rows of lighted lamps near her couch. She can't sleep in the dark any more. Not since that afternoon. *You see the sun went out when my guards executed Him.* That's what I said! I don't know how or what. I only know I was there, that though it was midday it turned as black as the tunnels of hell in that miserable city, while I tried to compose Claudia, and explain how I'd been trapped, and she railed at me with her dream. She's had the dream ever since when she sleeps in the dark. Some form of it. That there was to be a new Caesar, and that I killed Him.

Oh, we've been to Egypt, to their seers and magicians. We've listened by the hour to oracles in the musty temples of Greece, chattering their inanities. We've called it an Oriental curse that we're under, and we've tried to break it a thousand ways. But there's no breaking it. Except—and even *that* might not, you see.

But do you know why I've kept going? Deeper than the curse is the haunting, driving certainty that He's still somewhere near. That I've unfinished business with Him. That, now and then, as I walk by the lake He's following me. And much as that strikes terror, I wonder if that isn't the only hope. You see, if I could walk up to Him and this time salute! Tell Him I know now, whoever He is, He was the only Man worth the name in all Judaea that day. Tell Him I know I wasn't trapped, that I trapped myself. Tell Him here's one Roman who wishes He were Caesar! I believe that would do it. I believe He'd listen, and know I meant it, and that at last I'd see Him smile!

Yes, quiet tonight, isn't it, Gaius? Not a breeze stirring down by the lake. Yes, good night. You had better run along. No, no, I think—will you waken the slave outside the door and tell him to bring me a cloak, my heavy one. I believe I'll walk by the lake. Yes, it is dark there, but I won't be alone. I guess I never really have been alone. Yes, goodnight, Gaius!

EDMUND A. STEIMLE

And How Does It All End?

Man that is born of woman is of few days, and full of
trouble.
He comes forth like a flower, and withers;
*   he flees like a shadow, and continues not.*
And dost thou open thy eyes upon such a one
*   and bring him into judgment with thee?*
Who can bring a clean thing out of an unclean?
*   There is not one.*
Since his days are determined,
*   and the number of his months is with thee,*
*   and thou hast appointed his bounds that he*
cannot pass,
look away from him, and desist,
*   that he may enjoy, like a hireling, his day.*

—Job 14:1-6 RSV

We wish you not to remain in ignorance, brothers,
about those who sleep in death; you should not
grieve like the rest of men, who have no hope. We
believe that Jesus died and rose again; and so it will
be for those who died as Christians; God will bring
them to life with Jesus.

For this we tell you as the Lord's word: we who are
left alive until the Lord comes shall not forestall
those who have died; because at the word of
command, at the sound of the archangel's voice and
God's trumpet-call, the Lord himself will descend
from heaven; first the Christian dead will rise, then
we who are left alive shall join them, caught up in
clouds to meet the Lord in the air. Thus we shall
always be with the Lord. Console one another, then,
with these words.

—I Thessalonians 4:13-18 NEB

From *From Death to Birth* by Edmund A. Steimle (Philadelphia:
Fortress Press, 1973).

Early one summer morning, a New York policeman delivered a child in a dimly lighted Brooklyn tenement, and, less than three hours later, and only six blocks away, shot and killed a stick-up man who was pulling his gun on him. At the end of the day both the child and the gunman were still nameless. Anonymous birth and anonymous death—and the whole mystery of life and what it's all about caught up in a story of a policeman's tour of duty early one summer morning.

What *is* life all about? What's your life all about? And that question remains unanswered until you have faced up to the end of it. We may think that we know how the gunman's life ended but how will that new baby's life end? And yours? And mine?

The Bible—as realistic a book as you'll find anywhere—presents two possibilities. The first is in the mouth of Job: "Man that is born of a woman is of few days and full of trouble. He comes forth like a flower and withers. . . ." That is a dark picture, of course. We can say it came out of Job's depression and bitterness and may well reflect our moments of bitterness too. But it's more than that. What of the death of the gunman? Or of the peasants at My Lai? Or drop in on a ward for terminal illness or into any shoddy nursing home. And, frankly, what does it look like? "Man that is born of a woman is of few days and full of trouble. He comes forth like a flower and withers. . . ."

But Paul, of course, gives us a brighter prospect: "We wish you not to remain in ignorance, brethren, about those who sleep in death; you should not grieve like the rest of men, who have no hope. We believe that Jesus died and rose again; and so it will be for those who died as Christians; God will bring them to life with Jesus."

But isn't that pretty much whistling in the dark these days? For who can really believe any longer in a resurrection from the dead or in a life after death? Remember: Paul is not talking about an immortal soul that goes on living no matter what, some untouchable part of me which is indestructible. Paul is talking about a miracle; that we die, as Jesus died, every last bit of us. And then the miracle: "We believe that Jesus died—and rose again." And as for the rest of us who die: "God will bring them to life with Jesus."

And that's absurd, isn't it so? At least that's not where we are most of the time: thinking about a resurrection from the dead as if it were the most important news about your life and mine.

How was it with you this morning? A whole new day breaking upon us, like a new lease on life. Well, if you're anything like me, you didn't bound out of bed to greet the morning. I reluctantly pulled myself out of bed and brushed my teeth and sat down to orange juice and coffee with the sports page spread out before me. And after a bit, I began to wake up and think about what I'd be doing between breakfast and lunch: the jobs that had to be done, the telephone calls, the deadlines to be met. Never once did I give even a passing thought to the resurrection from the dead. As Helmut Thielicke puts it, "We don't *think* that way . . . The bird of a cheerful breakfast in the hand is worth more than a couple of resurrections in the bush." That's the way we operate.

But All Saints' Day comes around each year—and in November, too—and suggests that we do think a bit, at least, about this business of the resurrection from the dead. Normally we don't hear much about it even in church except once a year on Easter. But on Easter we are conditioned by our expectations of hearing the inevitable sermon on resurrection or immortality or life after death. On Easter we are conditioned to put death and resurrection into the parenthesis of Easter, out of touch with ordinary life the rest of the year. And we are also conditioned by the circumstances of the spring of the year, full of hope and buds and new blossoms . . . the spring of the year is all promise! So resurrection as a miracle doesn't really cut much ice with us in the spring. But in November? The season of dying and death, a long cold winter ahead with dull skies and rain and ice? Maybe it's a good thing to take a look at the resurrection from the grave when the days are short and the darkness deepens.

But it's not just a Sunday in the church year, All Saints' Sunday, which prods us to think about the mystery of a resurrection from the dead. The facts of life today keep pressing the question of death and what lies beyond. For one thing, as someone has noted, "Old age as we know it, did not exist prior to this century." He goes on, "When those now over 65 were born, the average man worked about 70 hours a week and died at age 40. A man now works 40 hours a week and has a life expectancy of 70." Thus for increasing numbers of people, "death" is no longer the abstraction preachers talk about on Easter; it is a fact all caught up with growing old . . . and dying.

And that puts resurrection from the dead into a new and not particularly pleasant perspective. Almost everyone, I suppose wants to "live a long time." But practically no one wants to "grow old and die." And yet both phrases mean exactly the same thing.

Moreover, growing old and dying today raises the specter of the very real possibility of poverty, or at least seriously shrinking income, and chronic illness and nursing homes and dependency—all of which we abhor. And that prospect seems far closer to Job's assessment of life and its destiny: "Man born of a woman is of few days and full of trouble. He comes forth like a flower and withers. . . ."

So what can the Christian faith say to those increasing numbers of us who not only will live a long time but who will also grow old . . . and die? This challenges our easy platitudes about the "dignity of life." It is far easier to become concerned with a poverty-stricken child, for example, because he at least has a future and our helping may possibly be rewarded in time. But what of the "dignity of life" for the very old and the dying? We haven't really wrestled with the full implications of the Christian faith until we have wrestled with the "resurrection from the dead" in the context of growing old . . . and dying.

But beyond all that, when we are utterly honest with the New Testament, we simply cannot avoid the fact of the resurrection from the dead. I know how we keep trying to edge away from that central fact. I live most of the year with young theological students who, to say the least, are embarrassed by that central miracle in the New Testament and interpret it in all sorts of easier ways but come up short when faced by the naked fact of death and what may come afterward.

But not only theological students. Ministers and their people all over the land tend to shy away from this central fact in the New Testament and instead talk endlessly about the teachings of Jesus, or his high moral example, or the miracle of new life here and now reborn out of the old, or the idea that Jesus and his great "principles" could never die, or that he lives on in the memory of Christians who commit their lives to him—and on and on. But the New Testament—if you are honest with it—centers around something else: not new life out of the old, not moral values or principles, not Jesus as the great example for living but, rather, that Jesus died and rose again from the dead. Apart from that miraculous fact, there would be no New

Testament, no church, no Christian faith, and possibly only the meagerest remembrance of Jesus of Nazareth caught up in a few pages of some musty history of ancient Jewish religion and its sects.

But without that central fact in the New Testament, believe me, I'd really have nothing to say to you. Because I don't get much of a charge out of high moral principles—do you? And what would I have to say to those who are growing old and dying other than to echo Job: "Man born of a woman is of few days and full of trouble. He comes forth like a flower and withers. . . ."

But because Jesus died . . . and rose again, I do have something to say. I can say to those who are growing old and dying that God has been there, in the darkness, in the despair, in the loneliness, in the death—and all is well! Darkness and death do not have the last word. The end is not death but life.

Moreover, you can't divorce the love of God here and now from the great hope that death and darkness do not have the last word. As someone has said, "What we believe about life and what we believe about the end of life are the same thing." For how can you talk about the love of God here and now, evident in nature, or in the love of parents for children, or in the fight for justice for the poor and the blacks and the third world, apart from the love of God when a man faces death and the darkness beyond?

Let's be specific. One big danger in talking about death and resurrection is to leave it as an abstraction—true for everybody and therefore nobody. Moreover, I don't know about you, but I'm not primarily interested in my own assurance of life after death for *me*. I know how readily that can become simply a selfish concern. And, after all, I've been fortunate. I've had a long and full life already, with far more love and fulfillment than I could ever deserve. So let's be specific. Let's look squarely at a baby in the arms of its mother lying dead in a ditch at My Lai. Well? What shall we say about God's love for that child? No chance for fulfillment, its life snuffed out before it even had a chance to bloom and wither. If there is a love for that child in the heart of God, that love is utterly meaningless apart from the hope that there is more in store for that dead baby.

For me, at least, the great hope for the resurrection from the grave speaks most eloquently for those whose lives never had a chance: blasted by illness or mental disorder or—like that baby at My Lai—by violent death. Then to speak of the love of God apart from the hope that the resurrection brings, is to speak of a meaningless love. You can't separate out the love of God in life from the love of God in death.

So here we are in November, the days shortening, the darkness deepening, a long winter's death ahead. Nothing in nature to speak to us of new life and the flowering and the hope. But on All Saints' Day we can sing out our hallelujahs because the Lord God omnipotent reigneth, with more power and more conviction than on Easter. Because the end of it all is not a withering away into death, life's interminable "No." The end of it all is God's triumphant "Yes." Therefore, "We should not grieve like the rest of men, who have no hope. We believe that Jesus died . . . and rose again; and so it will be for those who died as Christians; God will bring them to life with Jesus."

JAMES S. STEWART

Why Go to Church

*Ye are come unto mount Sion, and unto the
city of the living God, the heavenly Jerusalem, and to an innumerable company of
angels, to the general assembly and church of
the firstborn, which are written in heaven,
and to God the Judge of all, and to the spirits
of just men made perfect, and to Jesus the
mediator of the new covenant, and to the blood
of sprinkling, that speaketh better things than
that of Abel. See that ye refuse not him that
speaketh.*

—Hebrews 12:22-25

What this writer is doing is to describe what it felt like in those
early generations to belong to the Christian community—and
what it ought to feel like to belong to that community still today.
He is trying to give some idea of the amazingly rich inheritance
which is ours in the Church, the Body of Christ. "When you
meet in your places of worship," he says in effect, "with whom
are you meeting?" And then he proceeds to tell them. He tells
them first negatively, casting his mind back to the old days
before God in the fullness of time had sent forth His Son. "You
have not come unto the mount that might be touched, and that
burned with fire, nor unto blackness, and darkness, and
tempest": you have not come, that is, to Sinai, to the voice of
thunder that might freeze the blood and terrify the soul; not
come to the old rigid system of exclusion, where only Moses
could see the face of God, and common sinners had to keep their
distance and tremble in their God-forsakenness—you have not

From *The Wind of the Spirit* written and copyright © 1968 by James
Stewart. Published by Hodder & Stoughton, 1968; by Abingdon Press
(Apex paperback) 1975.

come to that! All that, having served its day, is past and finished. And then he goes on to tell them positively. "You have come to Mount Zion, to myriads of angels in festal array, to the Church of the firstborn written in heaven, to the God of all who is Judge, to the spirits of the blessed departed, and to Jesus and His saving blood." This is your Christian heritage, declares this man to his readers, and says it still to you and me; this is the truth about the Church at worship. And notice precisely how he puts it. He does not say "You shall come," forecasting something dim and far away, in another world beyond the grave. He says, "You have come": meaning, "This is what actually happens every time you meet for worship. This is the fellowship into which you enter." If only we could realise the riches of our heritage!

It is an amazing wealth of suggestion that this writer has piled up here in disorderly profusion. Can we get some order out of it? I think we can. He is saying five things about our fellowship of Christian worship in the Church.

He begins with this: it is *a spiritual fellowship.* "You have come unto mount Zion, the city of the living God, the heavenly Jerusalem." "You Christians," he means, "have direct touch with that invisible spiritual world which is the only ultimate reality. You are not prisoners behind the bars of a narrow earthbound existence, where men push and jostle one another for their tawdry, perishable prizes, and breathe the suffocating, poisonous air of a materialist philosophy. You are done with that! You have had your horizons stretched immeasurably. You are breathing the ampler air of spiritual truth. You have come unto mount Zion." For the bedrock reality of the universe is spiritual.

Let us be clear, however, what this means and what it does not mean. There is a frequent error we must guard against here. Far too often the spiritual has been set over against the secular as though these were different realms. This is a complete misunderstanding of the biblical revelation. The spiritual world is emphatically not something apart from the world of mundane affairs and the ordinary workaday life of men. How could it be, seeing that it is precisely in that world and its relationships that God keeps drawing near to us? It is ultimately there we have to find and acknowledge Him, if He is ever to be found at all. Therefore to isolate the sacred from the secular, as is so often done, is thoroughly alien to the intention of the gospel. The final rebuke to such a false division is the incarnation itself, when spirit and matter were for ever united by the fiat of God, and the Word was made flesh.

But now notice: so far from making acts of worship unnecessary, this renders them all the more essential. For we are not likely to go on believing for very long that God is with us in every common task and duty, including the hours when we cannot consciously be thinking of Him at all, unless we made room for times and seasons when we think of Him above everything else, and deliberately "stay our mind upon Him." "All life ought to be worship," declared William Temple; but he went on to add, "We know quite well there is no chance it will be worship unless we have times when we have worship and nothing else."

Now you know, as I know, how this highway of the spirit tends to get blocked by the dust and drudgery of life. The great Indian mystic, Rabindranath Tagore, once wrote a poem in which he compared our daily life to a narrow lane overhung with high buildings, between which there could be seen above a single strip of blue sky torn out of space. The lane, seeing the sun only for a few minutes at midday, asks herself—Is it real? Feeling some wayward breeze of spring wafted in from far-off fields, she asks—Is it real? But the dust and rubbish never rouse her to question. The noise of traffic, the jolting carts, the refuse, the smoke—these she accepts, these she concludes are clearly the real and actual things of life; and as for that strange strip of blue above, she soon ceases even to wonder about it, for so manifestly it is only a fancy, nothing real. This, says Tagore in effect, is precisely the truth about our ordinary mundane existence. The near things, the tangible, material things—these we accept, these we say are obviously the things that matter, they are solid, substantial fact: not recognising that it is that streak of blue above, that far glimpse of the spiritual, which is the essential reality for which every soul of man is made, and which alone gives meaning and perspective to all life's tasks and relationships.

Yes, we forget it; and yet sometimes, thank God, it comes back to haunt us. Sometimes, as Browning knew, "a sunset touch, a fancy from a flower-bell, someone's death" will disturb our too confident security. And specially in the worship of the Church, and above all through the mystery of Holy Commu-

nion, the world unseen may break right in upon us. Eternity
then stirs within our hearts, and we can doubt the spiritual
realities no longer, and we know we are going to be restless
until we rest in God. God grant that this may happen every time
we come up into His courts. "You have come unto mount Zion,
the city of the living God, the heavenly Jerusalem."

I pass to the second fact our text underlines concerning the
fellowship of Christian worship: it is *a universal fellowship.*
"You have come to the Church of the firstborn, who are written
in heaven." The writer is thinking there not of the Church in
glory but of the actual Christian society. In other words, this is
the magnificent idea of the beloved community. You who
belong to Christ, he declares, are no longer isolated and alone.
You are members of the greatest fellowship on earth, the
Church universal.

Now, of course, it is a great thing to be loyal to one's own
congregation, to be able to say that the very stones of the
building where you worship week by week are dear to your
heart. That is splendid. But do let us remember the greater
heritage and the wider horizon! Think of belonging to a
fellowship which from its small beginnings in an upper room has
grown and extended until today it is as wide as the world. Dead
must he be of soul who does not feel the thrill of belonging to a
fellowship like that!

Faber in one of his hymns complains—"We make God's love
too narrow by false limits of our own." He might have said the
very same thing about the Church. We made God's Church too
narrow by false limits of our own. Too often men have built
again with mistaken zeal the very barriers Christ came to level
to the dust, racial barriers, class barriers, barriers of sect,
denomination and government, of taste and temperament, until
the whole fellowship ideal has been pitifully impoverished and
restricted. But in the providence of God, such has been the
innate vitality of this ideal that not all the excesses of militant
nationalism, not all the outbursts of racial bitterness, not all the
mad follies of the sectarian spirit, not all the pathetic spiritual
exclusiveness which has claimed a monopoly of the grace of
God, have ever been quite able to destroy it. It is a tremendous
fact, the universal fellowship. Surely it does mean something to
us all that the hymns we sing here in church are being sung in
Africa, in India, in China, in the islands of the furthest seas. It
does mean something that a Kagawa in Japan, a Schweitzer in

Africa, a Bonhöffer in Europe, could feel themselves to be blood-brothers in Christ. It does mean something to me to receive, as I did in the days just before the last missionaries had to withdraw from China, a letter from the city of Sian in the province of Shensi, telling me of a great open-air gathering of young Chinese students and others who had come together to listen to half a dozen of their own number speaking of—what do you think? Communism? Nonsense! "What Jesus Christ means to me." And it does matter mightily that you and I within this church today should know that we are not isolated units brought together by the fact of meeting beneath the same roof or belonging to one congregation, but that outside these walls there is a great unnumbered host worshipping the same Lord Christ, feeling towards Jesus just as we feel towards Him, thanking God for Jesus just as we thank God for Him, pledged to stand up and fight for Jesus just as we are pledged to stand up and fight for Him.

There is no other fellowship—social, political or international—which can compare for a moment with this. Some of you may remember those dreadful militaristic demonstrations which we could hear broadcast from Europe occasionally before the war, thousands of voices shouting fanatically *"Sieg, Heil!"*—yelling it in menacing unison, *"Sieg, Heil!"* There is a louder chorus than that across the world today, if only we were able to hear it. And if I could stand in this pulpit and shout the words "Christ is risen" across the thousands of miles to Nigeria, Uganda, Bengal, Manchuria, Brazil, Jamaica, back would come the cry, drowning all other sounds, "Yes, He is risen indeed! Hallelujah!"

It is an incomparable thing, this universal fellowship. And every time you come to church, says this writer to the Hebrews, this is the fellowship you enter. "You have come to the Church of the firstborn, who are written in heaven."

I pass to the third description he gives of our fellowship in Christian worship. It is *an immortal fellowship.* "You have come to myriads of angels in festal array, and to the spirits of just men made perfect." He is away now, you see, across the river in the Church invisible and triumphant. He is away in that other world where all the celestial hosts sing to the Lord, ten thousand times ten thousand uniting in the great Te Deum of heaven: "Worthy is the Lamb that was slain to receive power, and riches, and wisdom, and strength, and honour, and glory, and blessing." And what he says is immensely important for all of us who here on earth have had to face the sorrow of separation, all for whom the poet in his bereavement spoke:

> Thy voice is on the rolling air;
> I hear thee where the waters run;
> Thou standest in the rising sun,
> And in the setting thou art fair.

For what this writer says to us is this: "When you Christians are at worship, bowing in prayer before the throne on high, then your loved ones on the other side are very near to you, and the cloud of witnesses is all round about you. In coming to commune with the world unseen, you are come to the spirits of just men made perfect—the immortal fellowship."

There is a lovely old Greek play, the *Alcestis* of Euripides, which tells how the hero Heracles, the Samson of the Greeks, once met and conquered death. There was a day when Heracles on a journey came to the palace of King Admetus; and there he found everyone desolate with grief because Death, that bitter tyrant, had carried off the fair young Queen Alcestis. Whereupon Heracles, who in his day had fought and tamed many wild beasts and dangerous monsters, the lion and the bull, the Hydra and Cerberus, offered to go out to the grave and face this last grim enemy and rob him of his prize. Away out to the lonely tomb he went; and there he met the monster Death, and grappled with him and vanquished him, and set his victim free. And the most beautiful scene in the drama is that in which Heracles comes leading by the hand someone completely covered with a white veil, and stands before the heartbroken King, and cries

> Look on her, if in aught she seems to thee
> Like to thy wife. Step forth from grief to bliss.

And he lifts the veil, and there is Alcestis, alive and fair and smiling as of old. "See, O King, I give her back to thee." Of course the Greeks knew that it was myth and fable. That kind of thing does not happen in this world. But come across into Christianity, and it is no myth nor fable now. A greater than Heracles is here. Our Master has met the last enemy and vanquished it for ever: so that today from across the river there comes, blown back to you, the sound of singing:

> Ev'n as a bird
> Out of the fowler's snare
> Escapes away,
> So is our soul set free:
> Broke are their nets,
> And thus escaped we.

"See," says Christ to you whom death has robbed, "I give him back—I give her back—to you!" And with that, you know that your loved one is alive for ever and intimately near you still.

No, they are not far away, the spirits of just men made perfect; and those who love God never meet for the last time. They are still watching over us who are left journeying and battling here, still rallying our faint hearts to cheer us on our way. It is said that when Napoleon with his Grand Army was crossing the Alps the troops at one point began to mutiny, refusing to march further, giving up the whole adventure in despair, beaten by the cold and the toilsomeness of that frightful journey. But someone suddenly had an idea: why should the band not play the Marseillaise? As soon as the notes of that thrilling, jubilant melody were heard, there in the wilds of the Alps, the light flashed back into listless eyes, and the strength returned to weary limbs, and they went on and breasted the summits and turned defeat to victory. So our dear ones, from where they dwell with Christ in glory, still cheer and urge us on; and every echo of the new song they sing is a thing to bring the light to our eyes and strength to our fainting hearts. And remember, says this writer to the Hebrews, when you come together for worship they are very near to you then. It is just as if they were holding Christ's right hand, and you His left. They are as near to you as that. "You are come to the spirits of just men made perfect"—the immortal fellowship.

Fourth, it is *a divine fellowship.* "You have come to the God of all who is Judge, and to Jesus the Mediator of the new covenant." In your worship, he tells them, reaching now the very heart of the matter, you have come to God as revealed in Jesus. And, indeed, without this all the other great things he has spoken of would be insufficient and unavailing. But beyond all these, he now says, deeper than all these, you have come right through to Christ.

It is said that a friend of Leonardo da Vinci's, looking at the unfinished picture of the Last Supper, was entranced by the loveliness of two silver cups on the table in front of Jesus, and immediately exclaimed at the artistic skill of their design. Leonardo's retort was to take his brush and paint them out. "It is not that I want you to see," he exclaimed, "it is that Face!" And is there anything we need to see but just that face of Jesus?

For never a congregation meets for worship but some are present perplexed and baffled and oppressed by the difficult problems of life; and the inarticulate longing of their hearts is—"Sir, we would see Jesus." Are there indeed any of us exempt from this experience? Somewhere, we feel sure, there must be a solution to the vexing enigmas of our life, somewhere a transfiguring light across all its meaningless frustrations, somewhere an interpretation of all the discipline we have to bear. And no mere philosophy of life is adequate, no stoic abstract view can finally avail. It is a divine heart we want to speak to, a Friend who will understand, a living love on which we may confidently lean. "Sir, we would see Jesus."

There is a characteristic little story which is told about Dr. John Duncan. He was scholar, mystic, theologian. He knew the Hebrew language like his mother tongue. It was rumoured among his students that when "Rabbi" Duncan said his prayers at night he prayed to God in Hebrew. One day two of them resolved to listen outside his door at the time of prayer: they would hear those flights of mysticism and theology going up to God in the Hebrew tongue. They listened, and this is what they heard:

> Gentle Jesus, meek and mild,
> Look upon a little child,
> Pity my simplicity,
> Suffer me to come to Thee.

There is nothing deeper than that. We would see Jesus. We are all one in this critical, final need. Suffer me to come to Thee!

And those happy souls who do in fact discover Christ—how different life looks to them! You know the kind of testimony they can bear. "I was battered by trouble, and Christ was my strength and stay. I was lost and groping, and Christ was my guiding light. I have trembled in the fierce fury of the storm, and Christ came to me over the waves and held me up, delivering my soul from death and turning the tempest into calm." This is the testimony.

When the earthquake broke on Philippi, and the prison walls were shaken and the doors burst open, and the gaoler rushed in on Paul and Silas, crying "What shall I do?"—I do not read that the apostles answered, "Run, man, for your life! Quick, before the walls crush you!" What they did say—and the words ring like a trumpet—was "Believe on the Lord Jesus Christ and thou shalt be saved." This is our deepest need. "If there be one of you," cried a Covenanting preacher to his flock dispersing across the moors when the approach of the enemy was signalled, "if there be one of you, He will be the second. If there be two of you, He will be the third. You will never, never lack for company." And every time you come to worship, says this writer to the Hebrews, you can be quite certain you are coming to Jesus. Do you think any of us could stay away from church if we realised that?

One other fact about our fellowship in worship he adds, and so makes an end: it is *a redeeming fellowship.* "You have come to the blood of sprinkling, that speaketh better things than that of Abel." For when all is said and done, it is sin that is the trouble. It is these weak-willed, wayward hearts of ours that are so desperately undependable. It is not only the stubborn sway of the sins of the flesh; it is even more the satanic subtlety of the sins of the spirit, which make us amid all our religious profession so terribly unlike Jesus—the pride of intellect patronising simpler folk, the pride of judgment imputing motives, the pride of religious life making us feel that we are doing rather creditably and certainly a good deal better than many others. It is these things that make our very virtues shabby and our righteousness like filthy rags; it is these which, when we come alive to them, may well reduce us to despair as we realise the devastating truth that even at our best we are bankrupt utterly, and that all we have ever done or can do is nothing.

But, says this man, "you have come to the blood of sprinkling." Where should any of us be if that were not true? If Christianity were not above everything else a religion of redemption?

And, he goes on, it "speaketh better things than that of Abel," or as it might more accurately be translated, "it cries louder than that of Abel." "The voice of thy brother's blood," said God to Cain in the old story, "crieth unto Me from the ground"; our secret sins, our frequent defeats, go crying up to God in heaven. If this were all, hope would be gone, and we could never lift our heads again. But here enters the gospel. For when our sins cry out to God for punishment and vengeance, something else also happens, declares this writer to the Hebrews: the blood of Christ cries louder, overbears and drowns and silences the very crying of our sins, and God for Christ's sake forgives.

There is a moving scene in Ian Maclaren's *Bonnie Brier Bush,* where the old country doctor MacLure, who for more than forty years had been a familiar and well-loved figure in the glen where he had gone his rounds, has come himself at last to the end of the day. Beside him in the gloaming there sits his friend the farmer Drumsheugh. The dying man asks him to read aloud to him out of the old Book; and Drumsheugh opens the Bible at the fourteenth of St. John. "Ma mither aye wantit this read tae her when she was weak." But MacLure stopped him. "It's a bonnie word, but it's no for the like o' me. It's ower gude; a' daurna tak it. Shut the buik an' let it open itsel." The farmer obeyed. He shut the book, and it opened of itself at a much thumbed page—the story of the penitent sinner in the temple who "would not lift up so much as his eyes to heaven"—and through his tears he read these words: "God be merciful to me a sinner."

And whoever we are, and whatever we are—minister, elder, deacon, church member, social worker—we all come to that at last. God be merciful to me a sinner. And the only question that ultimately matters is, Can God be merciful to such a one as I am, who must have wearied His mercy so often? Can His patience indeed hold out to the end? Let me answer it, not in my own words, but in words that have gone on singing their way down three hundred years from the Elizabethan age, since first they were written by John Donne, Dean of St. Paul's, in his *Hymn to God the Father:*

> Wilt Thou forgive that sin where I begun,
>   Which was my sin, though it were done before?
> Wilt Thou forgive that sin, through which I run,

And do run still, though still I do deplore?
When Thou hast done, Thou hast not done,
For I have more.

Wilt Thou forgive that sin which I have won
Others to sin, and made my sin their door?
Wilt Thou forgive that sin which I did shun
A year or two, but wallowed in, a score?
When Thou hast done, Thou hast not done,
For I have more.

I have a sin of fear, that when I have spun
My last thread, I shall perish on the shore;
But swear by Thyself, that at my death Thy Son
Shall shine as He shines now, and heretofore;
And having done that, Thou hast done,
I fear no more.

And every time you come to church, says this man, you are
coming to the blood of sprinkling, that forgives—everything.
Everything!
"See that ye refuse not Him that speaketh."

JOHN R. W. STOTT

I Believe in God

Do you find it difficult to believe in God? Perhaps you've never found it easy; or maybe you did once believe, until some shattering experience shook your faith. I want to help you if I can . . .

"I believe in God." That's how the Creed begins. We call it the Apostles' Creed, not because it was composed by the twelve Apostles of Jesus, but because it is a faithful summary of what they taught. And what did they teach? Well, the very foundation of all their teaching was that there is a God, an infinite yet personal Being. And before we can go on to think about what this God is like, we must be clear in our minds that He exists. Let me concentrate today on two things about the Christian faith in God.

Faith Contrary to Reason?

First, *faith in God is rational.* I know many people don't realize this. H. L. Mencken, for instance, the antisupernaturalist critic of Christianity, who taught that it was more civilized to doubt than to believe, wrote this: "Faith may be defined briefly as an illogical belief in the occurrence of the improbable." Now, that's an amusing definition of faith, but it is not an accurate one. Faith is not contrary to reason. Indeed, there are many arguments which make Christian faith perfectly reasonable. Let me suggest three of them.

The first is this. I believe in God when I look at nature, at its beauty of color and form, and at its intricate design. Are we really to suppose that the universe is the product of a series of chance accidents or of some blind force and not of a master mind? Let me illustrate what I mean. One of the best known buildings in London, the city in which I live and work, is St.

Paul's Cathedral, the Mother Church of the Anglican Communion. You will know that it was built by Sir Christopher Wren after the Great Fire of 1666 had destroyed the medieval cathedral. Wren died before it was completed. His body is buried in the crypt but he has no memorial in the cathedral. Instead, a plaque on his tomb bears a Latin inscription which means: "If you seek his monument look around you." In St. Paul's Sir Christopher Wren needs no monument. His memorial is the cathedral itself, which bears eloquent witness to the architect's existence and consummate skill. Can we not say the same of Almighty God, the great architect of the whole universe? "If you seek His monument, look around you." As St. Paul wrote, "ever since the creation of the world his [God's] invisible nature, namely, his eternal power and deity, has been clearly perceived in the things that have been made" (R. 1:20 R.S.V.). This argument from the fact of the universe and from the evidence of design within it still has its power today. A distinguished London surgeon, a Fellow of the Royal College of Surgeons, wrote to me about this last year. He said that our knowledge of intracellular physiology had only just begun. He went on with these words: "I am filled with the same awe and humility when I contemplate something of what goes on in a single cell as when I contemplate the sky on a clear night. And in addition, the coordination of the complex activities of the cell in a common purpose hits the scientific part of me as the best evidence for an Ultimate Purpose."

Next, I believe in God when I look at man, not of course at the cruelty and bestiality of which man is capable, but when I look at his highest faculties. Think of what we call our conscience, the imperious inner urge which tells us we *ought* to do something, the voice which applauds us if we do it and condemns us if we don't. Or think of man's sense of awe and wonder; his awareness of an order of existence above and beyond the material world of his five senses; his desire to worship, so that all over the world men have been found to be worshipping some deity. What is the meaning of these moral and spiritual aspirations in man? Can we really be so cynical as to imagine they are merely an illusion and cannot be satisfied? Isn't it more reasonable to suppose that they are part of the divine image which God has stamped upon man; that these longings in man correspond to something real in God who can satisfy them? Man's conscience is a reflection of the moral law of

God, and the thirst in man's soul is an indication that there is a God who can quench it.

First, I believe in God when I look at *Jesus Christ*. In two weeks' time I am going to talk about the evidence for the deity of Jesus of Nazareth, and I must not anticipate that now. But let me say that if you find it hard to believe in God, I strongly advise you to begin your search not with philosophical questions about the existence and being of God, but with Jesus of Nazareth. Most people, like myself, feel on more solid ground when we are thinking and talking about Jesus Christ. The concept of God as He is in Himself is beyond us. But with Jesus of Nazareth we are dealing with a historical person. Besides, we believe that this was God's purpose. God Himself is infinite in His being and altogether beyond our reach and comprehension. That is why He has taken the initiative to reveal Himself—for we could never come to know Him otherwise. And the climax of His self-revelation was the coming of His Son in human flesh. God means us to approach Him through Jesus Christ, not the other way 'round. So if you can't believe in God, let me urge you to read the four Gospels which tell the story of Jesus. I'm astonished how many intelligent people haven't read the Gospels since they were kids at school. But if you read again the story of Jesus, and read it as an honest and humble seeker, Jesus Christ is able to reveal Himself to you, and thus make God the Father real to you. Jesus once said: "No one knows the Father except the Son and any one to whom the Son chooses to reveal Him" (Mt. 11:27 R.S.V.). . . .

This, then, is what I mean when I say that Christian faith is rational. Christian faith is grounded upon evidence, evidence which comes to us as we look at nature, at man and at Jesus Christ. Of course this evidence falls short of conclusive proof. The existence of God is not capable of mathematical demonstration; otherwise men would be compelled to believe. But this does not mean that Christian faith is irrational or illogical.

Let me put it like this. Let's imagine that God is like a beautiful garden totally enclosed by a very high wall. Two men are determined to scale the wall and discover God. One man is called Reason, and the other Faith. Reason, a rather stolid, matter-of-fact fellow, manages by herculean effort to climb slowly and cautiously a short distance up the wall, where he gets stuck. Faith, a nimble and imaginative creature, is wildly impatient with Reason's laborious progress. He takes a flying leap into midair, trembles for a few moments near the top, precariously suspended in space, and then crashes painfully to the ground. Dismayed by their failure to scale the wall independently, Reason and Faith resolve to cooperate. Reason plants himself at the foot of the wall, with both feet firmly on the ground. Then Faith climbs onto his shoulders, and from this vantage point springs neatly over the wall. God, you see, is apprehended by faith, but the faith which apprehends Him is grounded upon reason.

Is Faith in God Personal?

Having tried to show that faith in God is rational, I want to make a second point, namely that faith in God is *personal*. True Christian faith is not only based on reason, it also issues in commitment. Faith is not the same as credence. When you say "I believe in ghosts, or fairies" or "I believe in the devil," you simply mean that you believe such creatures exist. But when you say "I believe in God" you mean (or ought to mean) more than that He exists. It is not even the same as saying "I believe in democracy," which means "I'm convinced of its rightness and of its influence for good and am willing if need be to live and die for my conviction." No. To believe in God means more than assenting to the facts of His existence and His goodness. It means that I have committed myself personally to Him in Jesus Christ as my Saviour, my Lord and my God.

Perhaps I could elaborate this by a simple equation that Christian faith equals belief plus trust. Faith is a belief of the mind leading to a trust of the heart, an intellectual conviction which becomes a personal commitment.

I may believe that a certain plane is airworthy, that the airline operating it is reliable, that the pilot and crew are skilled and experienced. But none of this is faith. I do not exercise faith until I translate my belief into trust, until I actually step on board and commit myself personally to it.

Let me illustrate the meaning of faith from the experience of John G. Paton, who was a famous Presbyterian missionary in the middle of the last century. He and his family landed on the 5th of November, 1858 on the island of Tanna, one of the New Hebrides group of islands in the Pacific. The inhabitants of the island were very primitive savages, so that when John Paton began to translate St. John's Gospel into the native language, he was immediately in difficulties over the expression "to believe in," so common in the fourth Gospel. How was he to translate this? The islanders were cannibals. Nobody believed in anybody else. There was no word for faith or trust in the language. As he worked at his desk, he asked a native to describe to him what he was doing, and got the answer: "You're sitting at your desk." Lifting both his feet from the floor and leaning back in his chair, he asked the same question, and in reply the native used a verb meaning, "you are leaning your whole weight upon" your chair. And *this* is the expression John Paton used throughout St. John's Gospel for "to believe in," so that John 3:16 would read, "God so loved the world that He gave His only begotten Son that whosoever leans his whole weight upon Him should not perish but have everlasting life."

Personal Commitment

This is in fact what the New Testament Greek expression to "believe in" means. It implies personal commitment and not merely intellectual credence.

Bishop Westcott, one of the greatest of all New Testament Greek scholars, wrote: "A Christian is essentially one who throws himself with absolute trust upon a living Lord, and not simply one who endeavours to obey the commands and follow the example of a dead teacher." And again: "The Apostles' Creed is *personal* in its object. It expresses not the conviction that something is true, but that some One is the stay of life. We do not say 'I believe that there is a God,' that 'Jesus Christ came to earth,' that 'the Holy Ghost was sent to men.' In this sense, as St. James says, 'the devils believe and tremble.' But we say 'I believe in God the Father,' 'I believe in Jesus Christ,' 'I believe in the Holy Ghost.' That is, I do not simply acknowledge the existence of these Divine Persons of the One Godhead but I throw myself wholly upon their power and love. I have found and I trust without reserve Him Who made, redeemed, sanctifies me. I have gained not a certain conclusion but an unfailing, an all-powerful, Friend. 'I believe in Him.' He can help me; and He will help me."

I do hope you can say that too.

HELMUT THIELICKE
translated by John W. Doberstein

Journey Without Luggage

*And he came down with them and stood on a
level place, with a great crowd of his disciples
and a great multitude of people from all
Judea and Jerusalem and the seacoast of Tyre
and Sidon, who came to hear him and to be
healed of their diseases; and those who were
troubled with unclean spirits were cured. And
all the crowd sought to touch him, for power
came forth from him and healed them all.*

*And he lifted up his eyes on his disciples,
and said:*

*"Blessed are you poor, for yours is the
kingdom of God.*

*"Blessed are you that hunger now, for
you shall be satisfied*

*"Blessed are you that weep now, for you
shall laugh."*

—Luke 6:17-21 RSV (cf. Matthew 5:1-9)

When Jesus had taken his place and saw the great crowd of
people gathered around him he began to read what he saw in the
multitude of eyes directed at him.

What was written in those eyes?

It was probably a mingling of hope and fear, of anxiety and
covert expectation.

To begin with, there was the host of the miserable, the
guilt-burdened, the lonely, the incurably ill, the careworn, the
people who were hagridden by anxiety. They gaze at him with
inscrutable eyes that can be fathomed only by the Savior
himself.

From *Life Can Begin Again* by Helmut Thielicke, trans. John W.
Doberstein (Philadelphia: Fortress Press, 1963). Used by permission of
Fortress Press.

Normally, we never see the miserable gathered together in this way. Suffering and sorrow usually creep away and hide themselves.

Just suppose that suddenly all the hospitals and asylums were emptied. Could we bear the sight of the crippled and mutilated, the pallor of death, the hopelessness? Could we bear to listen to the shrill cacophony of mumbling, babbling, lunatic voices, the shrieks of people tormented by persecution delusions and demonic possession?

So all these miserable, burdened people are gathered here around Jesus; for in some mysterious way Jesus attracts the miserable. He draws the sinners and sufferers from their hiding places like a magnet. Undoubtedly, the reason for this is that men sense in this Figure something they do not see in any other man.

For one thing they see (and we all see) that he stands among us as if he were one of us; he stands the test of misery. He does not act as do the influential "upper ten thousand" of this world, who build exclusive residential districts where they cannot see the world's misery, who send a monthly check to an institution for the destitute, but whom ten horses could not drag to the place where they would prefer to send their unfeeling money by itself. They are afraid to expose their hearts or even their nerves to all this. They fear that their Persian rugs would begin to burn beneath their feet and they would no longer get any pleasure out of them. They are afraid that their gleaming chandeliers would no longer be able to sweep away from their eyes the darkness they would have to gaze into there.

So these people are grateful to the Savior for coming to their miserable slum, grateful that he does not close his eyes as the vast army of those who are shadowed by suffering passes by.

At the same time, however, they see in him something else, which is far more incomprehensible and, put alongside of their first observation, almost inconceivable: the fact that the powers of guilt and suffering cannot touch him, that, mysteriously, these powers retreat as he comes by. To be sure, his heart, too, shuddered beneath the onslaughts of hell in the wilderness; for, after all, it was his will to possess a human heart, to which nothing human, no temptation, no dread, is alien. But sullen Satan was defeated and left the arena without having accomplished anything whatsoever. The same thing happened on the Cross. There, too, he was clutched and clawed by physical pain and the dread of dereliction; but again his spirit burst through the deadly encirclement and found the way to the Father's hand.

So they all sought to get near to him. They gazed with wistful longing at his hands that could do so much good and never wearied of blessing and healing.

But now his hands were at rest. Now he seated himself and began to speak.

We wonder whether they were not a little, perhaps even greatly, disappointed. People generally prefer "practical Christianity, the religion of action." They would much rather have him satisfy their hunger, bind up their wounds, and drive the mad fear from their minds.

But here he is opening his mouth to speak. Why does he turn to speech when all this misery cries out for action? Now, these people think, now come the theories and the doctrines that never feed and heal a man, that never warm a man's bones, that never bring back a dead son, never fill the dread emptiness of the future.

But even more: perhaps what he says will only make us more sick than we were before. Haven't people always been claiming that this is so? All respect to practical brotherly love! But have not the "dogmas" of Christianity brought miseries upon miseries to the world? Hasn't it constantly been creating separations between people? Hasn't it broken up communities, unleashed wars, troubled consciences, and robbed us of peace of mind?

So these people here may be thinking too. What will he have to say?

Probably what everybody already knows anyhow: that the misery and suffering gathered there before him represents a *judgment,* that the whole creation is corrupt, and so on. Oh, we know that old story of the preachers!

At any rate he'll be calling us to repentance, as John the Baptist did not long ago. He won't have anything else to say except to go on repeating with painful monotony: The ax is laid to the root of the trees and the Last Judgment is near.

These people who are gathered around Jesus know, or at least think they know, what is coming when Jesus opens his mouth: God's declaration of war against man, denunciation of sin, painful, scrutinizing exposure of those innermost thoughts with which God is not pleased.

The preachers are always beating this same old track. Everybody knows this. These people know precisely what is coming. And this in itself is very distressing and tiresome. Nor will they be able to contradict it, for this preacher of penitence from Nazareth is certainly right. But this only makes it more painful and depressing. That stuff never gets you anywhere. Nobody is helped by negatives, even when they are true.

Then Jesus opened his mouth and something completely unexpected happened, something that drove these people to an astonishment bordering upon terror, something that held them spellbound long after he ceased speaking and would not let them rest. Jesus said to the people gathered around him, people who were harried by suffering, misery, and guilt: "Blessed are you; blessed are you." The Sermon on the Mount closes with the remark that the crowds were astonished and frightened, even though it was a sermon on grace. But this is what always happens when God unveils his great goodness. It is so immense, so far beyond and contrary to all human dimensions and conceptions that at first one simply cannot understand it and we stand there in utter helpless bewilderment. The shepherds at Christmas were also unable at first to exult over the great light that broke through the darkness over the earth but could only fall to their knees in fear and scurry for cover.

When Jesus preached repentance, when Jesus wept over Jerusalem, which even then would not recognize the things that make for peace, he did so in a voice almost choked with tears. How is it that the language of the Bible, which is normally so strong and unsentimental, should at this point speak of tears? Jesus wept not only because these were *his* people who were lurching so unavertibly toward the abyss. No, Jesus wept because he knew the power of the Seducer, the menacing mystery of the devil, who seizes even the upright, the respectable, the morally intact people by the throat, and grips them in such a way that at first even they themselves (if they do not have the gift of distinguishing between spirits) have no premonition of the dreadful slopes to which they are being edged by a consummate cunning.

This is, after all, the ghastly mystery of the terrible twelve years in which we are dealing with this dark power in Germany, years in which the devil proved himself to be a master of every ruse and camouflage. In those years that lie behind us he did not appeal to the *base* instincts of our people, but challenged the sacrificial spirit and devotion of men. He caught hold of youth at the point of their idealism and their love for their country and, posing as an angel of light, played his diabolical games with the best attributes of our people.

Only because Jesus knew this power of the Seducer and because he grieved over those who were being seduced are we brought to the point where he wrests from our hearts the innermost willingness to *accept* judgment from *him*.

This is rather an amazing thing. For can there be any harsher judgment than that of the Cross of Golgotha, surrounded not only by the hangman's myrmidons and the masses roused to the pitch of sadism, but also by the best and most moral examples of humanity? And yet all of them together constitute a chorus, giving appalling expression to megalomania, their vanity, and their bad conscience. The fact is that we are all represented in the furious mob around the Cross. "Mine, mine was the transgression, But thine the deadly pain."

And yet we accept this judgment that comes from Golgotha. Simply because we sense that here a man died for those whom he himself would have to accuse, that here a man gave his life for those who have forfeited their lives, that here a man stood at bay, in his own flesh and blood, and therefore in an ultimate comradeship with us all, against the powers that would torment and destroy us.

The hard judgments which the Sermon on the Mount hurls upon us all, relentlessly unmasking the deepest secrets and urges of our hearts, are spoken by a Savior who in the very midst of judgment calls out to us "Blessed are you," a Savior who does not only fling out the cry "Woe to you," but invites us to the Father's house. These judgments are spoken by a Savior whose hand is not clenched into a smashing, repulsing fist, but is opened in the gesture of blessing, and as he blesses we see the wounds he suffered for our sake.

This leads us to the second point at which the utter difference between the judgments of God and the way in which we men are accustomed to judge and condemn becomes clear.

No man has ever yet been healed by judgment and punishment. Always the merely negative only makes us sick. What good does it do if in the midst of the judgment and retribution that comes to us we must say it serves you right; you can't kick; you made your bed and now you must lie in it.

I ask: What good does it do to have this insight into judgment? Obviously, none at all. It only pitches us into deeper hopelessness and inner paralysis, and in not a few people stirs up the horrible and sinful desire to end it all by violence.

The judgment by itself is no help at all if there is nothing else besides. Therefore God too is never the judge, but always, in the midst of judgment and in the midst of personal, vocational, and family catastrophe, he is the seeking God, the God who is seeking to bring us home, the "Savior," the restoring God. God is always positive, even in the very worst of the judgments and terrors that he must permit to come upon us.

That's how the beatitudes are to be understood: a hand stretched out to us in the midst of suffering and care, a hand that makes it clear that God still has a design for us and that he wants to lead us to goals so lovely that we shall weep for joy. God never merely stops with our past, though he does not let us get away with anything and puts his finger upon our sorest wounds. He is always the Lord who is concerned about our future, paving the way to save us and guiding us to his goals.

If we really want to learn to evaluate and rejoice in this positive side of judgment and be able to reach out for it in every time of need and suffering we shall have to guard against two misconceptions.

The *first* is this. We all know that familiar saying of Goethe: "Blessed is he that cuts himself off from the world without hatred. . . ." All of us have gone through hard, desperate, fear-scourged, hopeless hours of life, times in which we have tried to escape on the wings of dreams to some region where, to use Adalbert Stifter's phrase, the "gentle law" still reigns. At such times older folks may dream of the days of their youth when things were different and youth may dream of a future when things will be different. But is that true blessedness, true happiness? Isn't it only a shot of morphine that makes us dependent and unfit and only throws us back more helplessly into hard reality?

Jesus says something altogether different to us in his beatitudes. For he addresses his call specifically to those who are in a predicament, the poor, those who are suffering because of their own shortcomings and failures, the guilty, the grieving, the persecuted, the hungry and thirsty. Why should he call these, of all people, blessed? Is this merely cruel irony? What would someone who had been told yesterday by the doctor that he was suffering from cancer say if you called him "blessed"? What would a woman who had been betrayed by her husband and robbed of her dignity say? Or a mother who sees her child going wrong? Or a young man who lives in desperate loneliness in a rented room somewhere in a big city?

Isn't it sheer mockery to call these "blessed"—whether in Goethe's sense or even in the sense of Jesus of Nazareth?

But now, listen to this.

When we are dealing with the beatitudes of Jesus, we must not leave out of account *him* who spoke them; we dare not assess them as sentences or maxims of a general philosophy of life which are to be measured by whatever truth they contain within themselves.

In all of these utterances Jesus is secretly pointing to himself. And if we hear them addressed to us today by him who has been exalted to the right hand of power and looks down upon us from the glory of his eternity, then this is what he is saying to us:

"The first reason why you who are miserable and afraid are to be called is simply because *I* am in the midst of you. You complain because you must suffer? Look, I myself found my real mission and learned obedience in what I suffered. You complain because you have to drink a bitter cup? Look, when I myself was compelled to drink the most ghastly draught any man ever faced I learned to say, 'Not my will, but thine, be done.' So I found peace in unconditional acceptance of the will of my Father. You complain that in all your sufferings the face of God has vanished, that you cannot feel his presence at all, and you are left so dreadfully alone? Look, *I* too had that feeling of Godforsakenness; it found its vent in that terrible cry of dereliction, and the sun was darkened because it could not bear the extremity of that loneliness. But while my tortured body drooped, but was held and could not fall because of the burning nails, suddenly the Father's hand was there beneath me to break my fall and snatch my spirit from the anguish.

"Don't you understand this, my brothers? The first beatitude is that *I* am in the midst of you and that, because you are suffering my sorrows, I will also lead you to my fulfillments and my blessings."

Then the *second* reason for blessedness.

We should not think that Jesus merely wanted to give us a

few maxims of practical wisdom, that he merely intended to talk about the blessing of suffering and poverty and console us by telling us that suffering would make us more mature. Jesus knew all too well that it can turn out just the opposite, that a man can break down under suffering, that it can drive us into cursing instead of prayer, and that its ultimate effect will perhaps be bitter complaining and accusing of God for his injustice.

No, because it is *he* who is present, because he is in the midst of us, he comes not as a teacher but as the Savior. These are not just words, words, words; something *happens* to us.

For now we have a signature, sealed with blood and sanctified by the Savior's suffering, declaring that heaven has been opened to us, even when everything around us is locked tight, even if there should never again be any improvement, any future, any merriment or laughter in our lives. We have the signature which certifies that "in *everything* God works for good with those who love him" and that now (but actually only because that signature is valid) it is precisely the empty hands that shall be blessed, because they have long since lost all human hopes and consolations; that the worst sinners shall be comforted, because even the last shreds of any illusions as to their own consequence have been stripped away from them and now for the first time God has a chance to work in them. Now we have the assurance that those who come with nothing in their hands will learn, to their humiliation, that God is *everything* to them. When they hold the hand of God they learn that fabulous certainty with which we can step into the uncertainties of each succeeding day. We have the signed statement, sealed by the sufferings of Christ, that now those who go aimlessly stumbling through life are literally surrounded with joyful surprises, because they will learn (on this *one* condition, that they really dare to trust God) how God is always there, that his help is supplied with an almost incredible punctuality. They learn how he sends some person to help us up again; how he allows us to catch some word (which need not even be in the Bible) to which we cling; how he brings money into the house and bread to our table; and how in the hour of our greatest sorrow he may perhaps send the laughter of a little child.

He who dares to live in this way, in the name of this miracle, in the name of this opened heaven will see the glory of God, the comforting stars of God shining in the darkest valleys of his life and will wait with all the joyful expectancy of a child for the next morning where the Father will be waiting with his surprises. For God is always positive. He makes all things new. And the lighted windows of the Father's house shine brightest in the far country where all our "blessings" have been lost.

Blessed are you—not because the far country cannot take away from you the dream of home and better times to come. No, blessed are you because the door is really and truly open and the Father's hand is stretched out to you—as long as he who came in the name of the Father stands among us and proclaims, nay, fulfills, the words, "Blessed are you!"

GEORGE W. TRUETT

Why Do Souls
Go Away from Jesus?

Then said Jesus unto the twelve, Will ye also go
away? Then Simon Peter answered him, Lord to
whom shall we go? Thou hast the words of eternal
life.   —John 6:67, 68

In a very frank way, and with a deep desire to help you, I should
like to ask you, one by one, the personal question, What are
your relations to Jesus, the Savior and Master? Everyone must
have personal relations with Him. We must be His friends or
His foes. We must be for Him or against Him. What are your
personal relations to the Lord Jesus Christ? Are you for Him or
against Him?

Once when He was here among men in the flesh, and the
multitudes were following Him, and He was teaching them
pungently what following Him meant, the crowds were
depleted, and grew less and less before His searching teaching,
and finally He turned to the twelve apostles, who were
following Him, and put to them this plaintive question: "Will ye
also go away?" Then Simon Peter answered Him, "Lord, to
whom shall we go? Thou hast the words of eternal life."

Our text this morning is that searching question Jesus asked
the twelve: "Will ye also go away?" The text suggests two
burning questions for us this morning. Why do people go away
from Jesus? Where do they go? God give us to face faithfully for
a little while at this midday service these two weighty
questions.

Why do people go away from Jesus? The fundamental reason
is want of grace in the heart, the lack of true faith, the absence

From *A Quest for Souls* (Dallas: Baptist Standard Publishing Company,
1917).

of vital Godliness. The Apostle John tells us: "They went out from us, but they were not of us; for if they had been of us, they would no doubt have continued with us: but they went out from us that they might be made manifest that they were not all of us." But we are back to that searching question, Why do people go away from Jesus? Many do go away from Him. Why? Now, the outward reasons for their going reveal what is in their hearts, and we may glance this morning at some of these outward reasons why people go away from Jesus.

Here, on the occasion of our text, they went away from Him because they objected to His teaching. Through the long centuries, again and again, many have manifestly gone away from Jesus because they objected to His teaching. Read the context here in the sixth chapter of John's Gospel, and you will hear the multitudes as they cry out under His teaching: "This is a hard saying; who can hear it?" And so they turned away from Him because they objected to His teaching. The gospel of Jesus Christ, my friends, is very humbling to poor human nature. Pride revolts at the gospel of Christ. And yet such gospel is not designed to please man, but rather to save him. Jesus comes in His appeal to men, and puts before them the clear demand: "If you would have me for your Savior, I must come first, before father or mother or children or dearest loved ones, or your own property or your own life. I must come first." That is not easy. That is death to self. That is self-crucifixion. And yet you would not have it any other way. Let us make religion easy and we will play it out. Let us make religion hard, even with the hardness of the terms of discipleship laid down by Jesus, and it will be triumphant anywhere in the world.

Why do people go away from Jesus? Full many a time they go away from Him because of the fear of man. That is indeed a biting saying in the Bible, where it is declared: "The fear of man bringeth a snare." Pilate was not the only man who betrayed Jesus, and in that same act betrayed himself through the fear of man. All about us the fear of man plays the most desperate havoc in human life. All through the social order, in the world intellectual, and the world of business, and the world political, and the world social, the highest interests are betrayed, and the supreme call of Christ set aside, through the fear of men. There comes in the tragic power and peril of influence. What can some men mean, and women, by the tragical misuse, the desperate waste, of their highest influence? One waits for another, and one acts because of another, or one does not act because another does not, and all through the social order the fear of man is one of the ravaging wastes of the highest influence that comes to human life. They tell us that in the capital city of one of the older States, in the long ago, a marvelous meeting was led by the eminent American evangelist, Charles G. Finney, probably the ablest evangelist that America ever saw. He preached there some three months, and thousands came to Christ. When he was preaching there one night, the story goes that there slipped into the great audience to hear him the Chief Justice of the highest court of New York State. The learned Justice came out of sheer curiosity to hear a plain, pungent, powerful speaker. It was not his custom to go to church. Not for years had he been at any public service religious, and yet this evening the preacher brought his message to bear on the conscience of this man, taking for his text: "No man liveth to himself," and when the minister had finished his message, he said: "Now, I ask, appealing to your judgment and your conscience"—that is Christ's appeal always—to men's judgments and to men's consciences—His religion does not need any other kind of appeal—when the minister had finished his appeal, he said: "Now, is some man's judgment convinced, and is his conscience searched by the truth spoken to-night, and will he, for his own sake, and for the sake of everybody else whom he may influence, make his public surrender to Christ?" And down the long aisle came the Chief Justice, to make his confession of Christ. When he took the minister's hand, the Justice said: "If you will allow me, I should like even now to turn and speak some words to this waiting audience." And facing them, the dignified Justice said: "If I have any influence over anybody, I beg him to do as I have done, to yield life and all, utterly and now, to Christ." And he called for God's forgiving mercy, that he himself had so long delayed to make that great surrender. It is said that many lawyers at the bar, there assembled in that vast audience, came down every aisle, and stood around the great minister and Chief Justice, and said to the Judge: "Oh sir, because you have come, and because of your appeal, we, too, will make our surrender to Christ." What if the great Judge had not come? O my soul, I know the man, and you know him, who has not come, and yet, because he has not, there shelter behind him others, who perhaps will continue thus to hide behind him as long as he shall stay away from Christ.

Why do people go away from Jesus? Full many a time they go away from Him, through captious doubts and questions concerning religion. Many people ask, What if this and that be not so? What if the Bible be not trustworthy? What if Christ be not divine? What if there be no immortality for the soul? What if there be no heaven for Christ's friend, and no hell for those who will not have Christ? What if those things be not so? And with question marks like that, they turn away from the vital verities of faith, and miss the way of life. Do I speak this midday hour to some man or woman who is in the grip of some serious religious doubt? Then I call to you, do not trifle with that doubt. Probe that doubt, I pray you, to its very depth. Superficial dealing with doubts in the realm of religion is utterly inexcusable. Well has some one said that "doubt is the agony of some earnest soul, or the trifling of some superficial fool." Do not trifle with your doubts. You have too much at stake, if you have doubts, in this lofty realm of religion, to go along carelessly with such doubts. Doubt is caused in various ways and comes from various sources. There is the doubt of the head. Nathanael had such doubt. "Can there any good thing come out of Nazareth?" he asked, and the answer was given him: "Come and see," and he came and saw.

There is the doubt of the heart. Some disappointment comes, beating us into the dust. Some poignant sorrow comes to blind us and to smite us and to check us. John the Baptist had such doubt. Those fine plans and hopes that swept through his mind and heart seemed all crushed as he lay there in the jail, and he sent some of his men to ask the pitiful question of Jesus: "Art thou He that should come, or do we look for another?" Be patient with somebody in doubt, when the dark and cloudy day is on, when the black Friday presses down upon the spirit with its fearful pressure. But I have come to believe, my fellow-men, that doubt is caused by a wrong life more than by anything else in all the world. Time and again when I have come into close quarters with the man who spoke out his doubts and paraded them and defended them, I have found on careful inquiry, full many a time, that underneath and behind that doubt, and evidently occasioning that doubt, was some wrong life. If a man will come with right attitude in the sight of God, he shall be delivered from every doubt, which leads me to call your attention to that great challenge Jesus has given. Notice it: "If any man willeth to do His will, he shall know of the teaching, whether it is of God." That is as broad as the race. That is as comprehensive as humanity. "If any man willeth to do the will of God, he shall know of the teaching, whether it is of God." Let any human being, no matter what the question, what the fear, what the doubt, what the difficulty, assume a perfectly honest attitude toward God, saying: "I want light, and if thou wilt give it, no matter how, I will follow it," such person surely shall be brought into the light. Time and again you have seen, as I have seen, that challenge of Jesus frankly accepted and frankly proved, and men have been brought out of the darkness into the glorious liberty and light of the children of God.

I was in an Eastern city, some years ago, for some two weeks in a daily mission, and every evening when I would finish my message, I said, as was their custom: "If there are interested men and women, who would tarry behind for personal dealings touching personal religion, they will pass through this door into the smaller auditorium, and the rest may go while we are singing the last hymn." I stood there at the door, to greet the people as they passed into the smaller auditorium for more careful and for closer personal dealings, and along with the men who came this particular evening, there came an attractive looking man some thirty-six or thirty-eight years of age, and he tarried at the door to speak with me, fairly trembling as he did so, and yet putting on a brave face. He said to me as he tarried there at the door: "Well, sir, I do not believe a word you said to-night." I replied: "Then, pray, why do you tarry? My invitation was for serious people. My invitation was for men and women in earnest, for those with a desire deep and true to find light and to get help. Why do you tarry?" "Oh," he said, "I thought I would like to see you at close range, and to hear what you said to these men in this room, and therefore I have come along." I felt that I could see underneath all that brave exterior an interest deeper than he was willing at all for me to know, and I said: "You tarry, and when the others are gone, then I should like to have some words with you alone." And so he did, and when the other service was finished, I had him alone, and as I sat beside him I asked him: "What brought you into this place? What gave you these doubts? Whence came all this uncertainty in your spirit concerning religion?" He told me a story that I have neither the time nor the inclination here to repeat. He was the son of a minister in old Virginia. He was reared like a boy ought to be reared, and yet he had gone far away from all that rearing, having been absent from home some fifteen years. Then I said to him: "If these things I preach to you tonight are true, wouldn't you like to know the truth of it all?" He made quick response: "Certainly, I should like to know the truth of it all." Then I said: "You can know it. Here is the challenge of Jesus: 'If any man willeth to do His will, he shall know of the teaching, whether it is of God.' " I said: "Now as I bow my head, I will speak to your father's God and to my God, and I will ask Him just to lead you on, and to fill you with desire and purpose to follow His leading." And when I had finished the prayer I said, as we were bowed there at our chairs: "Let us remain bowed, and you try for a moment to pray." He started back and said: "Why, man, I would not know how to begin. I have not tried even in a dozen years." Think of a man's going a dozen years without calling on God! It seems impossible. "I would not know how to begin," he said. I answered: "Then I will frame a sentence for you, like I would frame it for my little child, and you say it after me." And so I did, and he repeated it, and I framed a second sentence, and he repeated that, and a third sentence, and he repeated that, and then I paused and said: "Prayer, sir, is the sanest thing in the world. Prayer is the outcry of a little, needy, finite, mortal being, to a great infinite, omniscient, omnipotent, all powerful, all merciful Being. Tell Him what you would like. Tell Him like you would tell a man something you should hasten to tell him, without any reserve." And then, timidly and tremblingly and haltingly he began his prayer. In a moment or two his words came faster. In a moment or two his sentences rushed like a torrent. He was confessing his sins. He was bewailing his dreadful decline, and memory was burning like fire, and it blazed and burned, as he recalled the old home, with the family prayer, and the father as a preacher, and the mother singing the simple songs of faith. And then he went on and said: "I remember, Lord, the last sermon I heard good father preach. He preached from that text, the cry of the publican: 'God, be merciful to me, a sinner.' " He said: "That is my prayer. Be merciful to me, a sinner. I give up to thee. Help thou a helpless sinner!" And then he was still, and then in a moment more he was on his feet, and I looked up at him and waiting for him to make his pronouncement, and then he looked down earnestly at me, with his outstretched hand, and said: "I have found the light!" Of course he had found the light.

Any man on the earth who will assume the right attitude toward Jesus shall be brought into the light.

My indictment against the skeptic who prates against the things of God is that he will not be candid about it and go deep enough. Any man in the world, doubter, skeptic, atheist, materialist, whoever he is, who will assume a perfectly candid and obedient attitude toward God, shall surely be brought into the light.

Why do people go away from Jesus? Full many a time they go away from Him through the power of sensual enjoyments. There are two Scriptures that set forth that truth. Here they are: "The pleasures of sin for a season," and this other: "Lovers of pleasures more than lovers of God." Through the power of sensual enjoyment, full many a time men and women miss the upward way and go the downward way to doom and death. And yet this world has in it nothing that can really satisfy the ache of the human heart. That brilliant Frenchman, Sabatier, was right, when he said: "Man is incurably religious." And then the Bible comes on, with its revealing statement, telling us that God hath set eternity in the human heart, and therefore nothing less than the eternal can satisfy the human heart. Temporal things, no matter how many, cannot satisfy the human heart.

> This world can never give
>   The bliss for which men sigh.
> 'Tis not the whole of life to live,
>   Nor all of death to die.
>
> Beyond this vale of tears
>   There is a life above,
> Unmeasured by the flight of years,
>   And all that life is love.

Nothing short of the infinite and the eternal can satisfy any human heart.

Why do people go away from Christ? Full many a time they go away from Him through the simple, fearful, fateful power of procrastination. They tell us that procrastination is the thief of time, and so it is, but, oh, it is so much more than that. Procrastination is the thief of souls! All about us are men and women who intend somewhere, sometime, to focus their thoughts on the things of God, and to say "Yes" to the call of Christ, and yet through the power of procrastination they are hurried on and daily lulled the more deeply to sleep, and the conscience is deadened, and the days go by and the highest things are lost. All about us there are men and women who, when we approach them concerning personal religion, will tell us that they intend to say yes to Christ, that they desire to be saved, that they fully expect this important matter of personal salvation to be settled a little later. But it is a little later than they say. It is to-morrow. It is by and by. Down yonder on the Mexican border, where I have often and joyfully preached to the cattlemen through the passing years, I have heard one cry escape the Mexicans' lips which is revelatory to a remarkable degree of the Mexican character. It shows why Mexico is so belated in the development of her civilization. That little word that the Mexican uses so frequently is this: *"Manana!"* To-morrow! You may crowd upon him this duty, or that, or the other, and he will consent to what you are saying, but in an undertone he will say: *"Manana! Manana! Manana!"* To-morrow! To-morrow! To-morrow! And so it is Satan's supreme cry to the human soul concerning religion—*"Manana! Manana!"* To-morrow! To-morrow! And as he cries it, men and women are beguiled and cajoled and deceived, and thus the battle is forever lost for the human soul. May God now arouse this audience from the awful peril of procrastination, that you may turn to God and be saved!

I am coming to our second question briefly. I have asked you, Why do people go away from Jesus? Now to the second question more briefly, Where do they go? Echo answers, Where? Where do they go? Well, if they are Christians and go away from Jesus, as many of them, alas, do, they go into backslidings. Oh, what stories could be told in this fair city about us, and in any other, of drifting Christians, if only hearts were revealed, and we could read all that in them is. Backslidden Christians! David went away from his Lord, and, oh, the hurt of it! Samson went away from his Lord. Oh, the hurt of it! Simon Peter denied the Lord. Oh, the shame of it and the hurt of it! And through the long years the friends of Jesus have listened to siren voices and have gone away from the right path into backsliding. How they have harmed religion! How they have harmed souls for whom the Savior died! How they have harmed themselves! How they have grieved Jesus! Do I speak to somebody here today who is a backslidden Christian? Oh, I exhort you, I summon you, I beseech you, for your own sake and for the sake of everybody else, hasten back to Christ!

I ask you this other question: Where do people go when they go away from Jesus, those that are not saved at all, those that are not born again, where do they go when they go away from Jesus? Jesus tells us in language unmistakable. "Ye shall die in your sins," He said to some who cavilled at His teachings, "and whither I go ye cannot come." You ask me if I believe in the fact of hell. I believe in the fact of hell as much as I believe in the fact of heaven, and I believe in the fact of the one for the same reason that I believe in the fact of the other. The one clear teacher concerning destiny, concerning the hereafter, was Christ Jesus the Lord, and He teaches that every man dying "shall go to his own place." Moral gravity is as real in the world of morals as physical gravity is real in the world natural and physical about us. Every man shall go to his own place when he leaves this world. If a man says to Jesus: "I will go on without you," where Jesus is, such man shall not come. If a man says to Jesus: "I disdain all else, frail as I am and sinful, and I believe on Christ, I can do nothing else, God help me," when such man goes hence, he will go to be with Christ.

Now, if you go away from Christ, pray look at what you give up. If you go away from Jesus you must give up this Book. Christ and the Bible are indissolubly linked together. If you can get rid of the Bible, you can get rid of Christ. If you can get rid of Christ, you can get rid of the Bible. The one is the complement and counterpart of the other. Christ and the Bible are the binomial word of God. If you get rid of Christ you get rid of the Bible, and if you propose to get rid of the Bible, sing no more by the open grave that shepherd's psalm, the twenty-third. Sing no more by the open grave, when you hide your loved ones from your sight, the glorious fourteenth chapter of John: "Let not your heart be troubled." You are done with Christ, if you are done with the Bible, and if done with Christ, you are done with the Bible.

What else do you get rid of when you get rid of Christ? You discredit the testimony of every friend that Jesus has ever had in all the world, and He has had friends many, both great and small. Many of the world's most capable minds have been the devoutest friends and followers of Jesus. Gladstone said he knew sixty of the greatest minds of his century, and that fifty-four of them—scientists, statesmen, mighty men in all callings—were the devoutest friends of Jesus that he ever saw. Oh, this gospel that we preach, my men and women, is not a collection of cunningly devised fables for people silly and thoughtless. The sanest thing on the face of the earth this Thursday morning is for a man or woman to be pronouncedly the friend of Christ—that is the sanest thing of all. Jesus is the needed Savior for the great as well as the weak. Will you look over the world's great names? In the list you will find many friends and followers of Jesus. Look yonder at the list of scientists, and in that list you will see Miller and Agassiz and Proctor, bowing obediently at the feet of Jesus. Look at the world's astronomers, and you will see Copernicus and Kepler and Newton showing their devotion to Jesus. Look at the world's first statesmen, and you will see Washington and Gladstone and others like them, showing their devotion to Jesus. And so through the centuries you will see the earth's first minds devotedly following Christ.

But I would bring the truth nearer you than that. There in the little circles where you and I live, are some whose names never get into the newspapers at all, but you and I believe in them as we believe in nobody else in the world, and they tell us that they have tried Jesus and found Him true. Yonder in the United States Senate some time ago, when a group of senators were at a dinner, as the story was told me by one who knew, one senator looked across to the chiefest senator at that time in the Senate, and said to him: "Senator, do you believe in that old doctrine that a man must be born again to get to heaven?" The senator after a moment's pause made serious reply: "I certainly do. I am grieved to have to tell you that I am not a Christian myself, but I believe in the doctrine of the new birth as preached by Christ." Then the first senator, wincing under the remarkable answer, said to the second, after a moment more: "Pray tell me why you believe in that old exploded doctrine of the new birth?" The senator waited a moment, and his face was serious and a tear was in his eye, as he said: "My mother and my wife have both told me that they surrendered to Christ, and have been born again, and they both live like it is so." You cannot answer that!

I detain you for a final word. If you go away from Jesus you are left baffled and broken in the presence of the three greatest mysteries of all, and I name them, and then we will go. If you go away from Jesus you are left broken and baffled in the presence of sin. You have no Savior if you reject Jesus. He is the only Savior. And the most terrible and obtruding fact on the earth this Thursday morning is the fact of sin in human life. If you get rid of Jesus you have no Savior from sin.

And if you get rid of Jesus you are left beaten and broken, with all the sorrow that is regnant in human life. Pause anywhere and you will hear the undertone of sorrow—anywhere. If you get rid of Jesus you have no delivering friend from the thralldom of sorrow.

And still more, and most of all, if you get rid of Jesus you are left in the presence of death, without light and without hope and without life, broken in the presence of death. When you come to the grave you will need a Savior. Plato and Socrates merely speculated as they looked into the open grave. So did Caesar when he stood up in the Roman Senate. Job asked the question: "If a man die, shall he live again?" Only one person has answered that question. Only one can answer it, and His name is Jesus. He came and bowed His head to death, and went into the dark chambers of the grave, and on the third day after they laid Him in Joseph's tomb, He pushed the grave door open and came out, saying: "Because I live all who trust me shall live forever." Oh, you must not dare to live or die without Jesus!

'Tis religion that can give
Sweetest pleasure while we live.
'Tis religion must supply
Solid comfort when we die.

After death its joys will be
Lasting as eternity.
Be the living God my friend,
Then my joys will never end.

Tell me, are you for Jesus? I would be for Him, were I in your place today, if I had to go through flame and flood to follow Him. Be for Him before it is too late! Does He call you today? Follow Him, trust Him, yield yourself to Him whatever your condition or case may be, and His word for you is sure: "Him that cometh to me, I will in no wise cast out."

GERHARD VON RAD
translated by James W. Cox

The Blessing of God's People

And the Spirit of God came upon him, and he took
up his discourse, and said, . . .
"Blessed be every one who blesses you."
—Numbers 24:3, 9 (RSV); also chapters 22–24

A short while ago, I read in a newspaper a prayer that went like
this: "God grant me the serenity to accept things I cannot
change, courage to change the things I can, and wisdom to know
the difference." Anyone who knew that in every situation—where one must change and where one must put up with
something—would be indeed a wise man! In the story that we
want to consider for these moments, we are told about how
Israel had to put up with a situation in a most remarkable way.
All will-to-change lay far, far beyond all human ability. Walking
in deeds of honor and of shame before the face of God, Israel had
tremendous experiences. Anyone who has not been through
this can learn from the story of Israel, that whoever knows
about God will experience the world and man in quite different
dimensions. Then it is that we really see man for the first time.
That was the secret of the story of Israel: the more intensively it
spoke of God, the more intensive, the more realistic did man
and the world in which man lives, become. That, of course, is
not just a happy accident for Israel. Much reflection, much
concentration is behind the narrative. One could compare the
Israel that tells this story to a man who, due to circumstances in
his youth, has long remained silent and kept matters locked up
within himself perhaps for decades, until now he breaks loose
and begins to talk about it. It seems that our Balaam story is
like that. There is much to consider here—much more than we
can bring out in one sermon.

Used with permission of Chr. Kaiser Verlag, Munich. Taken from
Gerhard von Rad, Sermons, Munich 1972, pages 161 ff.

After long wandering in the wilderness, Israel has arrived at the outskirts of civilized country. The Moabites are frightened: "This horde will now lick up all that is round about us, as the ox licks up the grass of the field." They regard the people of God coming upon them as a barbaric horde. But their king Balak knows what to do. The situation is not hopeless. Over yonder, of course, there is still the widely known magician and sorcerer Balaam. He must be summoned. He alone—and indeed just by using destructive words—can annihilate Israel. This Balaam is the main character in the story, down to its last sentence. But what was this man, then? The Bible says that he could curse. Perhaps nobody today understands that aright. What do we think of now as cursing? Naughty words which a man gives way to if he loses self-control. And if he can then serve up a stream of swear words, we roar with laughter. However, if a curse was anywhere involved—as the ancients saw it—it was no longer a laughing matter.

Who, then, was Balaam? I am going to put it this way: Balaam was a godless man. I know, of course, that we today do not like to pass such severe judgments. On the defensive about our faith, we feel that we are not authorized to make these statements, and this reticence is surely commendable. But still that does not take care of the matter. This problem did not let go of the great Dostoyevsky as long as he lived: What is actually a godless man? What is the outlook of such a person, and what goes on inside of him? Now, the specifically psychological problem, as it manifests itself in the innermost being of such a man, hence the problem as it has to do with his specific sufferings and conflicts—this does not interest our biblical narrator. What is of interest to him is the question of what one like this does, how he operates. Now if he is a real man, he always operates on a large scale. That is one thing. But he always operates destructively. Wherever his influence is felt, he leaves behind a charred ruins in which all good life withers. And that is precisely what the ancients had in mind when they said that such a man brings about a curse. I am convinced that the ancient Israelites, and the ancient Greeks as well, were wiser and more sensitive than we are about experiences of evil. They were more realistic. In those days, they had quite specific questions: What kind of instruments does evil seek for itself? How does it operate? In what way does it usually circulate among men? Many times there are men who are carriers and agents of something altogether evil. Most men happen to have nothing at all to do with this primitive evil, simply because they live just an average existence. They happen to have just as little to do with that as with primitive good. But many times there are men who have a mysterious contact with what is totally evil; they can produce and direct it, and it even follows them. Of course, always but a little way, and never without its drawing them down at last into its night.

That is the kind of man Balaam was. He was a specialist in this profession, a technician who thoroughly understood complicated machinations. Balaam had done everything but let himself be carried away or lose his self-control. He was, on the contrary, concentrated. He set out to do a job that he was determined to do neatly and precisely. And then something remarkable happened. Like so many specialists, this Balaam was also, no doubt, in some ways a limited man. Whoever has become such a competent technician of evil becomes blind to all that comes from God. And that is what happened in the famous scene in that hollow where the angel of the Lord stepped into the road. Balaam saw nothing at all. But his mount, the ass, saw the angel and could not be compelled with blows to go even one step farther. The God-blindness of Balaam was so deep that God, to begin with, had to open the mouth of the little animal, and then for the first time Balaam saw something. We must take care lest we promptly forget the picture that the narrator draws for us: this technician of evil, on his way to carry out an evil design, angry about opposition standing in his way, beats the animal, and finally a nice sum of money will pop out—but we are all too well acquainted with all of that.

If our story read like some edifying narratives, we would at this point hear how the angel of the Lord punishes Balaam, how he sends him home or soundly thrashes him. That, however, is not permissible, for such narratives are all untrue at certain points. But something quite different happens, something incredible. The angel lowers his sword; he steps aside and lets Balaam pass! He must say only what he is given to say. Now Balaam may have thought that that was past and done with and have recovered quickly from his fears. But who can grasp what occurred at that point? The angel lowers his sword and the horrible man may pass! But that is how it is: all Balaams are free to go their way!

Therefore, he goes on, arrives, is greeted in a somewhat

unfriendly manner, due to his delay, and immediately makes preparation on a mountain to do the work that he, like no one else, understands. But everything turns out badly for him. He is not in his usually great form. How strange: he hears himself saying not words of cursing, but words of blessing. Balak is amazed. He refers to the large sum of money that he has invested in this venture. But Balaam can only answer:

How can I curse whom God has not cursed?
How can I denounce whom the Lord has not denounced?

Something, therefore, has intervened, which all at once causes things to go quite differently. Balaam received it, of course, not as an experience to be grasped or understood at all. It was what the Bible calls God's blessing.

With that the narrator has now come to the heart of the matter. Here, right at this point, he wants our ear. But perhaps we no longer know even in the case of the word *blessing* precisely what we should mean by it. Do not these lines come to mind, lines which we like to sing on New Year's night, something that the narrator wants to tell us in our text?

> O Thou who dost not slumber,
> Remove what would encumber
> Our work, which prospers never
> Unless Thou bless it ever.

That is really a somewhat radical statement; but I believe that it comprises the totality of Christian consolation. Yet who, for such a reason, takes it with complete seriousness today? We could cite a whole catalogue of works, and it would certainly be wrong to question their seriousness and the willingness to sacrifice involved in them. But do you believe we could do even the most limited thing, regardless of our best intended "doings," if we could not bring it to pass in the shadow of a greater power. What do you think would come of it, if we could offer nothing for our eternal proneness to resignation but our good or often merely half-good willing? If we did that, we would have achieved what the ancients called blessing and be quiet about it. Perhaps many quickly come to terms with that: we today do not believe that we should be any longer bound to ancient biblical or Christian ideas in general. We today see the world differently. Oh, this "we today"! That of course has its good meaning in its place. But just as surely it is turned in less than no time into an intolerable impudence, where one, without any qualms, pushes aside a knowledge of the world, of man, and even a knowledge of God, which we today unfortunately lop off. Does this mean then that for the first time in our life the true reality of our life has been seen correctly? Let us put the question very simply. On which side then do the better realists now stand? Are those who so pretentiously say, "We today," the better realists? Or does our narrator take the lead when he regards the blessing of God as a reality, as a power by which we live unconsciously day and night, and that we are lost if we could not take shelter in it? Here, for the first time, the nature of the true reality of our life is settled.

But we are not nearly finished with Balaam. It is remarkable, the narrator tells us, that Balaam has not even once seen Israel; he has seen only Israel's outskirts. However, when he yielded himself to blessing, then he saw Israel totally—encamped tribe by tribe. A remarkable thing! So one can see God's people. It can also be true that one sees God's people but indistinctly, perhaps only their outskirts. Thus it is possible to speak of them, write about them, turn against them—with hardly a glimpse of them. In the very moment when Balaam saw the people of God, his mouth was opened for the first time to pronounce extravagant words of blessing:

> how fair are your tents, O Jacob,
>   your encampments, O Israel!
> Like valleys that stretch afar,
>   like gardens beside a river,
> like aloes that the Lord has planted,
>   like cedar trees beside the waters.
> Water shall flow from his buckets,
>   and his seed shall be in many waters. . . . (RSV)

This is how one can speak about God's people. It is not the style in vogue today. Today one hears only biting words on that subject. But here it almost sounds as if Balaam loved God's people, as if Balaam were bathed in the splendor of pure divine goodwill. Gardens beside a river, cedars beside the waters, his seed shall be in many waters. How fair are your tents, O Jacob! But in these times we do not surrender so quickly. Is all of that true? Where then can we see any evidence of such extravagant blessing? But it may be that is is only a matter of our simply not seeing the people of God as a totality, but merely their fringe. In truth, we do not even know whom God numbers among these people of his. "Who can count the dust of Jacob?" We do not see, of course, the thousands of daily deliverances that God grants us. We know nothing of the illuminations in simple hearts which no intellectual history records—nothing of consolations experienced, of good works in distant lands; no, we do not hear the good word, at which perhaps only God rejoices, spoken by good men who do not think of themselves at all as good, yet from whom a power and a light goes forth. Oh, let us enter a little more into this delight of God in his people! We would surely see more of the people of God from day to day and would not have to move along as sullenly as we do.

Today men like to represent the church of Christ in such fashion that it almost looks a bit spooky in our modern technological world. But our story of Balaam shows us for once what is on the opposite side. This king Balak with his worry and his money—doesn't he have something spooky? And the famous authority Balaam, who on the contrary is so completely in the hand of God, even he has something spooky. But God's people are dwelling in their tents in the valley; they know nothing at all of what has been taking place there. Not once have they succumbed to the state of fear! And the hand that God has held over them they have not seen. For them this day was no day of salvation: it was a day like any other day!

As for Balaam, so the narrator obviously imagines the incident, he wanted to pronounce curses, but he was utterly astonished to hear himself pronouncing blessings. Therefore, something happened, so to speak, between his will on the one hand and the words of his mouth on the other hand, something that our narrator without question regards as a miracle. But where on earth has one experienced anything like that? If we wanted to wait for that, then this narrative would perhaps contain only scanty comfort. But—for the information of anyone who may wonder—perhaps it was even at that time different, and Balaam actually cursed, just as he has continued to do for thousands of years. Perhaps he shouted to God's people: "I hate you; everything about you makes me sick. And you are still wretched, for you cannot take yourselves the least bit seriously. All of your cleverness lies in the fact that you are occupied with big words. Whatever is modern you pursue with the ridiculous dread that you might not be thought to be completely modern." Yes, perhaps that is how it was. Might it not have been like that? But in the presence of God it sounded as if he said, "How fair are your tents, O Jacob, like valleys that stretch afar, like gardens beside a river!" Might it not have been like that? Who discovers the secrets of such a cryptic narrator? How peacefully, how relaxedly is everything narrated, many times even with a touch of cheerfulness. Thus, it is as if the narrator breathes an altogether different air than that which is polluted by curses, as if he had something crucial behind him which still stands in front of most of us as an immovable stone wall.

For a change, our sermon text has not one time challenged us today to Christian action, but only that we very quietly let something good and healing happen to us. Even then we might be expectantly busy. We would then open our eyes a bit wider and the leaden boredom that afflicts many of us would fall away. For the reality of our life is abysmally mysterious, and powers of blessing which are never sufficiently recognized carry us. We could quietly also sometime talk about that. Whenever we ourselves cause it to be healthy but just once in a world polluted by curses, whenever we enter into a joy, whenever we entrust ourselves to something good, then we are living already on the resources of the faith in the blessing of Balaam. Dietrich Bonhoeffer became aware of these powers of blessing even in his prison cell: "By good powers wonderfully hidden, we await cheerfully, come what may."

LESLIE D. WEATHERHEAD

Key Next Door

John 13:7 *Jesus said, "Thou shalt understand hereafter."*
1 Cor. 13:12 *Now I know in part; but then I shall know fully.*

(R.V. margin).

I remember once wanting very much to see over a house. It was an empty house standing in its own grounds and that made the next house a good deal farther on. I went up the drive of the house I wanted to look over. The doors were shut and barred and the windows tightly fastened. I took the liberty of looking in through the ground-floor windows, and I could see a little. By walking round the house I could get some idea of its general plan. But, of course, from the outside one could really only have the vaguest idea of what the house might contain and what in detail had been the plan of the architect. One could only "know in part."

Then I noticed that there was a card in the window of a downstair room facing the front gate, and on the card were the words: "Key Next Door." So I had to go farther on, obtain the key and come back and enter the house. Then a good many things that had been obscured from me were made plain. The beauty and design of the house were revealed. The plan of the architect could be appreciated.

It seems to me that this is a parable. The house of life's meaning is like that. So many doors are shut, so many windows fastened. We peep in and we get glimpses of meaning. By walking round we may get a general idea of the lie of the house but there are bound to be many things that puzzle us and upon which no clear light shines. Yet, if I may press the parable, there is a notice that says, "Key Next Door." We may have to go farther on, perhaps even into the next phase of being, and indeed, perhaps the next phase after that—for there must be many stages of spiritual progress—before we can understand all, but we are promised that at last we shall understand. "Thou shalt understand hereafter."

* * *

You can imagine the setting of our text. The words were probably spoken on the very night before our Lord's death. Let us look at the situation. The disciples are very puzzled. They have tried to follow Him and they have left a good deal to do so, but He has talked about going away and even said that that was expedient. He has told them that He has many things to say to them, but they cannot bear them now. He has said, "What I do thou knowest not now," and then He has offered them the golden promise of our text: "Thou shalt understand hereafter." They had peeped through the windows. They had seen glimmerings of light. They had begun to understand, but they so badly wanted to see more. "Show us the Father," clamoured one of them, "and it sufficeth us." But He could only show them Himself. Often they must have been bewildered to the point of being dismayed, just as we are, but there was given to them, and we may say given to us also, the gracious promise, "You shall understand afterwards."

* * *

It is a message we need, for life to most thoughtful people is incomprehensible. It contains so many puzzles. There are such terrible inequalities in it; experiences that look like injustice at the heart of things, or even carelessness. Cruel things happen to people, frustrating things that do not make sense, and sheer accidents that alarm us. Things of enormous importance seem to depend on things that look like luck or chance. Big doors swing on such tiny hinges. What are we to do in the face of the problems that we cannot solve?

I want to say first that it is an act of faith to believe that there is a key anywhere. It is an act of faith based on the nature of God. If there is a God at all, He cannot be a cruel fiend, for if He were, we should be His superior, for we _know_, if we know anything at all, that kindness is better than cruelty, love is better than hate, goodness is better than badness, humility is better than pride, and unselfishness is better than egotism. If we know anything at all, we are sure of our fundamental moral values. We hardly need the poet to tell us that

> A loving worm within its clod
> Were diviner than a loveless God.

If there is a God at all, in whose being are included the moral values man treasures, He could not create a creature capable of asking such questions and yet incapable of ever finding out the answers. I believe that though evil is very powerful, it cannot keep the key out of our hands for ever, even though now we have to say that the key is next door. "Then I shall know fully."

* * *

I wonder if you feel that it is a feeble thing to say the key is next door. I wonder if you are put off by the very phrase. Are you in your mind thinking, "He is giving us the old religious dope, talking to us as parents sometimes talk to children, and saying, 'Of course, you cannot understand now, but you will one day' "? Few things, I think, are so aggravating to the eager, questioning minds of children than to be given that sort of dusty answer. Is it a kind of variation of 'pie in the sky when you die' to say to people, "Well, one day you will understand and all will be made clear"?

I used to think it was, but, after all, if you go to the theatre to see a play, you do not rise up at the end of the first act and say, "What a rotten play! What a feeble affair! What a stupid plot! What a meaningless business!" If I took you to the theatre and you said things like that at the end of the first act, I should say, "Sit down and see it through! You cannot judge a play at the end of the first act."

I must have quoted to you before the famous words of Gheyserlink: "If a cinema film of the history of the earth were to be produced, and if that film were to last twenty-four hours from midnight to midnight,then the first twelve hours of the film would show a history not yet discovered, and *man would not appear until the last five seconds of the film.*"[1] Well, if that is true, we have not got to the end of the first act yet, have we?

[1] *The Restless Earth* p. 101 (Scientific Book Club).

Though man is made in the image of God and every individual is infinitely precious to God, this does not deny the truth that at the present stage in the world-drama we call history, man is only a very little child. I am holding in my hand a little bar of steel with a knob at one end. It is three and a half inches long and is shiny because I have had it in my pocket for thirty years. You would never guess what it is. It is the axle of a little boy's engine, and when my second son was scarcely four years of age he was playing with it, holding it between his finger and thumb and putting the end of it in his mouth. He was nudged by his older brother and he swallowed it, and it lay jammed in the intestine. That experience with him taught me many things which I must not talk about now, but we had to take him to the Infirmary in Leeds and leave him there to be X-rayed every few hours. I shall never forget my feelings as I parted from him. How on earth could I explain to a little boy of that age the necessity of being X-rayed every few hours? How on earth could I combat his own thoughts which might reasonably have been thus—"Here am I in pain. I thought Daddy was my friend. He takes me away from home to a strange building and into a terrifying thing called a ward, full of other children. He hands me over to a complete stranger called a nurse, and when I need him most he deserts me utterly and goes home to have tea with Mummy." What an illustration of the words, "I have many things to say unto you, but you cannot bear them now. . . . What I do thou knowest not now, but thou shalt understand afterwards." The key to the house of meaning for that little dearly loved son was farther on. Now he understands. He knows that love was my motive.

We must try to realise that man is apt to forget what a baby thing he is and what a tiny power he has to comprehend what God is doing. I admit that I often see unintended humour, but the other day I heard a woman praising her husband. She said he was marvellous. She said things about him that could not possibly be true of anybody! You would think that the business of the City of London would come to a standstill if anything happened to him! But as she talked, I saw the angels behind her giggle, and one nudged the other and said, "Just listen to her!" I suppose to the angels it was the sort of situation that we might be in if we overheard a female slug boasting to another that her husband left the finest streak behind him on the garden path of any slug in the garden. As the slug is to man, so is man to those higher beings who inhabit the unseen. Our bravest deeds, our noblest efforts must get quite a different perspective when viewed from the heights of heaven, and here is little man standing up and throwing out his chest with an egotism that must make all heaven laugh, and being hurt that he does not understand what God is doing. I am imagining a tiny ant creeping along the front of this pulpit and coming to this break in the cushions, and finding it a real problem, to know how to cross the gulf here, where my finger is, and get home in time for supper, and I am realising that he does not even know that he is in the pulpit of the City Temple! He has never heard of the City Temple! Poor little insect! What does he know of London, or England, or Europe, or the world, or its place in space? Even the name Krushchev means nothing to him!

Honestly, without diminishing man's importance to God because he is a loved object, our *mental* grasp of things is probably as fractional as an ant's grasp of the world. If the majesty and wisdom and power of God are infinite, as we glibly say, is it any wonder that I cannot understand what He is doing? Indeed, it is amazing that the One who had the greatest insight and saw farther than any of us, could tell us with His divine authority, "You *will* understand afterwards," and that Paul by faith could say, "I shall know fully."

* * *

After all, even with our limited vision there are glimmerings of meaning. I talked about peeping through the windows of the house of meaning and seeing a little. But, you see, if there is the faintest glimmer of meaning about anything, it must mean that there is mind behind everything. If there is anything in the universe that makes sense—such as the eternal value of human values—then there must be mind behind all phenomena. If your little boy threw out on the carpet a whole boxful of wooden bricks each bearing a letter of the alphabet, it is incredible that as they fell they would make a word, and if after a brief absence you came back and even found a word of three letters, you would say, "A mind has been at work." I must admit that the universe often seems to me quite incomprehensible, events seem unrelated, accidents happen, and sometimes you would think there is no more meaning in the world than there is in blocks thrown out by a child's hand on a nursery floor. Then suddenly, with insight rather than intellect, you become aware of meaning. Beauty, for instance, seems to me meaningful, or we get a glimpse of truth, or see an act of goodness, or regard a mother's love for a child. They make sense. I feel that I "know in part." So I say to myself that although I cannot understand much, there is Mind behind some things and therefore Mind behind everything. And I feel that that Mind, more than personal in any human sense of the word, is saying to us tiny children with the minds of insects, "I know you cannot understand, but hold on. You shall understand afterwards. The key is next door."

* * *

In my own philosophy of life I have a place for accidents. I do not mean that they cause surprise to God, but His knowing about them, even beforehand, no more causes them to happen than my knowing that you will go out of the doors of this church after the service, is the factor which causes you to do so. By accident I mean a thing that God did not intend and man could not foresee. Surely there must be such happenings in the criss-cross of human freewill.

A week yesterday at the Cup Tie Final at Wembley, Dwight got his leg broken. You read about it and perhaps saw it on television. I never read that Dwight sat down on the field and said, "Why should this happen to me?" or "What have I done to deserve this?" or "Why did God allow this to happen?" He probably said, "Well, it's bad luck, but it's just one of those things." Just as the rush of bodies together broke his leg, the rush of wills together has broken many a heart, and the criss-cross of freewills, acting sometimes through ignorance, or folly or sin, has brought seeming disaster to many lives.

But let us in our illustration leave the football field and come to the home. Let us imagine that you are bringing up little children. You do not pad the walls with eiderdowns and put foam rubber on the floor. Your little boy can meet with quite a nasty accident on the edge of the fender, perhaps, or the table leg. But you do not leave razor blades about, or saucers of sulphuric acid. In other words, as far as you are able, no situation arises so disastrous that you cannot deal with it. In this way you guard your home. In this way God guards His universe. Many troublous things can happen to us, but nothing with which He cannot deal. To change the figure, nothing can go so wrong that He cannot weave it into an overall plan, though when you rise up, as a child rises up, crying out in anger and even in despair, He cannot explain because you are too little. He comforts you and says, "You shall understand afterwards."

* * *

Frequently I find myself amazed at the degree to which, by peering through the windows, we *can* know in part and make sense out of life, and, in my reading, illustrations occur repeatedly that light up my theme this evening.

I remember so clearly going out "birding" in Yorkshire with a dear friend of mine. We watched some jackdaws apparently building a nest in the crevices of an old ruined tower. They gathered their material and they pushed it into the crevices. Apparently they could not realise that it was dropping right through the crevices on to the floor inside the hollow tower. If they can feel frustrated, they must have felt terribly frustrated about that. Believe me or not, when we walked into the tower, there was a heap of nesting material almost up to my shoulders. But when we went to a farmhouse adjoining the ruins, an old lady, crippled with arthritis, came out and talked to us, and she said this, "You know the jackdaws are doing me a wonderful service. They gather my kindling for me. I use what they push through the holes at the top of that ruined tower to start my fire."

I do not often attempt to write poetry, but I did make up this verse:—

> In my frustration make me sure
> That Thou, my God, art He,
> Who buildest something to endure
> From what seems loss to me.

Do you remember how blotting-paper was first made? In a large paper-mill an employee omitted one of the ingredients of writing paper and he came and confessed his fault to his employer. The employer tried to write on the paper and found that it was useless, but the way in which the ink ran suggested a new use of this type of paper. Up to then, fine sand had been used to dry the written page. The carelessness of an employee

was not willed by the employer. You might call it an accident.
You might call it ignorance, or folly, or sin. But it was the origin
of something very useful. Out of what looked like meaningless
accident, something useful was born.

Perhaps a more impressive illustration is offered in the
conquests of Alexander the Great (365-323 [B.C.]). Land after
land, people after people, fell to his conquering might, but
wherever Alexander went the Greek language was spoken and
good roads were put down. Over three hundred years later the
Gospel spread as it never could have done unless there had been
roads called the Greek language in men's minds, and roads
across the country called Greek roads. Many a slave, lashed by
tyranny into servile labour, was all unknowingly spreading the
Gospel of Christ, but he couldn't know it then. The key was next
door.

The Psalmist guessed that God might even use "the wrath of
man to praise Him," and as Principal Oman once said, "Without
a trust that God has a purpose He can make it serve, human
cruelty dethrones for us either God's goodness or His
omnipotence; and one is a mockery without the other."

We have not to go far in this church to see the perfect
illustrations of my theme. Look at that Cross. It is illuminated
from behind until late every night, so that any one passing by
and looking through the glass doors from the street can get a
glimpse of its meaning and significance, and feel that there is
light behind his cross too.

But when it happened, it looked like defeat, it felt like defeat,
it was called defeat. Did you say you were frustrated and that
you were hurt? What do you think He felt, and what did they
feel who had committed their lives to Him and risked
everything for Him? There was no key to get into that house of
darkness on Good Friday. The key was next door, or next door
but one. They found it on Easter Day and entered the house of
meaning.

Do look through the windows. Do gather any light there may
be now for your problem. But lest you become bitter or cynical,
take home with you this golden word of our Lord—Thou shalt
understand hereafter.

Some years ago I had a strange dream. I am not making this
up for the purpose of the sermon. I was passing through a time
of great difficulty and unhappiness, and in my dream I was to be
offered a personal interview with Christ, and I thought, "Ah, I

will ask Him this. I will ask Him that. Now I shall get an answer to all my questions and the key to all my problems." Believe it or not, in the glory of His presence it was not that I forgot to ask Him anything. It seemed utterly unnecessary and meaningless. Somehow I had an overwhelming feeling that even He would not be able to explain to me because my mental grasp was so tiny, but there came an overwhelming feeling of supreme joy that questions no longer needed to be answered. It was sufficient to know there *was* an answer. I knew that all was well and somehow I know that all was well for everybody. Another text came to my memory: "In that day ye shall ask me nothing" (John 16).

* * *

As we close, have in your mind again, if you will, the picture with which we started, of the house shuttered and fastened and standing in its own grounds. Imagine that you and I are together at the gate. Then recall the words that our late King George VI loved so much. "I said to the man who stood at the gate . . . 'Give me a LIGHT that I may tread safely into the unknown.' But he replied, 'Go out *into the darkness* and put thy hand into the hand of God. That shall be to thee better than light and safer than a known way.'"

"What I do thou knowest not now, but thou shalt understand hereafter." The key is next door.

> I do not ask thy way to understand,
>   My way to see;
> Better in darkness just to grasp Thy hand
>   And follow Thee.

CLAUS WESTERMANN
translated by James W. Cox

The Call of Isaiah

Isaiah 6:1-8

What did you think when you listened a short time ago to the outcry in the middle of the story of the call of prophet Isaiah— "Woe is me! For I am lost; for I am a man of unclean lips and I dwell in the midst of a people of unclean lips"?

Did you think, "That story is about me"? Probably not—not one of you. Or did somebody, on the contrary, hear it with the dejected feeling, "Yes, I understand. I know why he said at this moment: unclean lips, people of unclean lips. I belong there—to this people of unclean lips." From our lips come our words. They are our gate to the world. And what all goes through this gate! Oh, to be sure, good, strong, pure words proceed from our lips, words of love and of trust. But there are the other words: words like poison, words like sewage; words that are dull and emit too much nonsense. None of us is absolutely free from them.

Isn't it perhaps true that our generation can understand this outcry of Isaiah in the presence of God even better than previous generations? We have experienced and continue to experience how to a monstrous degree words of men can be misused; how whole generations can be forced into mistrust of all words and how as our caution increases, confidence in the word of one another is buried deeper and deeper. We may know all of that; yet, only the man who himself suffers somehow in the same way can understand why Isaiah had to say that he belonged to the people of unclean lips.

But now precisely for those among you to whom this account is infinitely remote, I am repeating an old and honorable story

From *Verkündigung des Kommenden*. Old Testament Sermons. As delivered by Claus Westermann (Munich: Chr. Kaiser Verlag, 1958). Used by permission of Chr. Kaiser Verlag and Dr. Westermann.

of a world long gone, in which men were capable of experiencing something like that. Precisely when we see the story in this way one thing becomes clear: the man who reports that about himself has first of all actually perceived under the impression of this experience what is put into words in the outcry. In this experience he has obviously for the first time discovered the solid ground from which he can speak in such a way.

One can say that, therefore, only in the presence of God. If only we were capable of grasping that! There is but one place from which all such general and summary judgments about men or the words of men have meaning. Moreover, there can be a genuine and honest confession of sins only in the presence of God! All judging and condemning of others, all judging and condemning of ourself is an extremely questionable and extremely limited business and, in most cases, fruitless and destructive! But how splendid, how wonderful that men such as we, men who have counted themselves among the people of unclean lips, have caught sight of this place from which it became clear to them, how it actually is with us! One may believe that or not. One cannot ignore the fact that for the prophet Isaiah the seeing of that Other was a reality that changed his life. One cannot ignore the fact that something happened there.

Isaiah's lips were touched. One may picture that as he pleases; nothing depends on it. What is essential is that this event determined the life of Isaiah from then on. Now notice something very remarkable. A glowing stone was taken with tongs from the altar and touched his mouth; and there came to him along with that, at the same moment, a word that promised him the forgiveness of his sins.

Tongs, glowing stone, and altar—all these are the apparatus of the sacrifice. They are appurtenances of the procedure through which men everywhere in ancient times for centuries influenced their god or their gods. They belonged to an action that proceeded from man and was directed to the other side. In this story of the call of Isaiah it is reversed: the altar and its apparatus stand in the service of an action that proceeds from the other side and is directed to the man Isaiah. Here a transformation is pointed out to us which deeply influences the entire history of humanity. An epoch comes to its end, the epoch in which men believed that they could influence the transcendent powers in their favor through sacrificial offering of their goods. This story but hints that the action that can purify a man must proceed from the other side. Here it is the glowing coal that touches the lips of Isaiah. When the time was fulfilled, one came from the other side and took the death of shame upon himself, in order to accomplish purification for us.

Just as here it becomes possible for Isaiah to endure the presence of God through the action from the other side, to stand in his presence and hear him, even though he is a man like others, in the same way it became possible for the entire human race to endure the presence of God, to stand in his presence and hear him, by means of the action that took place in the life and suffering of the Christ.

What happened at that point is just as mysterious here as there. We can speak of it and tell others about it only as the mysterious center of a triad that determines this story of Isaiah's call and continues from there throughout the story. I say triad, for this transformation of Isaiah by the cleansing action of God precedes something and follows something.

This is what preceded: He has beheld God in his majesty. He has been surprised by something unspeakably glorious and mighty, which he can describe only with trembling and stammering. Strictly speaking, it is no description at all. He gives us only hints that point in the direction in which we should look. Yes, in the direction in which *we* should look! Just as the men to whom the story was told for the first time. How should we do that? Where should we look? Let us hear only what is said here. Where that which Isaiah saw touches our earth, two kinds of things happen: the threshold of the Temple trembles, and the man standing there is affected in his innermost being. *That* is the direction in which we should look—there to that point from which worlds are guided and worlds are overthrown, from which men are most radically influenced and transformed in their innermost being. And for that there are continually many possibilities; no world history and no church history can ever exhaust these possibilities that the holy God can choose to move the hearts of men and to move worlds.

The chorus of celestial servants shouts the *trisagion* to him: "Holy! Holy! Holy!" God is mystery; and woe to the poor man who no longer notices any mystery and who no longer knows anything mysterious. Where any of us go as far as we can, where we stand still, amazed and frightened or with pounding hearts, in the presence of a mystery, just there is where the skirt of his robe begins. We can see what the angels meant with their cry, of course, just when we are farthest removed from all miracles, when we are about to be swallowed up in everyday trifles and unending boredom; when dullness and depression squeeze the life out of us, when someone has disappointed us once more, when we ourselves have not lived up to expectations. Precisely then! Precisely then can we stretch forth our arms toward that which is beyond, toward the One who is beyond. That One is the holy One, and precisely then can we place ourselves beside this Isaiah who was a man like us and look in the direction in which he has pointed. Out of the midst of the tangle of egoistic dullness or under the hammer blows of brutal oppression we can endure simply because Christ has come to us from this holy God and gives us access to him.

However, the story that happened then with Isaiah continued. Something else followed—the third tone in the triad. God needed Isaiah. He did not need him as an angel, but as a man. He did not want Isaiah now to be continually singing hymns of praise. He left Isaiah among men and sent him to men. Isaiah could do it now. Not because he was at the moment better than others; he knew that God had done something to him, and that was enough. He could now be a messenger of the holy God. It is a limited office, the office of messenger! It does not depend on him, but on what he brings. So it was then, and so it is today. The more insignificant a messenger himself becomes and the more important what he has to bring may be, so much the better! The prophets in Isaiah's time actually grasped what it means to be a messenger. They wanted no fixed office for themselves, no title. They did not strive for honor and recognition, but had only the one burning determination, namely, to say to those to whom they were sent: God lives and God acts. With this message they went forth to men, out where they struggled and suffered, where they rebelled against God, and where they despaired of God—and were guarantors that God lives, in spite of everything.

This is how it has been throughout history. So in the fullness of the times, then, Christ came and in his own self revealed the holy God and suffered, because men could not tolerate it. But they recognized and believed it in those days, were sent out by him as messengers and have attested to what they heard and saw. Down to this very day and hour the message flows on and on and will continue to flow as long as the earth stands. For God acts, and they have the experience of it and must tell others about it. In this hour is said to you what you now hear: The bond between the holy God and this earth is not broken. You should listen to this statement, right where you actually stand and each of you as the person you actually are. It can happen today—and does happen—that somewhere in space a star explodes and a new star passes over into its orbit. It can happen today—and does happen—that a man learns with celebration or with trembling, that God lives and that he lives for him.

The overpowering rhythm in the three tones, which resound through the story of Isaiah's call, continues: the majesty of the holy God, the miracle of cleansing from sins, and the way of the message through the world. The church has this triad in mind in the doctrine of the triune God: the God who remains for ever the Other and Mystery; the God who nevertheless looks out of his heights into our depths, down to where we actually are, and has condescended to us; the God whose messengers and whose gathered people attest that God acts—yesterday, today, and up to the very end.

APPENDIX:
Guidelines
for Studying a Sermon

The following apparatus is the editor's adaptation of a scheme by Ozora S. Davis, as set forth in Davis' *Principles of Preaching*. It includes suggestions from Andrew W. Blackwood's *Protestant Pulpit*. In addition, it reflects some concerns of the editor and of two of his graduate students in homiletics, James M. Stinespring and James Mattison King.

In studying a sermon, these factors should be considered:
OVERALL IMPRESSION: Was the sermon interesting? Informative? Moving? Convincing?
ANALYSIS: Outline the sermon, giving main points and first subpoints. Include Introduction and Conclusion.
TITLE: Is it attractive? Clear? Honest? Related to main theme?
TEXT: Is there a single text, or are there multiple texts? Section, chapter, paragraph, sentence, phrase, or word? Used literally, analogically, typologically, or allegorically? Vitally related to sermon? Historical meaning accurately reflected?
CENTRAL IDEA: What is it? Is it formally stated? Where? Does sermon fulfill its promise?
INTRODUCTION: Does it seize attention at once? Relate theme or text to hearers? Is it too long? Too short? Irrelevant?
BODY: Are main points clearly stated? Related to central idea? A unity? Is there forward movement? Is each point given space according to its importance? Where is climax reached?
CONCLUSION: Does it summarize main points? Or reinforce main discussion? Or call for decision or action?

SUPPORTIVE MATERIAL:

Sources: *Percent*

Preacher's thought and experience

Bible

Biography

History and literature

Observation of contemporary life

Types:* Restatement? Examples—general, specific, hypothetical? Illustrations—anecdotes, parables, figures of speech? Argument? Testimony?

Quality: Varied? Apt? Fresh? True? Accurate? Right length?

TRANSITIONS AND CONNECTIVES: Varied? Natural?

UNITY: Does the sermon give an overall impression of wholeness?

STYLE: Is the style literary or oral? Abstract or concrete? Clear? Precise? Energetic? Natural? Beautiful? Individual? Are sentences varied in length and form?

GENERAL OBSERVATIONS: Does this sermon present a positive message? Is there an unusual format? What other striking features did you note? Was the appeal rational, affectional, ethical, or a combination of two or three?

---

* Definitions and examples of these terms can be found in the editor's books, *Learning to Speak Effectively* (London: Hodder & Stoughton, 1966; Grand Rapids: Baker Book House, 1974) or *A Guide to Biblical Preaching* (Nashville: Abingdon, 1976).

Biographical Notes

BAILLIE, DONALD M.: Born at Giarloch, Wester Ross, Scotland, in 1887. Died 1954. Educated at New Coll., Edinburgh, and at Heidelberg and Marburg, Germany. A Presbyterian. Pastor of Scottish churches from 1918 to 1934, including Inverbervie; Cupar, St. John's Ch.; and St. Columba's Ch., Kilmacolm. Taught systematic theology at Univ. of St. Andrews, 1934-54. He gave the Kerr Lectures at Glasgow in 1927, the Forwood Lectures at Liverpool in 1947, and the Moore Lectures at San Francisco in 1952. Success in ministry came rather late. Clarity of structure and simplicity of style were faithful vehicles of his profound theological insights. His books include the theological classic *God Was in Christ* (1947) and two volumes of sermons: *To Whom Shall We Go?* (1955), with a memoir by John Dow, and *Out of Nazareth* (1958). Another posthumous volume, *The Theology of the Sacraments* (1957), contains a biographical essay by his brother, John Baillie.

BARTH, KARL: Born in Basle, Switzerland, 1886. Died 1968. Educated at Univ. of Bern, Tübingen, Berlin, and Marburg. Reformed Church. Assistant pastor in Geneva, 1909-11. Pastor in Safenwil, 1911-21. Professor at Univ. of Göttingen, 1921-25; Univ. of Münster, 1925-30; Univ. of Bonn, 1930-35; Univ. of Basel, 1936-62. The preacher's task led him to write his commentary, *The Epistle to the Romans,* a volume that shook the theological world. His only visit to the U.S. was in 1962, when he delivered at the Univ. of Chicago and Princeton Univ. several of the lectures in *Evangelical Theology: An Introduction.* His lectures were written in full, as were his sermons. His sermons were characteristically in the homily style in simple, graphic language and illustrated by current happenings. His later sermons (preached in Basel to prisoners) had shorter texts than his earlier ones. His more than two hundred works include his monumental *Church Dogmatics* (12 vols. from 1936 to 1969); *The Preaching of the Gospel* (1963); sermons in *Come, Holy Spirit* (1933); *God's Search for Man* (1935); *Deliverance to the Captives* (1961); and *Call for God* (1967). A biography by Eberhard Busch, *Karl Barth,* appeared in English in 1976.

BUECHNER, CARL FREDERICK: Born in New York City in 1926. Educated at Lawrenceville Sch., Princeton Univ., and Union Theol. Sem. A Presbyterian. Taught English, Lawrenceville Sch.; creative writing, New York Univ. Chm. dept. of religion, Phillips Exeter Acad., where he was school minister. A successful novelist and poet. Recipient of numerous literary awards. His sermons reflect the imagination and excellent stylistic qualities that characterize his novels and poetry. His sermon volumes are *The Magnificent Defeat* (1966) and *The Hungering Dark* (1969).

BUTTRICK, GEORGE A.: Born at Seaham Harbour, Northumberland, England, 1892. Educated at Lancashire Independent Theol. Coll., Manchester, and Victoria Univ. (honors in philosophy). A Presbyterian. Pastor, First Union Congregational Ch., Quincy, Ill., 1915-18; First Congregational Ch., Rutland, Vt., 1919-21; First Presbyterian Ch., Buffalo, N.Y., 1921-27; Madison Avenue Presbyterian Ch., New York, N.Y., 1927-54. Preacher to the University and Plummer Prof. of Christian Morals, Harvard Univ., 1954-60. Harry Emerson Fosdick Visiting Prof., Union Theol. Sem., New York, 1960-61; Prof. of Preaching, Garrett Theol. Sem., 1961-70; Visiting Prof., Vanderbilt Div. Sch., 1970-71; Southern Bapt. Theol. Sem., 1971-. President, Federal Council of Churches of Christ in America, 1939-41. Lyman Beecher Lectures at Yale, *Jesus Came Preaching* (1930); E. Y. Mullins Lectures at Southern Bapt. Theol. Sem. (1943). Dr. Buttrick evinces in his sermons the acuteness of a penetrating mind working with issues of social and individual concern under the authority of biblical text and tradition. Wide reading and vivid imagination are incarnated in a down-to-earth style. Author of numerous books, including *The Parables of Jesus* (1928); *Prayer* (1942); *Sermons Preached in a University Church* (1959); *The Power of Prayer Today* (1970). Editor, *The Interpreter's Bible* (12 vols.) (1952), *The Interpreter's Dictionary of the Bible* (4 vols.) (1959).

CAMPBELL, ERNEST T.: Born in New York City in 1923. Educated at Bob Jones Univ., New York Univ., Princeton Theol. Sem. A Presbyterian. Frequent speaker on the Protestant Hour and the National Radio Pulpit. Preaching mission speaker in Alaska and Cuba. Frequent speaker on college campuses. Minister of Presbyterian churches in Pennsylvania and Michigan; minister of the Riverside Ch., N.Y.C., 1968-76. His preaching combines traditional evangelical concerns and keen social awareness and is couched in vigorous, graphic language. His books include *Christian Manifesto* (1970), *Where Cross the Crowded Ways* (1973), and *Locked in a Room with Open Doors* (1974).

CLELAND, JAMES T.: Born in Glasgow, Scotland, in 1903. Educated at Glasgow Univ. and Union Theol. Sem., N.Y. A Presybyterian. Taught at Glasgow Univ. Div. Hall, 1928-31; Amherst Coll., Mass., 1931-45. James B. Duke Professor of Preaching, Duke Div. Sch., 1945; Emeritus, 1968. Dean of the Chapel, Duke Univ.; Emeritus, 1973. Held numerous distinguished lectureships, including the Warrack Lectures in Preaching, 1964, *Preaching to Be Understood* (1965). Preacher at military bases; leader of seminars for chaplains; writer for "Preaching Clinic" in *The Chaplain*. Contributor to vols. of *Best Sermons* and *The Interpreter's Bible*. His sermons are clearly structured in a variety of patterns and make wide use of literary sources for illustrative matter. He exemplifiesthe theme of his lectures, "Preaching to Be Understood." He is the author of *The True and Lively Word* (1954), a book on homiletics; and *Wherefore Art Thou Come?* (1961) and *He Died As He Lived* (1966), both sermonic meditations.

FERRIS, THEODORE PARKER: Born at Port Chester, N.Y., in 1908. Died, 1972. Educated at Harvard Coll. and General Theol. Sem. An Episcopalian. Assistant minister, Grace Episcopal Ch., N.Y., 1933-37; Fellow and Tutor in General Theol. Sem., 1933-37. Rector, Emmanuel Ch., Baltimore, 1937-42; Trinity Ch., Boston, 1942 until his death. A delegate to the First Assembly of the World Council of Churches, Amsterdam, 1948. Guest on the National Radio Pulpit, the Episcopal Hour, TV Man to Man, and the Protestant Hour. His sermons were printed weekly and mailed to people in every state in the U.S.A. and in many foreign countries. These sermons had a warm, human quality that demonstrated the definition of preaching given by his illustrious predecessor in Trinity pulpit, Phillips Brooks: "truth through personality." He was the author of *This Created World* (1944); *This Is the Day* (1951); *Go Tell the People* (1951), a book on homiletics; *The Story of Jesus* (1953); *When I Became a Man* (1957); *The New Life* (1961); *Book of Prayer for Everyman* (1962); *What Jesus Did* (1963); *The Image of God* (1965). He also contributed the Exposition of the Acts of the Apostles, *The Interpreter's Bible* (1954).

FOSDICK, HARRY EMERSON: Born in Buffalo, N.Y., 1878. Died 1969. Educated at Colgate Univ., Union Theol. Sem., and Columbia Univ. A Baptist. Pastor, First Bapt. Ch., Montclair, N.J., 1904-15; Stated Preacher, First Presb. Ch., N.Y.C., 1919-24; Minister Riverside (nondenominational) Ch.,N.Y.C., 1926-46. Instructor in homiletics, Union Theol. Sem., 1908-15; prof. of practical theology, 1915-34; adjunct prof., 1934-46. Lyman Beecher Lectures, Yale Univ., *The Modern Use of the Bible* (1924). Preached on Sunday afternoons over a nationwide radio network on National Vespers, sponsored by the Federal Council of Churches of Christ in America. Regarded as a homiletician *par excellence* by both conservatives and liberals. His sermons are largely life-situational and raise personal counseling to a group level. *Riverside Sermons* (1958) brings together representative sermons from his numerous sermon volumes. His last volume, comprised of sermons preached after retirement, is *What Is Vital in Religion* (1955). His autobiography: *The Living of These Days* (1956).

GRAHAM, WILLIAM FRANKLIN (Billy): Born at Charlotte, N.C., 1918. Educated at Florida Bible Sem. and Wheaton Coll. A Baptist. Pastor of First Bapt. Ch., Western Springs, Ill., 1943-44; first v.-p. Youth for Christ, International, 1945-48; pres. Northwestern Schools, 1947-52; preacher for nationwide evangelistic campaigns since 1949; radio and television preacher; founder and pres. Billy Graham Evangelistic Assn.; editor-in-chief of *Decision* since 1963. He has been the recipient of numerous awards. His sermons make large use of the Bible, have clear structure, and employ simple language.

They emphasize the need for personal regeneration and show deep concern for righteousness in society. His books include *Calling Youth to Christ* (1947); *Peace with God* (1953); *The Secret of Happiness* (1955); *World Aflame* (1965); *The Jesus Generation* (1971); and *Angels: God's Secret Agents* (1976).

GUINN, G. Earl: Born at Mossville, Miss., 1912. Educated at Louisiana Coll., Southwestern Bapt. Theol. Sem., and New Orleans Bapt. Theol. Sem. A Baptist. Pastor of First Bapt. churches in Sterlington (1937-41), Jennings (1941-45), and Bossier City (1945-48), all in Louisiana. Chm. Dept. of Preaching, Southwestern Bapt. Theol. Sem., 1948-51. Pres. Louisiana Coll., 1951-74. Prof. of Christian Preaching, Southern Bapt. Theol. Sem., 1975-. Frequent speaker for denominational conventions and assemblies. Dr. Guinn's sermons are prepared with great care and always follow a clear line of direction, whether oriented biblically or theologically, and are delivered with vigor and without manuscript or notes. He is the author of numerous journal articles. He co-edited *Southern Baptist Preaching* (1959) with H. C. Brown.

HAMILTON, J. WALLACE: Born on a farm in Canada in 1900. Died in 1968. He attended neither college nor seminary, but studied for three years at the Moody Bible Institute, Chicago. A Methodist. Pastor at Baileyton, Tenn.; then, at St. Petersburg, Fla., of the Pasadena Community Church, from 1930 to 1968, where at this "drive-in" church average attendance ranged from 2,500 to 10,000. He preached all over the United States: at 50 Methodist Annual Conferences and at conferences and assemblies of numerous demoninations. Speaker on the Protestant Hour radio network. His sermons were written word for word but were delivered without notes or manuscript, except for his quotations. His books include: *Ride the Wild Horses* (1952); *Horns and Halos in Human Nature* (1954); *Who Goes There?* (1958); *The Thunder of Bare Feet* (1964); *Serendipity* (1965); *Where Now Is Thy God?* (1969); *Still the Trumpet Sounds* (1970); and *What About Tomorrow?* (1972).

JORDAN, CLARENCE LEONARD: Born at Talbotton, Ga., in 1912. Died 1969. Educated at Univ. of Georgia and Southern Bapt. Theol. Sem. A Baptist. While a graduate student, he taught at Simmons Univ., then a black school, and was supt. of the Sunshine Center, located in the black ghetto; served as supt. of missions for a local Baptist association of churches, pioneering in work among blacks and whites in the Haymarket section of Louisville (1939-42). He founded Koinonia Farm at Americus, Ga., in 1942, as "an experiment in Christian communal living." Despite physical violence and economic boycott against Koinonia Farm, the people and work endured. Dallas Lee, a friend and associate, said of him, "When you heard him you didn't just get new information or a new scholarly angle on some theological issue. You encountered a man—a man who strove to live by what he was talking about; a tall, country man with a big Southern voice, an infectious sense of humor, and a penetrating social compassion that balanced his evangelical warmth with ethical dynamite." He spoke before many denominational conventions, ministerial groups, colleges, universities, churches, and at retreat centers in the United States and Canada. He translated/paraphrased parts of the New Testament in *The Cotton Patch Version* of Paul's Epistles and in his own versions of Luke and Acts, and of Matthew and John. A number of his sermons are included in *The Substance of Faith and Other Cotton Patch Sermons by Clarence Jordan,* ed. Dallas Lee.

KENNEDY, GERALD: Born at Benzonia, Mich., 1907. Educated at Coll. of Pacific, Pacific Sch. of Religion and Hartford Theol. Sem. A Methodist. Pastor of First Congregational Ch., Collinsville, Conn., 1932-36; Calvary Meth. Ch., San Jose, Cal., 1936-40; First Meth. Ch., Palo Alto, Cal., 1940-42; St. Paul Meth. Ch., Lincoln, Neb., 1942-48; bishop of Meth. Ch., Portland area, 1948-52; Los Angeles area, 1952-72. While a bishop he served as pastor of First Meth. Ch., Pasadena, Cal., beginning in 1969. Pres. Council of Bishops of Meth. Ch., 1960-61. Lyman Beecher Lectures at Yale, 1954 *(God's Good News)*. Frequent lecturer at colleges and universities. Bishop Kennedy's sermons characteristically are clearly structured, aptly illustrated with fresh—often humorous—material, and couched in simple language and were delivered in a rapid-fire style with a deft touch of the prophetic spirit. He edited three volumes of sermon illustrations: *A Reader's Notebook* (1953); *Reader's Notebook, 2* (1959); *My Third Reader's Notebook* (1974). Other books include *His Word Through Preaching*

(1947); *Who Speaks for God?* (1954); *For Preachers and Other Sinners* (1964); *Fresh Every Morning* (1966); *Seven Worlds of the Minister* (1968).

KILLINGER, JOHN: Born at Germantown, Ky., 1933. Educated at Baylor Univ., Univ. of Ky., Harvard Div. School, and Princeton Theol. Sem. A Baptist. Taught English at Georgetown (Ky.) Coll. and was Dean of the Chapel; was Academic Dean at Ky. Southern Coll.; and is now Professor of Preaching, Worship and Literature at Vanderbilt Univ. Frequent speaker for church and military groups, college and seminary convocations, and ministers' gatherings. His books and addresses reflect appreciation of classical excellencies and contemporary moods. The author of some two dozen books, including *The Thickness of Glory* (1965); *The Centrality of Preaching in the Total Task of the Ministry* (1969); *Experimental Preaching* (1973); *The 11 O'Clock News and Other Experimental Sermons* (1975); and his most recent and widely known *Bread for the Wilderness, Wine for the Journey* (1976).

KING, MARTIN LUTHER, JR.: Born in Atlanta, Ga., 1929. Died, 1968. Educated at Morehouse Coll., Crozer Theol. Sem., and Boston Univ. A Baptist. He was active from his college days in the NAACP and led in the Southern Christian Leadership Conference from 1957, espousing a persistent and aggressive, but nonviolent, campaign for civil rights for blacks. In 1964 he won the Nobel Peace Prize. His sermons and other addresses were always to the audience and the occasion. He could stir intellectuals, meeting them on their own level, as well as the uneducated, to whom he preached in an idiom that better suited their tastes. His books include *Stride Toward Freedom* (1958), *Strength to Love* (sermons) (1963), and *Why We Can't Wait* (1964). His biography was written by Lerone Bennett, Jr., and is entitled, *What Manner of Man* (1964).

KNOX, RONALD A.: Born at Kibworth, Beauchamp, Leicestershire, England, 1888. Died 1957. Educated at Eton Coll., Balliol Coll., Oxford; and St. Edmund's Coll. Ordained a priest in Church of England in 1912; in the Roman Catholic Church in 1919. Chaplain of Trinity Coll., Oxford, 1912-17; Catholic Chaplain at Oxford, 1926-39. From 1939-50, he was engaged in translating the Bible into "timeless English" from the Vulgate. He wrote in several literary fields. His sermons show the same care in choosing the right word or phrase that characterized his style in his other work. There is a conversational tone, yet no wasting of words. "His sermons," said Evelyn Waugh, "were prepared, revised and rehearsed with every refinement of taste and skill." Several volumes of published and unpublished sermons were collected in *The Pastoral Sermons of Ronald A. Knox* (1960) and *The Occasional Sermons of Ronald A. Knox* (1960). A biography by Evelyn Waugh has been published, entitled *The Life of Ronald Knox*.

MACLEOD, DONALD: Born at Broughton, Nova Scotia, Canada, in 1913. Educated at Dalhousie Univ., Pine Hill Div. Coll., and Univ. of Toronto. A Presbyterian. Pastor of First Presb. Ch., Louisburg, N.S., 1938-41. Assoc. pastor of Bloor Street Presb. Ch., Toronto, 1941-45. Teaching fellow at Princeton Theol. Sem., 1946-47; asst. prof. of homiletics, 1947-53; assoc. prof., 1953-61; prof. of preaching and worship, 1961-. Founder and first president of Am. Acad. of Homiletics. Recipient of preaching awards. Editor of Princeton Sem. Bulletin. His sermons are constructed with the skill of a master craftsman and illuminated with choice supportive material, while they reflect careful textual exegesis. His books include *Here Is My Method* (1952); *Word and Sacrament* (1961); *Presbyterian Worship* (1965); and *Higher Reaches* (1971).

MARNEY, CARLYLE: Born at Harriman, Tenn., 1916. Educated at Carson-Newman Coll. and Southern Bapt. Theol. Sem. A Baptist. Served on committees and held offices with World Council of Churches, Bapt. World Alliance, and National Council of Churches. Minister at First Bapt. Ch., Austin, Tex., and Myers Park Bapt. Ch., Charlotte, N.C. Professor of Christian Ethics at Austin Presb. Sem. Frequent lecturer and chapel speaker at colleges and universities and preacher at many army and air force bases. His sermons reflect a wide range of reading in philosophy, theology, and ethics. The style Ksoften soars in cadences reminiscent of the King James Version of the Bible. His books include *Faith in Conflict* (1957); *Beggars in Velvet* (1960); *Structures of Prejudice* (1969); *These Things Remain* (1953); *He Became Like Us* (1964); *The*

Suffering Servant (1965); *The Carpenter's Son* (1967); and *The Crucible of Redemption* (1971).

MARSHALL, PETER: Born at Coatbridge, Scotland, in 1902. Died, 1949. Educated at Coatbridge Technical Sch. and Mining Coll. in Scotland and at Columbia Theol. Sem. A Presbyterian. Pastor, Covington, Ga., 1931-33; Westminster Presb. Ch., 1933-37; New York Ave. Presb. Ch., Washington, D.C., 1937-49. Elected Chaplain of U.S. Senate in 1947. He became known nationally for his often quoted pungent prayers. His preaching was colorful and dramatic, and his sermons were delivered with flawless diction of a Scottish flavor. Sermons were written in full in advance of delivery and presented from a well-mastered manuscript typewritten in a unique format suggestive of blank verse. His sermons are published in posthumous volumes: *Mr. Jones, Meet the Master* (1949); *A Man Called Peter* (a biography by Mrs. Marshall) (1951); and *John Doe, Disciple* (1963).

OATES, WAYNE E.: Born at Greenville, S.C., 1917. Educated at Mars Hill Coll., Wake Forest Coll., Duke Div. Sch., Southern Bapt. Theol. Sem. A Baptist. Pastor at Bunn and Peachtree Bapt. churches in N.C. Asst. pastor, Grace Bapt. Ch., 1942-43. Pastor of Union City (Ky.) Bapt. Ch., 1943-45; Broadway Bapt. Ch., Louisville, Ky., 1947-48. Chaplain, Ky. Bapt. Hosp., Louisville, 1945-46; Ky. State Hosp., Danville, 1946-47. Taught at Southern Bapt. Theol. Sem. 1945-74 in pastoral care and psychology of rel. Prof. in psychiatry and behavioral sciences, Univ. of Louisville Sch. of Medicine, 1974-. Guest lecturer and visiting prof. at Union Theol. Sem. (N.Y.) and Princeton Theol. Sem. Received the Distinguished Service Award of the Am. Assn. of Pastoral Counselors, 1959. His sermons reveal profound psychological depths as he exegetes both text and hearer. He is author of more than two dozen books, including *The Christian Pastor* (1957); *Anxiety in Christian Experience* (1955); *The Revelation of God in Human Suffering* (1959); *Confessions of a Workaholic* (1971); and *The Psychology of Religion* (1973).

PANNENBERG, WOLFHART: Born at Stettin, Germany, in 1928. Educated at Univs. of Berlin, Göttingen, Basel, and Heidelberg. A Lutheran. Taught at Univ. of Heidelberg,

Kirchliche Hochschule of Wuppertal, Univ. of Mainz, and is now prof. of systematic theology at Univ. of Munich. He has lectured at Harvard, Yale, Univ. of Chicago Sch. of Theol., and Claremont, Cal. It is his conviction that "dogmatic perspectives of particular denominations have no future in the renewed Church's proclamation and instruction." He does not regard the sermon as an authoritative word of God but as "an attempt to reformulate the substantial truth of the Christian faith." Thus the sermon must be related to all phases of human inquiry and experience. His translated works include *Jesus, God and Man* (1968); *Revelation as History* (1968); *Theology and the Kingdom of God* (1969); *Basic Questions in Theology* (1970); *Spirit, Faith, and Church* (1970); *What Is Man?* (1970); *The Apostles' Creed in the Light of Today's Questions* (1972); and a volume of sermons being translated into English.

PEALE, NORMAN VINCENT: Born at Bowersville, Ohio, 1898. Educated at Ohio Wesleyan Univ. and Boston Univ. Ordained to Methodist ministry. Pastor, Berkeley, R.I., 1922-24; Kings Highway Ch., Brooklyn, 1924-27; University Ch., Syracuse, N.Y., 1927-32, Marble Collegiate Reformed Ch., since 1932. Editor, *Guideposts*. President, Reformed Church in America, 1969-70. Television speaker on What's Your Trouble? and writer of newspaper column, Positive Thinking. His sermons are positive and affirmative, emphasizing psychological principles. They are simple in structure and style and make abundant use of stories that exemplify the principles inculcated. They are preached extemporaneously and often employ folksy humor. His books include *A Guide to Confident Living* (1948); *The Power of Positive Thinking* (1952); *The Tough-Minded Optimist* (1962); *Enthusiasm Makes the Difference* (1967); and *You Can If You Think You Can* (1974).

READ, DAVID H. C.: Born Cupar, Fife, Scotland, 1910. Educated at Daniel Stewart's Coll., Edinburgh; Edinburgh Univ.; Univs. of Montpellier, Strasbourg, Paris, and Marburg; New Coll., Edinburgh. A Presbyterian. Pastor of Coldstream West Ch., 1936-39; Chaplain to the Forces of the British Army, 1939-45; Pastor of Greenbank Parish, Edinburgh, 1939-49; first chaplain to Univ. of Edinburgh, 1949-55; Chaplain to the Queen in Scotland, 1952-55; pastor of Madison Avenue Presbyterian

Ch. since 1956. He was Warrack Lecturer on Preaching at Univ. of Glasgow in 1950-51 and Lyman Beecher Lecturer at Yale, 1973. His sermons are fully written before delivery. They do not follow a standard structural pattern but vary in style according to the subject matter and the objective, thus achieving sometimes unusual results. His books include *The Communication of the Gospel* (Warrack Lectures) (1952); *The Christian Faith* (1955); *Virginia Woolfe Meets Charlie Brown* (1968); *Sent from God* (Lyman Beecher Lectures) (1973); and *The Gospel According to Paul* (1974).

SANGSTER, WILLIAM E.: Born in 1900 at London, England. Died in 1960. Educated at Handsworth Coll., Birmingham; Richmond Coll., London; and the Univ. of London. A Methodist. Pastor in Bognor Regis, 1923-26; Colwyn Bay, 1926-29; Liverpool, 1929-32; Scarboro, 1932-36; Leeds, 1936-39; Westminster Central Hall, 1939-55. In 1955 he was appointed head of the Home Mission Department of the World Conf. of Methodists. While a pastor, he served as pres. of the Meth. Conf. of Great Britain and chairman of the Evangelical Comm. of the World Conf. of Methodists. He frequently preached and lectured in other countries, from India to the U.S., with great acclaim. His messages were informed with a deep piety and were characterized by clarity of structure, simplicity of language, and freshness, variety, and aptness of illustration. They were delivered with intensity of feeling. His books on preaching include: *Let Me Commend* (1949), *The Approach to Preaching* (1952), *The Craft of the Sermon* (1954), and *Power in Preaching* (1958). Sermon books include: *Why Jesus Never Wrote a Book* (1932); *He Is Able* (1936); *Can I Know God?* (1960); and *Westminster Sermons*, Vol. II (1961). Paul Sangster, his son, wrote his biography, *Doctor Sangster* (1962).

SCHERER, PAUL E.: Born at Mt. Holly Springs, Pa., 1892. Died 1969. Educated at Coll. of Charleston, S.C.; Luth. Theol. Sem., Mt. Airy, Pa. A Lutheran. Asst. pastor, Holy Trinity Ch., Buffalo, N.Y., 1918-19; pastor, Holy Trinity Luth. Ch., N.Y.C., 1920-45. His teaching career included the teaching of English and rhetoric for a year after college graduation, an instructorship at Mt. Airy Sem., and a professorship in homiletics at Union Theol. Sem. in N.Y., 1945-60. From 1961 until near the time of his death he was a visiting prof. at Princeton Theol. Sem. In 1943 he delivered the Lyman Beecher Lectures on Preaching at Yale, "For We Have This Treasure." From 1932 to 1945 he was heard by millions on National Vespers, a coast-to-coast radio network broadcast on Sunday afternoons. His sermons were usually written in full and were uniformly based on careful exegesis and profound theological conviction. The style evinces a vivid imagination, aptness and variety of illustration, and precision of language. His voice was capacious and well-modulated, and his delivery had a controlled dramatic quality. His sermon books include: *Facts That Undergird Life* (1938); *The Place Where Thou Standest* (1942); *When God Hides* (1934); and *The Word God Sent* (1965).

SCHWEIZER, EDUARD: Born in Basel, Switzerland, 1913. Educated at Univ. of Basel, Marburg, and Zurich. Member of the Reformed Church. Minister in Basel, 1936-37; Nesslau/St. Gallen, 1938-46. Professor of New Testament: Univ. of Mainz, 1946-49; Univ. of Bonn, summer, 1949; Univ. of Zurich, since fall, 1949. Rector (pres.) of Univ. of Zurich, 1964-66. Pres., Studiorum Novi Testamenti Societas, 1969-70. Guest prof., Colgate-Rochester Div. Sch.; San Francisco Theol. Sem.; Doshisha Univ., Kyoto; and Internatl. Christian Univ., Tokyo, Japan; Ormond Coll., Melbourne, Australia. Member of Faith and Order Commission, World Council of Churches, for several years. A regular preacher at the Cathedral of Schaffhausen. His sermons were normally written in full in shorthand after listening for ninety minutes to a discussion of the text by a representative group from the congregation that would hear the sermon. Schweizer used this "sermon seminar" method as a part of his preparation for the pulpit when he was a full-time parish minister and even after assuming his professorship at Zurich, as long as it was practical to bring together a group. Thus he takes seriously both scholarly opinion and the insights and questions of the hearers. He has written over 200 essays in scholarly symposia, festschriften, and periodicals. Besides a number of scholarly books on specific themes, he is the author of commentaries on Mark (1970) and Matthew (1975). *God's Inescapable Nearness* (1971) contains his sermons and an essay by James W. Cox analyzing his preaching theory and practice.

SHEEN, FULTON J.: Born in 1895. Educated at St. Viator Coll.; St. Paul Sem.; Catholic Univ. of Am.; Univ. of Louvain, Belgium; Sorbonne, Paris; Collegio Angelico, Rome. A Roman Catholic. National Director, Society for the Propagation of the Faith, Bishop of Rochester, and now Titular Archbishop of Newport, Gwent. Preacher on Catholic Hour radio broadcasts for 25 years. Lecturer on television series, Life Is Worth Living. Taught at Catholic Univ. of Am. for 25 years. Listeners of all faiths have been stirred by his pulpit oratory, which is born of a happy combination of scholarship and contemplation. He is the author of about 60 books, including *Philosophy of Religion* (1948); *Peace of Soul* (1949); *Life Is Worth Living* (1953); *Life of Christ* (1954); and *Those Mysterious Priests* (1974).

SOPER, DONALD OLIVER: Born in 1903. Educated at Aske's School, Hatcham; Cambridge Univ.; London Univ. A Methodist. Minister, South London Mission, 1926-29; Central London Mission, 1929-36. Supt., West London Mission, Kingsway Hall, from 1936. Conducted open-air meetings in Hyde Park and on Tower Hill, in London. In 1960, he gave the Lyman Beecher Lectures on Preaching, *The Advocacy of the Gospel* (1961). Other books include: *It Is Hard to Work for God* (1957) and *Aflame with Faith* (1963).

SPEAKMAN, FREDERICK BRUCE: Born at Chandler, Okla., 1918. Educated at Coll. of Emporia (Kan.), Univ. of Okla., Harvard Univ., and Princeton Theol. Sem. A Presbyterian. Pastor at Central Brick Presb. Ch., East Orange, N.J., 1946-50; Westminster Presb. Ch., Dayton, Ohio, 1963-72; twice at Third Presb. Ch., Pittsburgh, Pa., 1950 63, 1972 to present. He was awarded the Hugh Davies Prize as the outstanding preacher in his graduating class at Princeton Sem. and has preached widely at summer conferences and in college and university chapels. He has served as guest professor of homiletics at Pittsburgh Theol. Sem. He is recognized as a dynamic speaker with the gift of imagination and "a richness of expression." His books include *The Salty Tang* (1954), *Love Is Something You Do* (1959), and *God and Jack Wilson* (1964).

STEIMLE, EDMUND: Born at Allentown, Pa., 1907. Educated at Princeton Univ., Luth. Theol. Sem., Philadelphia, and Univ. of Pa. A Lutheran. Taught at Luth. Theol. Sem., Philadelphia, and Union Theol. Sem., N.Y.C., until retirement in 1975. Pastor in Jersey City, N.J., 1935-40; Cambridge, Mass., 1940-52. Preacher over radio on the Protestant Hour. Received honorary doctorates from Wagner Coll., Muhlenberg Coll., Roanoke Coll., Gettysburg Coll., and Hamilton Coll. His sermons are couched in clear, picturesque language and presented with a crisp, matter-of-fact delivery. His books of sermons include *Are You Looking for God?* (1957), *Disturbed by Joy* (1967), and *From Death to Birth* (1973).

STEWART, JAMES STUART: Born at Dundee, Scotland, in 1896. Educated at St. Andrews Univ.; New Coll., Edinburgh; Univ. of Bonn, Germany. A Presbyterian. Served as minister of three Ch. of Scotland congregations, the last being the North Morningside Ch., Edinburgh. Until retirement, he was prof. of New Testament language, literature and theology, Univ. of Edinburgh, New Coll., the title which he now holds as prof. emeritus. He has preached at religious assemblies and has held numerous special lectureships, including the Warrack Lectures, Edinburgh, and the Lyman Beecher Lectures, Yale Univ. He was Moderator of General Assembly of the Ch. of Scotland, 1963-64. His sermons are carefully structured and preached with intensity of language and delivery. His books include *The Life and Teaching of Jesus Christ* (1932); *A Man in Christ* (1935); *The Gates of New Life* (1940); *The Strong Name* (1940); *Heralds of God* (1946); *A Faith to Proclaim* (1953); *The Wind of the Spirit* (1968); *River of Life* (1972); and *King Forever* (1975).

STOTT, JOHN R. W.: Born in 1921, son of Sir Arnold and Lady Stott. Educated at Rugby Sch., Trinity Coll. (Cambridge) and Ridley Hall (Cambridge). Ch. of England. After serving a curacy, he became Rector of All Souls, Langham Place, London, in 1950. In 1959, he was appointed an Honorary Chaplain to the Queen. In 1975, he became rector emeritus of All Souls. Speaker for university missions, pastors' seminars, and student conferences in various countries. His writings and sermons are theologically conservative with a strong evangelical emphasis. His preaching has had wide appeal. His many books include *Basic Christianity* (1958); *The Preacher's Portrait* (1961); *Understanding the Bible* (1972); *Christian*

Mission in the Modern World (1975); and *Baptism and Fullness* (1975).

THIELICKE, HELMUT: Born at Barmen, Germany, 1908. Educated at Greifswald, Marburg, Erlangen, and Bonn Univs. A Lutheran. He taught at Erlangen Univ., then became a professor at Heidelberg Univ., a post from which he was dismissed by the Nazis. In 1940 he became pastor at Ravensburg. Subsequently, he taught at Tübingen and Hamburg Univs., serving both as rector. Though his speciality is systematic theology, he is known in the English-speaking world primarily as a preacher. His sermons are characterized by theological and ethical depth and by boldly imaginative treatment of issues of social and individual concern. His two-volume (in English) *Theological Ethics* contains the substance of his preaching. Best known among his sermon volumes are: *Our Heavenly Father* (1959), *The Waiting Father* (1960), and *How the World Began* (1961). His most recent work is his *Evangelical Faith,* Vol. 1 (1974).

TRUETT, GEORGE W.: Born in Clay County, N.C., 1867. Died, 1944. Educated at Baylor Univ. A Baptist. Founder and principal of Hiawassee Academy, Towns County, N.C., 1887-89. He planned to be a lawyer, but the importunity of fellow church members persuaded him to receive ordination. He was financial agent for Baylor Univ., 1891-93. Pastor of East Waco (Tex.) Bapt. Ch., 1893-97; First Bapt. Ch., Dallas, 1897-1944. Pres., Southern Bapt. Conv., 1927-30; Bapt. World Alliance, 1934-39. Every Sunday night Truett's sermons were beamed into the United States from a powerful radio station across the Mexican border and reached large sections of the country. His sermons were simply constructed and made large use of profoundly moving illustrations. He spoke extemporaneously with great vigor. With many Southern Baptists, his opinion on ecclesiology or theology was the final word. His political influence was immense, not because of direct addressing of issues, but because of personal ethos and spiritual conviction obliquely expressed. His sermon books include *We Would See Jesus* (1915) and *A Quest for Souls* (1917). His biography, *George W. Truett* (1939), was written by Powhatan W. James.

VON RAD, GERHARD: Born in Nürnberg, 1901. Died 1972. A Lutheran. Educated at Univs. of Erlangen and Tübingen. Taught at Univs. of Leipzig, Jena, Göttingen, and Heidelberg, where he was prof. of O.T. theol. from 1949 until his death. Guest professor at Princeton Theol. Sem., 1960-61. Received honorary doctorates from Univs. of Leipzig, Glasgow, Lund, and Wales. His preaching demonstrates a wrestling with the biblical text at the exegetical and existential levels, in line with his conviction that "we must reproduce the utterance of the Bible in our language (just as concretely *ad hominem*) as it was meant in the Bible." His books in English translation include: *Studies in Deuteronomy* (1953); *Genesis* (a commentary) (1961); *Old Testament Theology* (2 vols.) (1962-65); *The Message of the Prophets* (1968); *Deuteronomy* (a commentary) (1966); and *Biblical Interpretations in Preaching* (1977).

WEATHERHEAD, LESLIE: Born in London, England, in 1893. Died in 1976. Educated at Univs. of Manchester and London. A Methodist. Served churches in Madras, India; Manchester; and Leeds. From 1936 to 1960 he was pastor of the famous City Temple in London, where psychology in its relation to religion was practically implemented. In 1949 he delivered the Lyman Beecher Lectures on Preaching at Yale Univ. His sermons show a great variety of form and illustrative sources. Though somewhat eclectic theologically, "it is Weatherhead's distinction," says Horton Davies, "to have provided as the aim of each of his services of worship 'a glimpse of Christ.'" His sermon volumes include: *That Immortal Sea* (1953), *Over His Own Signature* (1955), and *Key Next Door* (1960). A biography has been written by his son.

WESTERMANN, CLAUS: Born at Berlin, 1909. Educated at Univs. of Tübingen, Marburg, and Berlin. Taught at Kirchliche Hochschule, Berlin, and at Univ. of Heidelberg, where he is prof. of O.T. His sermons unfold in timely exposition that makes the text transparent for the needs of present hearers. Many of his books, which deal mainly with O.T. subjects, have been translated into English and have found wide acceptance among serious Bible students. He edited a volume of O.T. sermons, *Verkündigung des Kommenden*, which has not been translated. His sermon that appears in *The*

Twentieth-Century Pulpit was taken from this volume. Some of his translated books are *The Genesis Accounts of Creation* (1964); *Handbook to the New Testament* (1969); *Handbook to the Old Testament* (1967); *The Old Testament and Jesus Christ* (1970); *Our Controversial Bible* (1969); *A Thousand Years and a Day* (1962).